THE DEVOUT LIFE

THE DEVOUT LIFE

Plunging the Depths of Spiritual Renewal

ROGER HELLAND

Foreword by Howard A. Snyder

WIPF & STOCK · Eugene, Oregon

THE DEVOUT LIFE
Plunging the Depths of Spiritual Renewal

Wipf & Stock
An Imprint of Wipf and Stock Publishers
199 W. 8th Ave., Suite 3
Eugene, OR 97401

www.wipfandstock.com

PAPERBACK ISBN: 978-1-5326-3664-6
HARDCOVER ISBN: 978-1-5326-3666-0
EBOOK ISBN: 978-1-5326-3665-3

Manufactured in the U.S.A. 10/05/17

CONTENTS

FOREWORD

Pietism was one of the most significant church renewal movements in history. Yet in our day few are familiar with it—the ways God's Spirit used this movement to renew the church and spread the Good News throughout the world. In some circles, the very term "pietist" is viewed negatively as though it meant an unhealthy inward focus, a turning away from the world.

Roger Helland's book sets the record straight. It can help contemporary Christians not only learn from history, but also discover how they themselves can experience God in their lives in ways that transform them and the world around them.

The aim of the book, Roger says, is "to help equip, empower, and renew church leaders and churches to thrive in missional disciplemaking. My fire is that pastors, church leaders, and churches would flourish!" The key to this is life centered in God, true Christian devotion. We get practical insights into such discipleship by reviewing the lives and impact of key figures like Johann Arndt, Philip Jacob Spener, August Herman Francke, Nicolas von Zinzendorf, and John Wesley.

While the author draws on key figures in the Pietist traditions, he shows that genuine Christ-centered devotedness is and has been found in other traditions as well, from Anabaptist to Roman Catholic. The heart of Pietism is a living faith—not "sterile orthodoxy" but living orthodoxy, based in Scripture and a vital, living relationship with Jesus Christ. Quoting Donald Bloesch, Roger writes: "What I call for is a marriage between Pietism and orthodoxy, a theology of Word and Spirit."

Roger shows that devotion and discipleship must go together. They are two interdependent parts of one whole. "Devoutness" is not just inward, a thing of the heart. It is also outward, touching every area of our lives in the church and in society. Holding the inward and outward together, the book shows that genuine love for God necessarily shows itself in active concern for our neighbor and our world.

This means that a devout life is one of "continuous Christian conversion." A life saturated by Scripture, prayer, the sacraments, Christian community, catechesis, confession and repentance, solitude and silence, and active engagement with society are all key components of a faithful devout life. God's Spirit turns these practices and disciplines into joy-filled living as we walk with Jesus the Head, nurture life in the church, Jesus' Body, and live out the mind of Christ in witness to the world.

Fulfilling our God-given mandate to be faithful stewards of God's grace (1 Pet 4:10) and the good earth (Gen 2:15), Roger Helland shows how from the roots of a healthy devout life.

—Howard A. Snyder

Author of *The Radical Wesley, The Problem of Wineskins, Salvation Means Creation Healed* (with Joel Scandrett), and other books. Howard has served as a pastor and has taught at Asbury and Tyndale Theological Seminaries, and other institutions, most recently as Visiting Director of the Manchester Wesley Research Center in England.

INTRODUCTION

A Pietist Posture for Spiritual Renewal

Everyone now endeavors to be eminent and distinguished in the world, but no one is willing to learn to be pious.[1]

(Johann Arndt)

I love the church—God's people—even with all her failures and foibles. And I love the Lord Jesus Christ, who inspires me to pour myself out on the sacrifice and service of his people's faith (Phil 2:17). That is why, for the rest of my days, I will be a relentless pastor-teacher committed to serving the Lord's church and cause in the world. As I write, I reflect on what drives my four decades of Christian ministry that spans vigorous spiritual service as a lay-leader, church elder, pastor, Bible college and seminary instructor, denominational leader, mentor, and author. It boils down to my central voracious passion—to help equip, empower, and renew church leaders and churches to thrive in missional disciplemaking. My fire is that pastors, church leaders, and churches would flourish!

However, the chilling remark sent from the beleaguered Apollo 13 spacecraft trumpets my concern: "Houston, we have a problem!" The frequent disheartening reports about the decline of growth and health in most North American denominations and churches, combined with reports of disillusioned Millennials who are leaving the church, and reports of those who are "done" with church (though not with Christ), reveal alarming trends. When the Canadian Bible Engagement Study reports that only

1. Arndt, *True Christianity*, 21.

one in seven Canadian Christians read the Bible once per week, that only one in four Christians believe the Bible is relevant to modern life, and that most Canadians, whether Christian or not, read the Bible seldom or never, we have a problem![2] Furthermore, according to the Barna Group, "Most people (66 percent) feel they have had 'a real and personal connection' with God while attending church. However, that means one-third of those who have attended a church in the past have never felt God's presence while in a congregational setting. Also, when asked about frequency, most of those who have attended church describe these encounters as rare."[3] Prayerless churches also diminish God's presence. Citing Findley Edge, Calvin Miller declares, "People will endure anything in a church except an absence of vitality."[4]

On *The State of Discipleship* in the United States, the 2015 Barna Report stated that only 1 percent of pastors say, "Today's churches are doing very well at discipling new and young believers." 60 percent feel that churches are discipling "not too well." Three-quarters of practicing Christians believe it is "very important to see growth in their spiritual life." But only 20 percent of Christian adults are involved in some sort of discipleship activity. The research revealed little correlation between activity and perceived growth, with a disconnection between how people think about their spirituality and what occurs in their lives. Pastors feel that the most critical elements of discipleship are *matters of the heart* rather than of structure.[5]

THE LOSS OF PIETY

Donald Bloesch, in *The Crisis of Piety*, addressed a similar demise prevalent in the church back in 1988. He wrote:

> Our age currently finds itself in a crisis of faith. One symptom of the breakdown in faith is the loss of *piety*. Spiritual disciplines such as prayer and fasting are foreign to most modern Christians . . . What is needed today is a *renewal of devotion* to the living Savior. Such renewal involves the very life of the church, which

2. Canadian Bible Engagement Study, "Are Canadians Done with the Bible?"
3. Barna Update, "What People Experience in Churches."
4. Miller, *Letters to a Young Pastor*, 19–20.
5. Barna Update, "New Research on the State of Discipleship."

> rests on an outpouring, and a rediscovery of the Holy Spirit in Christian faith and practice.[6]

Bloesch's conclusion matches today's problem, "It cannot be denied that modern Protestantism is troubled by the demise of genuine piety—heartfelt devotion and consecration to God. It involves a commitment that is total, one that affects every area of life—a synthesis of the love and fear of God."[7] One Sunday at a church service where I preached, we sang the hymn *I Surrender All.* I winced inside as the lyrics pierced my soul, because I had to admit that the heresy of my life did not always match the orthodoxy of the hymn: "All to Jesus I surrender, all to him I freely give, I will ever love and trust him, in his presence daily live." Do I, do we, have a commitment that is total? Do we surrender all with the love and fear of God?

The problem I observe with many beleaguered churches and church leaders that fail to thrive, is usually *spiritual* not *structural.* It is easier and more common (and perhaps a sign of entrenched *modernity*) for leaders to focus more on *structural* church renewal: design improved weekend services and programs, or develop better small groups, boards, leadership, vision, volunteerism, strategic planning, or even become "missional." There is value in structural renewal with an enormous oversupply of resources that can enhance the institutional aspects of church life. However, to merely change the structures is like someone who walks up to a tree full of monkeys and bangs the trunk with a bat. All the monkeys jump to different branches restructured. But remember, they are still the same monkeys! Deep inner change can elude you! It is tougher and less common, however, to focus on and sustain *spiritual* church renewal. We need a vibrant faith nourished by direct contact with God aglow with the Spirit's empowering presence.

Howard Snyder expresses a mediating position that combines institutional (structural) and charismatic (spiritual) renewal. We should value the theological and organizational aspects of the historic institutional Church and its stewardship of the Scriptures, the sacraments, and Christian theology. And, we should welcome the spiritual and charismatic aspects of church revitalization that sparks a renewed experience of God's grace and new life in Christ, and sprouts new growth. A partially deadened tree can send forth some new shoots (cf. Isa 11:1; Job 14:7–9). We need a renewing spirit and renewing structures, like new wine in new wineskins (Luke

6. Bloesch, *The Crisis of Piety*, 1–3.

7. Ibid., 25–26.

5:37–38).[8] But, remember, new functions *precede* new forms. And, like fire and the fireplace, we need both the dynamic Spirit to enflame and the durable structures to enshrine the devout life. But a tidy fireplace without a crackling fire inside will lack spiritual fervor (cf. Rom 12:11).

A key factor for spiritual renewal is the spiritual vitality of burdened pastors themselves. One afternoon I sat in the dean's office of a Canadian seminary. He excitedly said to me, "Roger, I have a new book for you to read. We're giving this out to pastors and denominational leaders. It's based on a seven-year research project in the United States that reveals what it takes for pastors to survive and thrive over the long haul. The authors discuss five themes required for effective ministry, and we want to do something about this."

He fetched the book from his bookshelf and handed it to me. The title is, *Resilient Ministry: What Pastors Told Us About Surviving and Thriving*. As I glanced at the white book, I paused for a moment and replied intuitively, "Before I open this book I'll tell you what I think it reveals as the number one issue. It's *spiritual formation*." I opened the paperback and bingo! There it was, *spiritual formation*—number one! The other four issues in descending order were: self-care, emotional and cultural intelligence, marriage and family, and leadership and management. It is not surprising that according to a Canadian research project, "an active spiritual life" is perched at the top of seven characteristics of a flourishing congregation.[9] This matches a similar conclusion, posted by Gary McIntosh of Talbot School of Theology, who places "spiritual dynamics" and "effective evangelism" as top factors of growing churches in North America.[10]

"As the leaders go, so go the people," right? I know first-hand that the foundation for pastors and church leaders to survive and thrive is *their* spiritual formation forged in the depths of a devout life. A pastor surveyed in *Resilient Ministry* remarked, "Look, I may be a pastor, but I'm an inch deep. My life is filled with incessant activity and little prayer. 'Contemplation' is foreign in my vocabulary and non-existent in my life."[11] To thrive as a church leader will require better major league pitches than "good to great leadership," purpose driven strategies, preaching, teamwork, or giftedness.

8. See, Snyder, *The Radical Wesley*, 129–42, *Signs of the Spirit*, 270–76, and *The Problem of Wineskins*.

9. Flourishing Congregations Institute, "Defining a Flourishing Congregation."

10. McIntosh, "The 6 Top Factors in Growing Churches."

11. Burns, et al., *Resilient Ministry*, 19.

It will require *piety*. Calvin Miller reflects, "And when you are hungry for Christ, there is a likelihood that you may seek him with all your heart. Will this save evangelicalism? Yes. It will save it when you are commited to the practice of your highest devotion."[12]

THE DEVOUT LIFE AND SPIRITUAL RENEWAL

What is your highest devotion? We all tend to devote ourselves to someone or something. Women generally devote themselves to their children and to their families and relationships. Men generally devote themselves to their work and to their sports and hobbies. In 1728, English Anglican devotional writer William Law wrote, "He therefore, is the devout man, who lives no longer to his own will, or the way and spirit of the world, but to the sole will of God; who considers God in everything, who serves God in everything, who makes all the parts of his common life parts of piety, by doing everything in the Name of God, and under such rules as are conformable to his glory."[13] Devotion is the feelings and commitments that surge from your heart, driven by what you love. What do you love? We get glimpses into the nature and affirmation of the devout life in Scripture:

- Hezekiah turned his face to the wall and prayed to the Lord, "Remember, Lord, how I have walked before you faithfully and with *wholehearted devotion* and have done what is good in your eyes" (2 Kings 20:2–3 NIV).
- Now there was a man in Jerusalem whose name was Simeon, who was righteous and *devout*, waiting for the consolation of Israel, and the Holy Spirit was on him (Luke 2:25).
- At Caesarea, there was a man named Cornelius, a centurion of what was known as the Italian Cohort, a *devout* man who feared God with all his household, gave alms generously to the people, and prayed continually to God (Acts 10:1–2).
- And one Ananias, a *devout* man according to the law, well-spoken of by all the Jews who lived there (Acts 22:12).

For Christians, what fuels the devout life is an ardent practice of dedication and commitment to love God and people through Jesus Christ *from*

12. Miller, *The Vanishing Evangelical*, 218.

13. Law, *A Serious Call to a Holy and Devout* Life, 13.

the heart. Helen Keller remarked, "The most beautiful things in life cannot be seen or even touched, they must be felt with the heart." The inner sanctuary of your heart will offer the fragrance and fruit of devotion and beauty. In 1609, in his *Introduction to the Devout Life*, French Jesuit bishop St. Francis of Sales describes it this way:

> All true living devotion presupposes the love of God, a very real love of God . . . Devotion is the sweetest of sweets, the queen of virtues, the perfection of love. If love is the milk of life, devotion is the cream thereof; if it is a fruitful plant, devotion is the blossom; if it is a precious stone, devotion is its brightness; if it is a precious balm, devotion is its perfume, even that sweet odor which delights men and causes the angels to rejoice.[14]

Donald Bloesch notes, "Karl Barth states in *Evangelical Theology* that there can be no theology apart from devotion" and Bonhoeffer affirmed, "'Our hearts have room only for one all-embracing devotion, and we can only cleave to one Lord. Every competitor to that devotion must be hated.'"[15] Can you name any competitors in your heart that sabotage your singular devotion? Bloesch continues, "Devotion, it should be said, means the service of Jesus Christ, not simply worship. A devout person is a consecrated person, not simply a religious person. Devotion entails *piety*, that is, the fear of God, but it also includes mercy, service to our fellow humanity."[16] A devout life is the foundation for spiritual and even missional renewal. Church renewal only occurs when pastors, leaders, and Christians are spiritually renewed! This should evolve into what I call a "missional spirituality"—an embodied love for God and neighbor expressed from the inside out.[17] One morning I received an email from a dear woman my wife and I have known for decades. Her husband died after a two-year battle with cancer. Rob and Lorna had just retired and moved to a new home and set their sights to serve the Lord in a new church, spend time with family and friends, and do some fishing. I will remember this winsome man who was devout *from the heart*, whose stellar beauty beamed through his love for family and friends. Lorna's breathtaking work as a professional photographer expresses that same beauty.

14. Francis, *Introduction to the Devout Life*, 12–13.
15. Bloesch, *Crisis of Piety*, 16.
16. Ibid.
17. See, Helland and Hjalmarson, *Missional Spirituality*.

The command center of the devout life is *piety*. This is an older word that refers to Christian maturity marked by holiness, reverence, and godliness. Picture a gentle, wise, and winsome Pope Francis or Elisabeth Elliot type Christian who radiates Jesus Christ. A pious person is not simply a moral or religious person, but a godly or devout person. An artesian well I will draw from for the devout life is *Pietism*—a spiritual renewal movement that arose within European Lutheran and Reformed State Churches in the late seventeenth and early eighteenth centuries. *Pietism* was "a Bible centered movement, concerned for holy living that flows from a regenerate heart."[18] It played a significant role in the beginning of evangelical movements in Britain, and the main themes of Pietism influenced the main themes of evangelicalism. Continental Pietist spirituality made its mark on almost every phase of the British and American awakenings.[19]

The Pietist movement, launched in the late seventeenth century, was a welcome reaction to lifeless Lutheran orthodoxy and spiritual atrophy. Imagine what it would be like if the sum of your Christian life was a series of rituals: the pastor baptized you as an infant; you sat through rote catechism classes; you attended church every week by law and listened to academic sermons and received communion; you went to confessional to seek forgiveness of your sins; and then you glugged your intake of beer and played cards or dice while your pastor haggled with other pastors, and everyone held to exact doctrine, even though rancid corruption seethed within.

Douglas Shantz writes, "The genius of Pietism lay in the adjectives it employed: *true* Christianity; *heartfelt, living* faith; a *living* knowledge of God; the *inward* Christ; and the *inner* Word; . . . the *new* man; *born again* Christianity."[20] Pietism stressed that *true* Christianity was a *practical* love for God and neighbor that integrated the head and the heart—doctrine and devotion—evidenced by the "fruits of faith" through ongoing repentance and conversion. Pietism focused on inner piety, religious experience, and renovation—*the regenerate life*. It placed the authority of Scripture above church creeds and dogmas as the source for the Christian life. Pietism embraced a love theology that promoted a missional emphasis on charity and good deeds fused with an activation of the spiritual priesthood of true

18. Lindberg, *The Pietist Theologians*, 4.

19. Noll, *The Rise of Evangelicalism*, 60.

20. Shantz, *An Introduction to German Pietism*, 284.

believers primarily practiced in small groups called "conventicles," viewed as "colleges of piety" and as "little churches within the church."

Pietism is a *religion of the heart*—the affective command center or nucleus of your life. Though the Puritans generally enjoy more attention in church history, there is a current rediscovery of the Pietists. I see classical Pietism as a mighty river of spiritual renewal with many tributaries and parallel streams that flowed into it and out from it. Though it is no longer a movement but a milieu or an ethos, its effects and expressions permeate much of evangelical spiritual life, with some mutations and distortions. Pietism was an eclectic mix of biblical theology merged with the ideas of numerous devotional writers. It developed into two primary camps—*church* and *radical*—with a variety of expressions such as Halle, Moravian, Württemberg, and Reformed. Throughout this book, I will cite various Pietist scholars and develop the ideas primarily of key *church* Pietist leaders, both early and modern, and others who influenced the Pietists or reflect Pietist ideas. Let me introduce a few Pietists to you.

The primary founder of Pietism was Philipp Jakob Spener (1635–1705), a forty-year-old German Lutheran pastor in Frankfurt. His book *Pia Desideria* (1675)—which means "Pious Desires"—became a driving force for Pietism. He criticized the corrupt conditions in the church that included defects in civil authorities, clergy, and the common people, suggested that better conditions were possible, and made six practical proposals to correct them through a "theology of hope." Though we may take his six proposals in *Pia Desideria* for granted today, they were revolutionary and controversial in his day.

A forerunner of Pietism was Lutheran pastor Johann Arndt (1555–1621). Through his book *True Christianity* (1605–1610), Arndt sought to apply Luther's theology and to *practice* the true Christian life of love for God and others. He was an initial influence for Spener, whose devout godmother had him read *True Christianity*. Influenced by Thomas à Kempis's *The Imitation of Christ*, and by other medieval mystics, Arndt argued for a mystical union with Christ, ongoing repentance, and a Spirit-activated faith expressed in strong social concerns based on love, which validate true from false Christianity. *True Christianity* "would become the most widely read and disseminated devotional book of the seventeenth and eighteenth centuries."[21]

21. Olson and Winn, *Reclaiming Pietism*, 27.

Spener's successor, who helped advance Pietism further, was pastor and professor August Hermann Francke (1663–1727). He taught at the University of Halle in Germany—the chief academic center of Pietism. One of his students was Count Nikolaus Ludwig von Zinzendorf (1700–60), Lutheran Pietist and reformer of the Moravian movement. Francke's older sister, Anna, encouraged him to also study Arndt's *True Christianity.* Francke developed the evangelistic, missions, and social side of Pietism. He reinforced the doctrine of true repentance that led to conversion, which results in joy and assurance.

Other past and present Pietist leaders whose imprint on evangelical spirituality I will reference, include Johann Albrecht Bengel, John Wesley, Stanly J. Grenz, Donald G. Bloesch, Richard Foster, Roger E. Olson, John Piper, and Glen G. Scorgie. I will also reference some leaders (such as Lewis Bayly) whose Puritan, Reformed, or other views support Pietist themes, or help develop my ideas. The devout life is broader than the Pietist tradition per se, but my goal is to explore and expand on key features of Pietism and apply them for spiritual renewal today.

THE LEGACY OF PIETISM

Influences of Pietism appear in phrases such as: "be born again, receive Jesus Christ into your heart as personal savior, cultivate personal devotions and the inner life, and experience God." If we value the priesthood of believers, small group Bible studies and prayer meetings, and say, "God spoke to me through that Scripture passage or sermon," or if we hold to the doctrine of the "illumination of Scripture by the Holy Spirit," we show Pietist influences. If we appreciate personal diaries and biographies, we are indebted to a genre peculiar to Pietism. If we hold that one's baptism, catechism, receiving communion, attendance at church services, and membership in the church does not constitute Christian conversion, we represent a Pietist posture. Bruce Shelley summarizes the aims of Pietism:

> The aims of the Pietists were twofold: First, they stressed the importance of personal faith. They left behind all dreams of Catholic Christendom and Puritan commonwealths. They believed that Christianity started with the individual. So, for the first time in Christian history, the idea of conversions of baptized Christians (as well as pagans) came to prominence. The essence of faith, said the Pietist, is a personal experience of God's grace in the believer's

> heart. Second, the Pietists wanted to shift the center of the Christian life from the state churches, in which a person was born and brought up, to intimate fellowships of those who had a living faith in God. Revitalized laymen from these centers were expected to spread the Word of God through all classes of men.[22]

Pietism has endured numerous criticisms that identify it with mysticism, individualism, subjectivism, legalism, and separatism. Rightly so, as it is hard to pin someone down who retorts in a Bible study, "Well this is what this text means to me," or "God spoke to me," or "I have a prophetic word from God for you." Similarly, it is hard to challenge someone who sings a hymn that somehow validates God's existence through personal experience: "You ask me how I know he lives, he lives *within my heart*." When Baptists teach "soul competency" or "soul liberty," which grants each believer freedom of the soul from outside compulsion to enjoy direct ability and accountability from God, the center of gravity for authority can lie with the individual. When some Christians retreat to their private worlds of spirituality and feelings, become anti-intellectual or otherworldly, and are branded as "Pietist," the term carries a misguided label for itself.[23] When narrow leaders determine who has correct biblical faith and doctrine, and instigate "rules of righteousness" to quarantine people from sin (and others judge this as Pietism), the term is sorely misunderstood. The word *piety* can even transmit stiff, stuffy, and strict notions.

However, mutations and mistakes that evolved in Pietism should not discredit its original intent and influence in evangelical spirituality. As with all renewal movements, criticism of Pietism is largely aimed at the extremes and the fringe.[24] When it "remains tethered to the vitalizing dynamic of Scripture, it continues to embody a fervent, relational, and holistic spirituality that resonates well with the spiritual longings of contemporaries disillusioned with rationalism, formal religion, and the depersonalizing dynamics of modernity."[25] Pietism stressed the Bible's teaching over the institutional church's teaching, and produced numerous hymns, devotional literature, small group Bible studies and prayer meetings, lay ministry, evangelism

22. Shelly, *Church History in Plain Language*, 345.

23. Shantz states, "The term *Pietists* came into common parlance in Leipzig in 1689 in the context of a student society devoted to practical Bible study led by August Hermann Francke," *Introduction to German Pietism*, 5.

24. For a defense against six major criticisms of Pietism, see Olson, "Pietism: Myths and Realities," 7–16.

25. Carlson, "Pietism," 674.

and global missions, cultural impact, and the call to Christian conversion. Pietists emphasized one's personal walk with God. They produced devotional materials and hymns that express Pietist themes.

Pietism influenced Charles Wesley's, Fanny Crosby's, and Nikolaus von Zinzendorf's hymns. It permeated the Moravians who influenced the Wesleys and the Methodist movement into many Wesleyan streams such as the Salvation Army, Church of the Nazarene, The Missionary Church USA, and the Evangelical Missionary Church Canada. Pietism also influenced Mennonites, Quakers, European Reformed Churches, the Evangelical Covenant Church, the Evangelical Free Church, the Baptist General Conference, and the Christian and Missionary Alliance. It made an enduring mark on Jonathan Edwards, Francis Asbury, George Mueller, Friedrich Schleiermacher, Søren Kierkegaard, Phoebe Palmer, D. L. Moody, Oswald Chambers, Hannah Whitall Smith, Andrew Murray, E. M. Bounds, R. A. Torrey, A. B. Simpson, Herman Bavinck, Keswick renewal in the UK, and the Holiness and Pentecostal movements in the US and Europe.

F. Ernest Stoeffler concludes:

> During much of the seventeenth, and throughout the eighteenth [centuries], Pietism engendered a new spirit of religious devotion . . . Religious faith began to be regarded as a live option by large segments of the population which had hitherto thought of it as little more than a cultural relic. Preaching and pastoral work were revitalized. An entirely new hymnody came into existence and devotional aids were made widely available for private and family worship. There was a new vision of a Christian's responsibility toward community and the nation, a new sensitivity to the needs of the disadvantaged, the sick, and the dying, and a new awareness of the dire necessity of adequate educational institutions. Not only that, but for the first time during its existence Protestantism began to think seriously of a worldwide witness to its faith in word and deed.[26]

Pietism was also *missional.* Dale Brown notes: "The Pietist milieu resulted in desires to transform the living conditions of the poor and oppressed, reform prison systems, abolish slavery, remove class distinctions, establish a more democratic polity, initiate educational reforms, philanthropic institutions, and missionary activity, obtain religious liberty, and

26. Stoeffler, *Continental Pietism and Early American Christianity*, 10.

propose programs for social justice."[27] Pietism "promoted a practical Christianity marked by personal transformation, programs for social betterment, hopes for Christ's kingdom on earth, and calls for an end to denominational strife. In short, Pietism sought to bring reformation to the reformation."[28]

Let me tell you about a reformation in my own reformation. I taught a course on "Missional Spirituality" at Bethel Seminary, San Diego. As a California boy, I was in heaven! That week, I had lunch with Dr. Glen Scorgie, professor of theology at Bethel. As we exchanged personal information and ideas over some tasty Mexican cuisine, all the planets lined up for me! I learned that Glen and I shared many things in common. He grew up in Canada, where I now live; he now lives in southern California, where I grew up. He teaches at a Baptist General Conference seminary with a passion for spiritual formation and missional life. I serve as the district minister of Alberta in the Baptist General Conference with a passion for spiritual formation and missional life. We both also share influences from the Wesleyan tradition. Go figure! Mid-way through lunch, I gazed into Glen's eyes and asked: "Glen, how can a man who grew up in Canada with Wesleyan roots, and now lives in California and teaches theology at a Baptist Seminary?"

With a smile on his face and without hesitation he announced, "I'm a Pietist!" Bam! Without thinking I immediately replied, "So am I!" I instantly resonated with him. It was if someone pulled the drapes open to let the early morning sunshine beam into the living room of my soul. Now I realized why I could traverse inter-denominational terrains as a pastor in the Vineyard, Mennonite Brethren, Christian and Missionary Alliance, and Baptist worlds. And why I can appreciate Wesleyan, Reformed, Anglican, Anabaptist, Catholic, Orthodox, and Charismatic traditions. I am a Pietist! Several years ago, I also began to explore the Swedish Baptist Pietist roots of the Baptist General Conference where I serve. Then I began to teach workshops and eventually graduate seminary courses on the devout life and the theology and history of spirituality, with applications to spiritual and missional renewal from a Pietist posture.

Lastly, for approximately three months, I led a weekly small group gathering in my home with my oldest son Joel and his friend Josh. Our goal, like a Pietist "college of piety," was to study, discuss, and pray through Scripture together in community. We chose the book of Matthew, which deals with discipleship. Each week we would read a few chapters privately

27. Brown, *Understanding Pietism*, 86–87.

28. Shantz, *Introduction to German Pietism*, 1.

at home and record our insights and questions along with our confessions and personal prayers, responses and applications, in our journals. We would gather for ninety minutes to share our journals and have discussion, followed by listening prayer based on the text of Scripture for that week. It was one of the most transformational small group experiences that each of us has ever had. During our last meeting, as we prayed for one another, my son offered what he sensed the Lord was saying to me. Joel seized my attention! Even before he shared it with me, I sensed the very same thing deep inside my heart and mind. He said, "Dad, I sense the Lord is saying that he's taking you *deeper*!" I felt a gravitational pull to go deeper in God as a devoted disciple.

Like an Olympic high dive athlete who plunges the depths of the tank below, the devout life will plunge us into the depths of God's Spirit, "For the Spirit searches everything, even the depths of God" (1 Cor 2:10). The Pietists advanced the *life* of salvation—regeneration or new birth with cleansing by the Holy Spirit, and *Spirit*-ual renewal. For, "when the goodness and loving kindness of God our Savior appeared, he saved us, not because of works done by us in righteousness, but according to his own mercy, by the washing of regeneration and renewal of the Holy Spirit, whom he poured out on us richly through Jesus Christ our Savior" (Titus 3:4–6). Christians can impede *Spirit*-ual renewal when they default to an incomplete theology and practice. Jim Cymbala warned that we must not simply believe in the Father, Son, and Holy Scriptures. We need the Holy Spirit. Pietist Johann Arndt offers a robust theological foundation for spiritual renewal:

> In this renewal in Christ, in this spiritual, heavenly, godly truth, everything is set. This is the end of all theology and the whole of Christianity. This is union with God (1 Cor 6:16), the marriage with our heavenly Bridegroom, Jesus Christ, the living faith, the new birth, Christ's dwelling in us, Christ's noble life in us, the Holy Spirit's fruit in us, the enlightenment and healing of the kingdom of God in us. Christ and faith are so united with one another that everything that is Christ is ours through faith . . . Where Christ's life is, there is pure love; and where love is, there is the Holy Spirit; and where the Holy Spirit is, there is the whole kingdom of God.[29]

What inflames my Pietist spirituality is a deep practical theology—Christology—heart-felt devotion and magnificent surrender to Christ Jesus as Lord. Another term for piety or devotion is *reverence*. Christ himself

29. Arndt, *True Christianity*, 277–78.

lived such a life with stunning results: "In the days of his flesh, Jesus offered up prayers and supplications, with loud cries and tears, to him who was able to save him from death, and he was heard because of his *reverence*" (Heb 5:7). While there are many valuable academic books available on Pietism, my goal is to offer an applied and practical one anchored in solid academics. As I will suggest, the devout life is a life of piety, nurtured by a certain posture and expressed by certain practices. Paul announces that God supplies his Spirit and works miracles among us [both present tense] by hearing with faith (Gal 3:5). Jesus promises that "out of our heart will flow [present tense] rivers of living water. Now this he said of the Holy Spirit" (John 7:38-39). While there is no uniform consensus on a definitive list of characteristics of Pietism, I will explore and expand on ten observable features for a devout life drawn from a Pietist posture. Let us release the river of renewal to gush from the headwaters of the word and Spirit, with piety and devotion. When it does, let us dive in together!

DEVOTIONAL EXERCISE

Reflect on Johann Arndt's opening remarks in *True Christianity*:

> To show simple readers wherein true Christianity consists, namely, in the exhibition of a true, living faith, active in genuine godliness and the fruits of righteousness, how true repentance must proceed from the innermost source of the heart; how the heart, mind, and affections must be changed, so that we might be conformed to Christ and his holy Gospel; and how we must be renewed by the word of God to become new creatures. As every seed produces fruit of a like nature, so the word of God must daily produce in us new spiritual fruits. If we are to become new creatures by faith, we must live in accordance with the new birth. In a word, Adam must die, and Christ must live, in us. It is not enough to know God's word; one must also practice it in a living, active manner. Many think that theology is a mere science, or rhetoric, whereas it is a living experience and practice. *Everyone now endeavors to be eminent and distinguished in the world, but no one is willing to learn to be pious.*[30]

30. Ibid., 21.

1

DEVOTION TO BIBLICAL PIETY

What is the chief purpose of mankind?
To know God, serve God, and glorify him forever!

(Roger Helland)

For most of my Christian life, I have suffered with a gnawing spiritual hunger. I have rarely felt like a "Spirit-filled" or "fully devoted" follower of Jesus. Have you? Sometimes I feel like a well-intentioned slouch, who makes yet another resolution to lose weight in January and then yields to the gravitational appeal of nachos, pizza, and ice cream in February. It is tough to maintain a diet when food is your favorite dish! Jesus resisted Satan's lure of physical food by his focus on spiritual food when he cited a memorized Deuteronomy 8:3, "Man shall not live by bread alone, but by every word that comes from the mouth of God" (Matt 4:4). I believe this; but to live it is another matter. I grew up in a non-Christian family where stifling words that came from parental mouths, tainted with demanding expectations of performance and perfection, scalded my soul. When you add my task-orientation into the dough, the chemical reaction can become a conflicted wrestling match between what is devotion and what is mere dedication.

Some years ago, I watched a captivating video by a preacher named Malcolm Smith entitled "Beware of The Yeast of the Pharisees," drawn from

Matthew 16:11–12. His central point was that a satisfying spiritual life in Christ—eating the True Bread from heaven—suffers contamination when the yeast of the fastidious legalistic teaching of the Pharisees is kneaded into it. To live a holy life, the rabbis believed, we need "fence laws." These were meticulous rules that defined holy conduct with lists of do's and don'ts to safeguard people from breaking the Torah. Some strict believers today have their own fence laws of do's and don'ts: don't smoke, swear, dance, expose yourself to secular movies or music, drink alcohol, work on Sundays, associate with sketchy people, read liberal writers . . . matched with do's: do read your Bible, pray, attend church, tithe, dress modestly, defend doctrine, serve, be committed. These are not all wrong. However, a legalistic approach neither works nor satisfies; it only imprisons you in a narrow dungeon of insecurity that wears you out.

Smith closed with the story about the everyman Christian who strives and feels a bone-weary sense of guilt and failure for not measuring up. Each Sunday sermon becomes another scolding reprimand to shape up—until that Christian realizes the solution is *not* one more fretful shuffle forward to the altar to "rededicate his dedication." Rather than lug the Pharisee's yoke of legalism on his aching shoulders any longer, he opts for Jesus's easy yoke of learning instead. He hears Jesus beckon, "Take my yoke upon you, and *learn* from me, for I am gentle and lowly in heart, and you will find rest for your souls. For my yoke is easy, and my burden is light" (Matt 11:29–30). That message stirred my heart for a life of bold devotion over bald dedication.

To *learn* from Jesus means I will focus on piety rather than on performance—to please him more than to please people. A devoted disciple is a life-long learner. I have discovered that my gnawing spiritual hunger is a tug from my sinful nature mingled with my propensity to strive. I aim to "taste and see that the Lord is good" as I come to Jesus who promises, "I am the bread of life; whoever comes to me shall not hunger, and whoever believes in me shall never thirst" (John 6:35). I also yearn to be like Barnabas, who was devout— "a good man, full of the Holy Spirit and of faith" (Acts 11:24). I know many Christians who are dedicated but are not devout—who serve in giftedness without godliness; who perform without piety. This is hazardous for the church. I want to be a part of the solution—with devotion to biblical piety. And you?

WHAT IS BIBLICAL PIETY?

The term *piety* is peculiar—rather outdated. A related term is *pious*. A pious person is one who possesses piety—reverence, devotion, virtue, or godliness. These are hefty words—noble words—that whisper elegance like a white swan. Piety is derived from the Latin *pietas*, which denotes loyalty, devotion, tenderness, goodness, and pity. There is a warm affective side to piety with gracious charm and humble radiance, not a stern or stiff side with pursed lips and a creased forehead. In today's language, we might use the terms *godliness* or *spirituality*. Greek has two words that carry similar meanings translated as *piety*: (1) *eulabeia*, which means, "good holding," in reverence for God, (2) *eusebeia*, which means, "good worship," godliness.

An example of *eulabeia* is Hebrews 5:7: "In the days of his flesh, Jesus offered up prayers and supplications, with loud cries and tears, to him who was able to save him from death, and he was heard because of his *reverence*." This is a colossal insight: God heard Jesus's prayers because of his reverence or piety! An example of *eusebeia* is 2 Peter 1:5–7, "For this very reason, make every effort to supplement your faith with virtue, and virtue with knowledge, and knowledge with self-control, and self-control with steadfastness, and steadfastness with *godliness*, and *godliness* with brotherly affection, and brotherly affection with love." There is power in piety, where some "have the appearance of *godliness*, but deny its power. Avoid such people" (2 Tim 3:5). Peter Davids remarks: "In this case 'godliness' or 'piety,' [*eusebeia*] a term that, when applied to 'life,' indicates a life that the deity would approve of."[1] It is a reverent posture of the *heart*, from which we seek God's approval.

First century Jewish historian Josephus remarks on the life of Pythagoras, a famous Greek philosopher and mathematician in the late sixth century B.C., "Pythagoras, therefore, of Samos, lived in very ancient times, and was esteemed a person superior to all philosophers in wisdom and *piety* towards God."[2] Piety is that fear or devotion we have toward God that he commends. Early in his *Institutes* John Calvin asserts, "Piety is requisite for the knowledge of God." He expands: "Indeed, we shall not say that, properly speaking, God is known where there is no religion or piety . . . *I call 'piety' that reverence joined with love of God which the knowledge of*

1. Davids, *The Letters of 2 Peter and Jude*, 168.
2. Josephus and Whiston, *The Works of* Josephus, AP, 1:22:162.

his benefits induces."[3] Peter exhorts: "But *in your hearts* set apart Christ as Lord" (1 Pet 3:15, NIV). Each morning I spend at least an hour in sacred quiet and solitude where I set apart my heart to the Lord in prayer and Bible reading. I enter my day consecrated.

Recently, I read through Proverbs to help me live as a wise person. Wisdom's foundation and fruitfulness is deeply theological and fulfilling, "The fear of the Lord leads to life, and whoever has it rests satisfied" (Prov 19:23). Proverbs mentions the *heart* over seventy times. Its relation to God influences just about every action and attitude. David Rowe comments: "Wisdom (or knowledge or understanding) becomes radically earthy, incarnate, and manifests in the gritty, everyday experience of the faithful. It is never mere shrewdness, 'street smarts,' or business acumen; wisdom characterizes the discerning heart that is both morally righteous and practically smart."[4] What stands out with blue-sky clarity is that Proverbs stations piety at the intersection of wisdom's principles and practices to live successfully. If you desire to be a successful parent, business owner, pastor, or civil servant, you must cultivate wisdom through piety. However, it is not just general piety, morality, or goodness, but piety governed by the Bible characterized by devotion to Jesus Christ. Modern Pietist theologian Donald Bloesch remarks,

> We must take care to differentiate biblical piety from all kinds of pseudo-piety. Biblical piety is first of all characterized by inward devotion to the Savior, Jesus Christ. It entails daily repentance under the cross of Christ and renewed dedication to the will of Christ . . . Holy Scripture, being the veritable vessel of the gospel, is the principal source of all piety. This is not to deny that other devotional writings may be used in our spiritual life as a supplement to Scripture, but they should be in full accord with the Bible.[5]

THE PRACTICE OF PIETY

As a physician practices medicine, and a lawyer practices law, a devout person practices piety. After all, *piety* characterizes a true Pietist! Roger E. Olson and Christian Collins Winn identify *conversional piety* as the fourth

3. Calvin, *Institutes of the Christian Religion*, 1, II, 1, 39, 41.
4. Rowe, "Wisdom," 840–41.
5. Bloesch, *Crisis of Piety*, 4–5.

hallmark of Pietism—a strong devotional life and a personal relationship with God through Jesus Christ crucified and risen.[6] They remark: "Of course, this hallmark is not unique to Pietism. The Puritans, for example, emphasized this as well. The distinctive Pietist expression of this concept appears in the phrase 'intimacy with the Savior'—a favorite phrase of Zinzendorf's to describe the true Christian life."[7] The evangelical theme of "intimacy with God," somewhat mystical, derives from Pietism.

Conversional piety requires holy living, practiced by what English Puritan Jeremy Taylor calls *purity of intention*, "That we should intend and design God's glory in every action we do as expressed by St. Paul" (1 Cor. 10:31). He argues that a holy end will sanctify our actions. We should reflect upon why we do things so that the means serve the ends. The purity of our hearts with impeccable and innocent desires to please God should monitor our motivations. Taylor warns that without purity of intention all religious actions like prayer, almsgiving, fasting, and humiliation, degenerate into secular, sinful actions.[8] As a young adult, this practice affected John Wesley: "In the year 1725, being in the twenty-third year of my age, I met with Bishop Taylor's "Rule and Exercises of Holy Living and Dying." In reading several parts of this book, I was exceedingly affected; that part in particular which relates to purity of intention. Instantly I resolved to dedicate all my life to God, all my thoughts, and words, and actions."[9] The practice of *purity of intention* now forms a critical part of my pursuit of the devout life. What about you?

To cultivate conversional piety requires that devout Christians not only practice piety, but also vigorously *pursue* piety. Let Peter's words simmer in your soul: "But as for you, O man of God . . . *Pursue* righteousness, *godliness*, faith, love, steadfastness, and gentleness" (1 Tim 6:11). A man or woman of God will flee the love of money (v. 10) and instead will continuously strive for, seek after, and aspire to righteousness and godliness—piety, from that Greek word *eusebeia*. A strong devotional life does not simply mean you will have morning "devotions" or that you will bring a "devotional" message before a board meeting. To practice and pursue piety fuels how you live out the Christian life—the devout life. You will strive to please God.

6. Olson and Winn, *Reclaiming Pietism*, 94.

7. Ibid., 94–95.

8. Taylor, *Holy Living and Dying*, 12–19.

9. Wesley, *A Plain Account of Christian Perfection*, 3.

What do you pursue—a career, a fortune, a name, a woman, a man, a position, a dream? What you love is where your devotion converts to passion, which then drives what you pursue. It is fine to pursue a career or a dream. However, if they become your single-minded focus in life, they can easily turn into idolatry and you can succumb to an empty pursuit of a mirage. I must make this adjustment regularly as part of my ongoing repentance. Remember the words of Zinzendorf: "I have but one passion, and that is he, and only he." Let me offer two key ingredients for the practice and pursuit of piety: theology and training.

Theology

My mother-in-law, affectionately called "Ma Handley," was a simple Saskatchewan farm girl who loved her family and her flowers. She modeled generosity, hard work, and hospitality, and always made time for people. When I was a Bible college student, interested in her youngest daughter, I would go over for supper or coffee and we would chat. After I eventually married her daughter, we would often talk about life, and as she aged, we would occasionally talk about death. She would reflect on "the dirty thirties" (the depression years) and would sound off about parenting, politics, and at times religion. She was a thinker, and in many ways a *theologian*. She knew some Bible and basic theology. In her peculiar way, she conceded to God's sovereignty and would retort, "Roger, if it's meant to be it will be!" That has helped me! She did not fear death and would muse, "When it's my time to go, I'm ready to go and face my Maker." She eventually died from cancer. Remarkably, as she drew her last breath in the hospital, I had kneeled beside her bed and literally prayed her to Jesus!

We are all theologians to some degree. Pietist theologians, Stanly J. Grenz and Roger E. Olson, state: "No one who reflects on life's ultimate questions can escape theology. And anyone who reflects on life's ultimate questions—including questions about God and our relationship with God—is a theologian."[10] *Theo/logy* comes from a combination of two Greek words: *theos* (God), and *logos* (thought, word). When we think, or talk about God, we engage in theology whether as a layperson, pastor, or scholar. Early Pietists embraced Protestant orthodox theology. However, Scripture was the primary authority over church creeds, confessions, or dogma. The goal of nutritious Christian theology is to direct us in a true knowledge of God

10. Grenz and Olson, *Who Needs Theology?*, 13.

and his benefits, which will enlarge our hearts and minds to shape our piety and discipleship. Calvin bears repeating here: "*I call 'piety' that reverence joined with love of God which the knowledge of his benefits induces*." Listen to the Psalmists: "What shall I render to the Lord for all his benefits to me?" (Ps 116:12), and "Bless the Lord O my soul, and forget not all his benefits" (Ps 103:2).

The first ingredient for the practice and pursuit of piety is to flourish in good theological reflection to increase your knowledge of God. Peter blends piety and theology: "His divine power has granted to us all things that pertain to life and *godliness* [piety], through the *knowledge* of him [theology] who called us to his own glory and excellence" (2 Pet 1:3). There is that Greek word *eusebeia* again, translated as *godliness* or *piety*. God's power grants the resources you need to shape your life and piety toward his glory and excellence through your *experiential knowledge* of him.

In Greek, the noun *gnosis* and its verb *ginosko* means comprehension, or what is known, information that is discovered or learned: "God is good." To know (*ginosko*) God and Jesus Christ whom he sent constitutes eternal life (John 17:3). And to know (*ginosko*) Jesus opens direct access to know and see God (John 14:7). The intensified noun *epignosis*, used in 2 Peter 1:2 and 3, is full, exact, personal knowledge or recognition. It overlaps with *gnosis*, but can mean, "coming to know" as knowledge that is gained in conversion not on one's own.[11] "I *know* God is good, first-hand!" If you only know about God through propositions like "God is love," you can consign him to an abstract idea like "the man upstairs" and create impersonal distance. God can be merely doctrine to you! You may know ice cream tastes good, but until you eat some your knowledge can be information. You must taste and see firsthand that the Lord is good (Ps 34:8).

In *Knowing God*, Puritan Anglican J. I. Packer asks: "What were we made for? To know God. What aims should we set ourselves in life? To know God. What is the 'eternal life' that Jesus gives? Knowledge of God (John 17:3). What is the best thing in life, bringing more joy, delight, and contentment, than anything else? Knowledge of God."[12] To know God is a matter of *personal dealing* and of *personal involvement*.[13] It is one thing to know *about* God through information, yet another thing to know *of* God

11. Davids, *The Letters of 2 Peter and Jude*, 165.

12. Packer, *Knowing God*, 29.

13. Ibid., 34–35.

through personal experience, as lovers know each other or as parents know their children. How do we make the shift? Packer suggests:

> We must seek, in studying God, to be led to God. It was for this purpose that revelation was given, and it is to this use that we must put it. How can we turn our knowledge *about* God into knowledge *of* God? It is that we turn each truth that we learn about God into matter for meditation *before* God, leading to prayer and praise *to* God.[14]

Lewis Bayly, an English Reformed Puritan, influenced early Pietists as well as Puritans. In 1611, he wrote a theological guide to the Christian life entitled *The Practice of Piety: Directing a Christian How to Walk, that He May Please God.* According to Dale Brown, Spener had read it by age fourteen.[15] According to Douglas Shantz, it was read and discussed at a Pietist gathering in Spener's Frankfurt home in the early 1670s.[16] Bayly covers lots of hefty ground with his advice, prayers, and meditations. Though it is wordy and dates from the 1600s, it displays enormous spiritual depth and is available online.[17] Bayly echoes Calvin's assertion: "And forasmuch as there can be no true piety without the knowledge of God; nor any good practice without the knowledge of a man's own self; we will therefore lay down the knowledge of God's majesty, and man's misery, as the first and chiefest grounds of the Practice of Piety."[18] Do you want to be pious, to know God? Let me suggest four ways for you to meet him.

The first way to know God is through continuous *conversion.* God "desires all people to be saved and to come to the knowledge [*epignosis*] of the truth" (2 Tim 2:4). Christians "have put on the new self, which is being renewed in knowledge [*epignosis*] after the image of its creator" (Col 3:10). To know the truth and the creator spawns initial and ongoing spiritual renewal in continuous conversion.

The second way to know God is through *Scripture.* If you wanted to get to know someone, you could read his or her letters, text messages, or emails. You would read what they have to *say* by what they wrote. You can read the transcripts of Lincoln's Gettysburg Address or Luther King's "I have a Dream" speech. Though they *spoke* these at a point in time, they

14. Ibid., 18.

15. Brown, *Understanding Pietism*, 16.

16. Shantz, *An Introduction to German Pietism*, 47.

17. Bayly, *The Practice of Piety.*

18. Ibid., 27.

continue to *speak* from them in print. God speaks in Scripture *to you*. Read Scripture *theologically* and observe what passages reveal about who God is in Christ, what he says and does, how and why. To know celebrities like Katy Perry or Justin Bieber, millions of fans read their daily online posts. Read and study Scripture daily, with an even greater interest to know God in Jesus Christ.

The third way to know God is through hearing *prayer*. Jesus said, "My sheep hear my voice, and I know them, and they follow me" (John 10:27). Each verb is present tense: we hear his voice, he knows us, and we follow him. Jesus knows you and speaks! Do you hear and follow him? God ordained prayer as the primary way for personal two-way communication to occur, for "people are meant to live in an ongoing conversation with God, speaking and being spoken to. Of course, talking to God is an almost universal practice . . . It is widely recognized that a major part of prayer is listening to God and letting God direct us."[19] We should also pray for *wisdom* and *revelation*, "that the God of our Lord Jesus Christ, the Father of glory, may give us the Spirit of wisdom and of revelation in the knowledge [*epignosis*] of him" (Eph 1:17).

The fourth way to know God is through *creation*. God's power and creativity are colossal as the universe trumpets his radiant glory: "The heavens declare the glory of God, and the sky above proclaims his handiwork" (Ps 19:1). Observe someone's living room or office and you will detect their values, interests, and personality by the pictures, books, artifacts, and handiwork there. My mother loved Hummel dolls. Those ceramic figurines reveal her heart. The creation and cosmos reveal God's heart, his stunning handicraft and intricate artwork. Like the breathtaking displays in the British Museum, God's wisdom is on display in the very fabric and engineering of creation (Prov 8:22–31; 6:6–8; Job 38–41; Rom 1:19–20). Adam McHugh reflects, "God spoke creation into existence, and now creation speaks of his existence."[20]

Observe an elegant falcon in flight, the stately palm trees of southern California, the jagged grandeur of the Rocky Mountains, or the golden hues of a summer sunset. Gaze at gleaming galaxies or dazzling meteor showers, the staggering magnificence of the Grand Canyon, the cheerful colors of daisies and daffodils, and finally, the dignity and design of your mother's face. The boundless mastermind, artist, and star maker, left profuse and

19. Willard, *Hearing God*, 21.

20. McHugh, *The Listening Life*, 112.

enthralling clues behind that beckon you with uplifted hands to "Behold your God!" On January 7, 1855, British Baptist preacher Charles Haddon Spurgeon, at age twenty, announced:

> No subject of contemplation will tend more to humble the mind, than thoughts about God. But while the subject *humbles* the mind, it also *expands* it. He who often thinks of God, will have a larger mind than the man who simply plods around this narrow globe. The most excellent study for expanding the soul, is the science of Christ, and Him crucified, and the knowledge of the Godhead in the glorious Trinity. Nothing will so enlarge the intellect, nothing so magnify the whole soul of man, as a devout, earnest, continued investigation of the great subject of Deity . . . Then go, plunge yourself in the Godhead's deepest sea; be lost in his immensity; and you shall come forth as from a couch of rest, refreshed and invigorated.[21]

Training

I work out at the gym usually three times per week. I walk and run on the treadmill, use different weight machines, do core exercises, swim laps, and then last and best of all, slink into the hot tub! I always feel improved after a hearty physical workout, which tunes up my body and lowers my stress. When I lapse in discipline and choose to sleep in or miss my regimen because of work travel or vacation, I start to feel sluggish and blunt. I envy fit, young, elite Olympic speed skaters and gymnasts, tennis pros and baseball sluggers. However, when I see them drenched by sweat and strain in their fitness and practice regimens, I appreciate that they only got there because of rigorous bodily training. And yet, Paul redirects me when I hear him bellow from the bleachers, "*Train* yourself for *godliness*; for while bodily training is of some value, godliness is of value in every way, as it holds promise for the present life and also for the life to come" (1 Tim 4:7–8). The devout life, like the Olympic life, requires that I train myself—in *eusebeia* (piety). Physical training is silver; spiritual training is gold. Notice Paul does not say *try* to be godly; but rather *train* for godliness. Without training you could never compete in the Olympics just because you tried. We must become "spiritual athletes."

21. Cited by Packer, *Knowing God*, 13–14.

Paul literally coaches, "*Gymnasium* yourself toward *godliness*." The word gymnasium, which refers to a fitness center or to a European academic secondary school, comes from the Greek noun *gymnasia*. The verb form is *gymnazō*. 1 Timothy 4:7–8 includes both words. Early Greek men exercised naked (*gymnos*), and the words *gymnazō* and *gymnasia* initially referred to physical exercise but broadened to mean training or discipline, and the structured processes of personal development through practice, including intellectual development. Hebrews 5:14 conveys the idea: "But solid food is for the mature, for those who have their powers of discernment trained (*gymnazō*) by constant practice to distinguish good from evil." Familiar to Timothy and the recipients of the letter, the gymnasium was the center of civic life in Greek-influenced towns.

Pietist Johann Arndt, in *True Christianity*, lists fifteen "Beautiful Rules for a Christian Life." To begin his section, he cites 1 Timothy 4:7–8 and comments:

> This verse is a description of the Christian life teaching us how a Christian is to carry out his life in the best possible way, namely, with godliness that contains all Christian virtues in itself. The apostle gives two significant motives. First, it is of use in every way. If man's godliness is in all his walks, works, and deeds, it makes everything good and chaste and blesses everything. Second, it has its reward in this life, as is to be seen in Joseph, Daniel, and others. In the eternal life we will reap without ceasing (Gal 6:9).[22]

Opponents hurled attacks against the Pietists, Puritans, and Methodists for their strident views on holy character for Christians. However, like spiritual fitness coaches, they originally formulated their rules and methods to help foster training in piety. It is impossible to become an elite athlete in the *gymnasia* without structure, discipline, and rules that govern such training. Procrastination, laziness, and the undisciplined soul will sabotage noble intentions. Proverbs refers to such people as sluggards who always make excuses to live idle lives. No one can slapdash their way to become a skilled golfer, pianist, or preacher, without discipline, rules, and practice. There is simply no progress in godliness without discipline, rules, and the practice of piety. Let us sign up for a spiritual fitness membership in the gymnasium of soul craft.

The word *training* can sound barren and arduous. Think of dog training, leadership training, fitness training, and job training. Think of piano

22. Arndt, *True Christianity*, 178.

lessons, with droning repetition, practice, and rehearsals. Think of first aid classes with two day's worth of mock training to save a plastic dummy's life. But when Paul urges Timothy to train himself for godliness, he urges present tense sustained development of the highest caliber—*to be like God.* This might be a summons to practice the spiritual disciplines. Although, Paul may have something more life-oriented in mind. Observe the fuller canonical context of this text:

> The Spirit clearly says that in later times some will *abandon the faith and follow deceiving spirits and things taught by demons*. Such *teachings* come through hypocritical liars, whose consciences have been seared as with a hot iron . . . If you point these things out to the brothers and sisters, you will be a good minister of Christ Jesus, *nourished on the truths of the faith and of the good teaching that you have followed*. Have nothing to do with *godless myths and old wives' tales*; rather, train yourself to be godly (1 Tim 4:1–7).

> Remind them of these things, and charge them before God not to *quarrel about words*, which does no good, but only ruins the hearers. Do your best to present yourself to God as one approved, a worker who has no need to be ashamed, *rightly handling the word of truth*. But avoid *irreverent babble*, for it will lead people into more and more *ungodliness*, and their *talk* will spread like gangrene (2 Tim 2:14–17).

Do you see the rancid problem that Timothy faced? False spiritual teachers, branded as hypocritical liars and heretics scripted by deceiving spirits and demons, infected the Ephesians. Their different doctrine and teachings—which wrangled in godless myths, old wives' tales, endless genealogies, and quarrels about words, irreverent babble, foolish and ignorant controversies that bred quarrels—ravaged the spiritual vitality of that church! This describes a sewage backup of "humonic" (human-demonic) words that putrefied God's words. Sick words cause sick souls. Paul commissioned Timothy to offer "sound teaching" or "healthy doctrine."

Have you ever suffered from tainted teaching, nitpicked words, and heated disputes? Have you ever found yourself entangled like a fly in a spider's web of irreverent babble, foolish controversy, and godless quarrel? At times the church can be a petri dish for malicious ministers who in the guise of "spirituality" and "truth" batter the faith and feelings of gullible or unguarded people. I experienced this when a group of church leaders met for three days to discuss the future of our conference. Well, it morphed from discussion to a mad mutiny, and from a mad mutiny to a boxing contest of combative personalities and philosophies of ministries—a dismal three days where one leader literally passed out on the floor! Another debacle occurred two years later at a board meeting where a heated vote was taken over a candidate. It did not go well. One leader commented to me a few weeks later, that he felt a demonic presence in both of those meetings!

With respect to church leaders, Spener addressed the issue of disputes and controversies in his day. He cites Lutheran theologian David Chytraeus, and advises, "That the study of theology should be carried on not by the strife of disputations but rather by the practice of piety." He cites Luther: "Truth is lost not by teaching but by disputing, for disputations bring with them this evil, that men's souls are, as it were, profaned, and when they are occupied with quarrels they neglect what is most important."[23] So, what is the application? Do not get entangled in corrupt and ungodly teaching, doctrine, controversies, babble, or quarrels. Rather, train yourself to be godly—*gymnasium* yourself for piety! Spener concludes: "How often the disputants themselves are persons without the Spirit and faith, filled with carnal wisdom drawn from the Scriptures, but not instructed by God! How often is unholy fire brought into the sanctuary of the Lord?—that is, an unholy intent, directed not to God's glory but to man's."[24]

What is the chief purpose of mankind?
To know God, serve God, and glorify him forever!

FOR REFLECTION AND PRACTICE

1. How would you define and describe biblical piety? How would you practice and pursue piety, through theology and training?
2. How does being entangled in or ensnared by corrupt teaching, controversies, or quarrels relate to your devotion to biblical piety? How can irreverent babble lead you into more and more ungodliness? Evaluate your interactions with people in terms of conversation or controversy. What changes and commitments might you need to make, when and how?

23. Spener, *Pia Desideria*, 50, 100.
24. Ibid., 100.

3. Evaluate your depth of devotion to biblical piety. If you desire for it to deepen, what is required? What changes and commitments will you make, when and how?

FOR PASTORS AND CHURCH LEADERS

1. Spiritual renewal of local churches is unlikely without the spiritual renewal of pastors and church leaders. As a pastor or church leader, the effectiveness of your ministry depends on the depth of your spiritual life—your piety. Evaluate your depth of devotion to biblical piety. What is required? What changes and commitments will you make?
2. The early Pietists pioneered innovative actions and teaching for spiritual renewal in the lifeless, institutional, corrupt church system of their day. If you desire to deepen the level of corporate devotion to biblical piety in your church, what are some specific measures, like Philipp Jakob Spener's approach in *Pia Desideria* (which you may want to read) that you might implement? How would you do it as leaders?

2

DEVOTION TO HEART RELIGION

Who is a Pietist? He who studies the Word of God
And accordingly leads a holy life.
This is well done, good for every Christian . . .
Piety above all must rest in the heart.[1]

IMAGINE THIS SCENE. ASSEMBLED before an aged king David is a vast bustling crowd of Israelite officials and warriors. This outgoing king delivers a stirring charge to his son Solomon, the nation's next king, and first Temple builder. Hushed leaders lean forward to listen. David counsels, "And you, my son Solomon, acknowledge the God of your father, and serve him with *wholehearted devotion* and with a *willing mind*, for the LORD searches every heart and understands every motive behind the thoughts" (1 Chr 28:9 NIV). The Hebrew phrase *wholehearted devotion* is literally "heart of shalom"—a whole, sound, and complete heart of peace. It matches a *willing mind*—literally, a "willing soul." The fuel of royal service is the devout life, which glows in the heart to acknowledge and serve God, with purity of intention. A royal prayer is for a united heart, "Teach me your way, O Lord, that I may rely on your faithfulness; give me an undivided heart,

1. A poem by Joachim Feller (1689), in response to an attack on "Pietists" by a University of Leipzig theology professor, Johann Carpoz, who intoned, "Our mission as professors is to make students more learned and not more pious," cited and translated by Dale Brown, *Understanding Pietism*, 13.

that I may fear your name. I will praise you, Lord my God, with all my heart; I will glorify your name forever" (Ps 86:11–12 NIV). The devout life fosters a renovated heart to fear a faithful God. Dallas Willard states: "We live from our heart . . . the greatest need of humanity—is *renovation of the heart*. That spiritual place within us from which outlook, choices, and actions come has been formed by a world away from God. Now it must be transformed."[2]

For Willard and the Pietists, piety and holiness require a renovation of the heart. It is not enough to staunchly defend purity of doctrine if we lack purity of heart. Like movie actors whose personal lives do not match their Oscar-winning performances, religion and ethics can default to external performances. Arndt argued, "True Christianity consists, not in words or in external show, but in living faith, from which arise righteous fruits, and all manner of Christian virtues, as from Christ Himself."[3] He asked, "What is Christian faith without a Christian life?"[4] There are dreadful cases where Christians can showcase attractive faith in public and yet commit unsightly actions in private. I know a pastor who is a remarkable preacher and thinker. He can charm people in meetings with his personality and ideas. But in private interactions, he can also bully people and gossip (likely a blind spot). He needs, as we all do, acute heart not just head renovation. Francke confessed: "I kept theology in my head and not in my heart, and it was much more a dead science than a living knowledge. I knew to be certain how to say well what is faith, regeneration, justification, renewal, etc. but of them all there existed nothing in my heart."[5]

The devout life fosters a renewal and strengthening of the *inner* self (2 Cor 4:16). We should pray, "that according to the riches of his glory he may grant us to be strengthened with power through his Spirit in our inner being, so that Christ may dwell in our hearts through faith" (Eph 3:16–17). To what degree does Christ reside in your heart? When the Spirit strengthens our inner person according to the wealth of God's glory, Christ will abide in us with his continual presence as we place our trust in him with an active faith. Arndt appealed: "Therefore, dear Christian! Let not your religion be confined to bare externals, but see that it proceeds from the more inward recesses of a heart endued with a true, living, and active faith, and with

2. Willard, *Renovation of the* Heart, 13–14.

3. Arndt, *True Christianity*, 23.

4. Ibid., 60.

5. Cited by Brown, *Understanding Pietism*, 73.

an unfeigned, inward, and daily repentance."[6] Is your heart endowed with a true, living, and active faith? Likewise, Jonathan Edwards taught, "True religion consists, in a great measure, in vigorous and lively actings of the inclination of the will of the soul, or the fervent exercises of the heart."[7] Is your will vigorous and lively with a fervent heart? Is it inclined and focused upward to behold God's spectacular glory with what John Piper calls a "Godward heart"?[8]

Your heart is the command center of your life—the deepest place of your affections, desires, and will—the sacred location of faith, feeling, and motives. What voice does your heart hear? Is it the voice of love, of poetry, of music, of art, of beauty? What stirs you—ideas that grab your mind or inspiration that grips your heart? Have you known someone who was heartless or have you ever suffered heartache? Have you had a heart-to-heart talk with someone or felt that your heart was not in a project? James K. A. Smith, a Reformed theologian influenced by Augustine, offers a compelling case where he asserts that you are what you love, and you are what you worship. He challenges the worldview that you are what you think. The heart is both a homing beacon and a compass that both orients and directs our loves. Our loves, which are more visceral and subconscious than intellectual, orient us toward a goal to fulfill our desires. Our loves are disordered through worldly cultural propaganda and practices. Discipleship is not chiefly an intellectual project where we acquire more information. Rather, "discipleship, we might say, is a way to curate your heart, to be attentive to and intentional about what you love."[9] Discipleship, then, is a transformational process that reorders and recalibrates the habits of your heart. Like a compass that always directs you to true north, your heart directs your life. Proverbs 4:23 advises, "Above all else, guard your heart, for everything you do flows from it" (NIV).

Puritan John Flavel bases his entire treatise on this verse in *A Saint Indeed or the Great Work of a Christian in Keeping the Heart in the Several Conditions of Life*. He wrote: "The *heart* of man is his worst part before it is regenerate, and the best afterwards: it is the seat of principles, and fountain of actions. The eye of God is, and the eye of a Christian ought to be, principally fixed upon it. The greatest difficulty in conversion is, to win the heart

6. Arndt, *True Christianity*, Christian Classics Ethereal Library, 237.

7. Edwards, *A Treatise on Religious Affections*, 14.

8. Piper, *A Godward Heart*.

9. Smith, *You Are What You Love*, 2.

to God; and the greatest difficulty after conversion, is, to keep the heart with God."[10]

Is your heart won to and kept with God? The English word *heart* occurs approximately one thousand times in Scripture, often disguised in translation, with an immense range of meaning.[11] In the Old Testament *heart* includes the *mind* (will) and the *spirit*. There is no specific word for *mind* in Hebrew as in Greek and English. The *spirit* is that immaterial empowered life principle part of you. The *soul* houses the heart and spirit, and refers to the whole person—to life—as when God breathed into Adam and he became a living soul—being, person (Gen 2:7). Like a computer operating system the soul interconnects all the dimensions of who you are. You express who you are at the deepest unified level with your heart and soul: "You will seek the Lord your God and you will find him, if you search after him with all your heart and with all your soul" (Deut 4:29).

THEOLOGIA CORDIS

Central to Pietism and the devout life is a love theology, a theology of the heart—*theologia cordis*. Paul writes, "The aim of our charge is love that issues from a pure heart and a good conscience and a sincere faith" (1 Tim 1:5). Piety requires purity of heart. Jesus promised, "Blessed are the pure in heart, for they shall see God" (Matt 5:8). Who you are influences what you see. The Greek for *pure* means, "unmixed or unalloyed." It is the quality of twenty-four carat gold, of corn without chaff, of a first-class army purged of cowards and critics. The pure in heart glow with humble brilliance like innocent newborns that beam as they gaze into their mother's eyes. The pure in heart have no deceit and no hypocrisy. Jesus said, "This people honors me with their lips, but their heart is far from me" (Matt 15:8), and "A good person produces good things from the treasury of a good heart, and an evil person produces evil things from the treasury of an evil heart. What you say flows from what is in your heart" (Luke 6:45 NLT). Glen G. Scorgie concludes, "As it turns out Jesus focused on the condition of a person's heart . . . The religion of Jesus remains a religion of the heart."[12] If we probed the treasury of your heart, what would we discover there—a tainted heart, an evil heart, a stubborn heart, a conflicted heart, a pure heart? Let us, "flee the

10. Flavel, *A Saint Indeed*, 12.

11. Elwell, "Heart," 938.

12. Scorgie, "Religion of the Heart," 6.

evil desires of youth, and pursue righteousness, faith, love and peace, along with those who call on the Lord out of a *pure heart*" (2 Tim 2:22).

We face a sober reality: "The heart is deceitful above all things, and desperately sick; who can understand it? 'I the Lord search the heart and test the mind, to give every man according to his ways, according to the fruit of his deeds'" (Jer. 17:9–10). The *Book of Common Prayer* expresses: "Almighty and most merciful Father, we have erred and strayed from thy ways like lost sheep, we have followed too much the devices and desires of our own hearts." We can harbor insincere hearts. Like tin, they are mixed and impure. Your home might appear sound on the outside, but home inspectors can discover concealed problems. In public, you might announce an undying love for your church, but in private you then malign it with icy criticism. Or you "sacrifice" your time and money for a mission trip to Mexico, or agree to be a church board member, but your heart craves recognition. These deeds appear noble, but God judges our heart.

Wide open to God's X-ray view, yet concealed from human inspection, are our inmost thoughts and intentions. God scrupulously judges what my deeds deserve. My heart and mind produce them. It is astounding that, "The same heart that can be 'deceitful above all things, and desperately wicked' (Jer 17:9) can also become the shrine of divine love and the Spirit (Rom 5:5)."[13] When we honestly probe the deep treasury of our heart, we will discover a complex montage of ingredients that includes our thoughts, intentions, desires, and emotions. It likely will not always be attractive. We may uncover some foul ingredients—suppressed mental and emotional habits and subtle inclinations that contaminate our lives, "for out of the heart come evil thoughts, murder, adultery, sexual immorality, theft, false witness, slander" (Matt 15:19). We can secretly commit these atrocities in our hearts without any visible actions.

There is widespread teaching these days that claims personal transformation is achieved through "emotionally healthy spirituality." The Pietists believed there was an overlooked emotional side to spiritual vitality. Spener, and especially Francke, stressed the *experience* of God's grace and truth as a catalyst for wholesome feelings associated with faith, joy, comfort, and especially repentance. Because Pietism stressed an affective side to faith, its theology of experience made it vulnerable to charges of emotionalism, individualism, and subjectivism. Yet Spener remarked, "True belief is not so much felt emotionally as known by its fruits of love and obedience to

13. Elwell, "Heart," 939.

God."[14] We know the heart generates a range of emotions from despair to joy, from anger to affection. Our hearts need healing. When David sinned with Bathsheba, he affirmed of God, "Behold, you delight in truth in the inward being, and you teach me wisdom in the secret heart" (Ps 51:6). Take heart!

Fortunately, God can renovate your heart. He achieves it through the word of the gospel with the gift of the Holy Spirit and cleansing activated by faith. Peter announces: "The Gentiles should hear the word of the gospel and believe. And God, who knows the heart, bore witness to them, by giving them the Holy Spirit just as he did to us, and he made no distinction between us and them, having cleansed [purified] their hearts by faith" (Acts 15:7–9). God offers us the combination of belief and faith that opens wide the dike to release the river of renewal that will flood our hearts with the transformational power of the word and the Spirit.

The zenith of *theologia cordis* is Mark 12:29–31, "Jesus answered, "The most important is, 'Hear, O Israel: The Lord our God, the Lord is one. And you shall love the Lord your God *with all your heart* and with all your soul and with all your mind and with all your strength.' The second is this: 'You shall love your neighbor as yourself.' There is no other commandment greater than these." Jesus cites Deuteronomy 6:4, the Jewish *Shema* (love God), and Leviticus 19:18 (love neighbor). This is Pietist love theology—devotion to heart religion. Arndt comments: "The love of God and the love of neighbor are one thing and must not be divided. The true divine love cannot be better noted or proven than in the love of neighbor (1 John 4:20–21) . . . Faith demonstrates that the love of God and man make a true Christian."[15] This is a missional spirituality—"an embodied love for God and neighbor expressed from the inside out."[16] Our love for God will parallel our love for others. "If we love our neighbors as we love ourselves, we shall want for them the treatment we should want for ourselves, were we in their place."[17]

We do not merely love God and others *with* our hearts as an instrument, but *from* our hearts as a region. Oscar Wilde commented, "Keep love in your heart. A life without it is like a sunless garden when the flowers are dead." When the artesian spring of a pure heart that loves God surges, it

14. Brown, *Understanding Pietism*, 76.

15. Arndt, *True Christianity*, 126–27.

16. Helland and Hjalmarson, *Missional Spirituality*, 31.

17. Wessel, *Mark*, 737, citing Mitton, *Gospel of Mark*, 99.

irrigates and quenches your soul, mind, and strength, and those around you. The two sections of the Ten Commandments reveal the structure of love for God and neighbor (Ex 20:1–11, 12–17). Love is the fulfillment of the law (Rom 13:8–10; Gal 5:14). Piety is *relational* (John 13:34). Jon Stewart said, "Remember to love your neighbor as you love yourself. And if you hate yourself, then please—just leave your neighbor alone."[18]

What is often overlooked here is the role of the *spoken* confession of theology and its inner work in our hearts that shape our piety: "*Hear* O Israel, the Lord our God, the Lord is One. You shall love the Lord your God with all your heart and with all your soul and with all your might. And these words that I command you today shall be on your *heart*" (Deut 6:4–6). And, "But you shall love your neighbor as yourself: I am the Lord" (Lev 19:18). We could say out loud, "Listen church, God is personal, supreme, and unique. Therefore, love him from your whole being. Etch these commands on your heart. And love others as yourself. He is the Lord!" In Scripture, to hear or listen also means to *obey*. To confess theology with our mouths and believe it with our hearts activates salvation—the obedience of faith (Rom 16:26). Paul teaches:

> But what does it say? "The word is near you; it is in your mouth and in your heart," that is, the message concerning faith that we proclaim: If you declare with your mouth, "Jesus is Lord," and believe in your *heart* that God raised him from the dead, you will be saved. For it is with your *heart* that you believe and are justified, and it is with your mouth that you profess your faith and are saved (Rom 10:8–10).

The Pietists developed a theology of regeneration. The regenerate life occupies the cathedral of the heart. Anglican John Wesley embodied a *theologia cordis*. He viewed Christian vocation as "faith working in love" with holiness of heart and life, informed by a love for God and neighbor. Observe his Pietist progress in the devout life:

> In the year 1726, I met with Kempis's "Christian's Pattern." The nature and extent of inward religion, the religion of the heart, now appeared to me in a stronger light than ever it had done before. I saw, that giving even all my life to God—supposing it possible to do this, and go no farther would profit me nothing, unless I gave my heart, yea, all my heart, to him. I saw, that "simplicity of intention, and purity of affection," one design in all we speak or

18. Quoted by Dark, *The Sacredness of Questioning Everything*, 9.

> do, and one desire ruling all our tempers, are indeed "the wings of the soul" without which she can never ascend to the mount of God. A year or two after, Mr. Law's *Christian Perfection* and *Serious Call* were put into my hands. These convinced me, more than ever, of the absolute impossibility of being half a Christian; and I determined, through His grace, (the absolute necessity of which I was deeply sensible of) to be all devoted to God, to give Him all my soul, my body, and my substance.[19]

THE CATHEDRAL OF THE HEART

Years ago, while in Paris, I visited Notre Dame Cathedral. It is considered one of the most famous and finest examples of French Gothic architecture. Construction began in 1163 during the reign of King Louis VII and was completed in 1345. The surface area of this cathedral is 5,500 square meters. The sanctuary stirs your imagination and emotions by its immaculate grandeur and colossal dimensions. Technically, a cathedral is the "seat of a bishop" for a diocese. But as its sacred function inspires your reverence, you conclude that this is a "house of God!"

Your heart is God's cathedral, the place of his indwelling (2 Cor 1:22; Gal 4:6; Eph 3:17). He has direct access to your will, thoughts, intentions, and emotions. Pray that God would "grant you to be strengthened with power through his Spirit in your inner being, so that Christ may dwell in your heart through faith" (Eph 3: 16–17). To *dwell* is a strong image. It means to take up residence, settle down, and inhabit. If you bought an old ramshackle house, settled in, and started to renovate it, that home would eventually reflect your personality and values. You would work on the kitchen, bathrooms, bedrooms, and living room and make them your own. Christ will renovate your old ramshackle heart and form it into a new cathedral to house his holy personality and values. In 1876 Jean Sophia Pigott composed a poem that reflects this idea:

> Make my life a bright outshining
> Of thy life, that all may see
> Thine own resurrection power
> Mightily put forth in me.

19. Wesley, *A Plain Account of Christian Perfection*, 3.

Ever let my heart become
Yet more consciously Thy home.[20]

Just as Notre Dame Cathedral underwent several renovations over the centuries, you need Christ to renovate the cathedral of your heart. Perhaps you attempted to get the project going. You tried inadequate methods like will power or positive thinking. Or you went forward to rededicate your life, or made an appointment to see a Christian counselor. You worked to change yourself. You resolved to be a better person this year. You read good books or took a course on spiritual formation. Like a contractor who merely paints over a wall damaged by water rather than first replace the drywall, you will not see true renovation. If you have gripping fear, anxiety, or lust, or if you have obsessive thoughts that compel you to make self-destructive choices, then at the source, you have a "heart problem." Behavioral modification or mere counseling will not renovate it. Let me suggest three biblical practices to serve as a blueprint for heart renovation.

First, "Keep your heart with all vigilance, for from it flow the springs of life" (Prov 4:23). The Hebrew is literally, "guard your heart with all guarding" or "keep watch over your heart with all watchfulness." Puritan John Flavel stated: "That the keeping, and right managing of the heart in every condition, is the great business of a Christian's life."[21] Slowly read this quote again. What do you think? To keep—watch, guard, protect—your heart requires that you cultivate a single-willed and single-minded attentiveness toward your life. "Purity of heart," Kierkegaard wrote, "is to will one thing." James says that a double-minded person is unstable in all his ways (Jas 1:8)—literally a person of "two souls"—a split personality! Like the adage, "It's hard to ride two horses at the same time." Even for Superman, Batman, or Spider-Man, it is an enormous challenge to live two lives.

Like an alert sentinel, do not sleep on guard duty. Watch! When that attractive married person enters the room, or enters your eyes from a website, and you feel that warm infatuation, at once your emotional default must say "no." When someone treats you with contempt, check your inner world and surrender that rising anger and vengeance to the Lord, by the Spirit. Hold your tongue and forgive. When you feel that chronic fear, compulsive greed, or critical spirit begin to engulf you, choose the opposite spirit. Watch your heart often. John Flavel says:

20. Cited by Carson, *Praying With Paul*, 165.

21. Flavel, *A Saint Indeed*, 13.

> Frequent observation of the frame of the heart, turning in and examining how the case stands with it; this is one part of the work: carnal and formal persons take no heed to this, they cannot be brought to confer with their own hearts; there are some men and women that have lived forty or fifty years in the world, and have scarce had one hour's discourse with their own hearts all that while: it is a hard thing to bring a man and himself together upon such an account; but saints know those soliloquies and self-conferences to be of excellent use and advantage.[22]

Second, maintain a soft, believing, purified heart towards the Lord. It is common, if not watched, for our hearts to become cynical and despondent toward God. Trials and misfortunes can lead to disappointment and disbelief. Hard knocks can form hard hearts. The book of Hebrews offers another set of practices to cultivate devotion to heart religion. The writer addresses a group of Jewish Christians who suffered severe trials, persecution, and ridicule because of their new Christian faith (Heb 10:32–36). The infernos of trial were so unbearable that they wanted to jettison Jesus. They needed to *hear* God's voice and persevere in faith. The author cited a parallel issue that Israel faced under Moses during the wilderness wandering in the book of Numbers. At the crazed intersection of unbelief and hard hearts is bad theology. He also cited Psalm 95:

> Therefore, as the *Holy Spirit says*, "Today, if you hear his voice, do not harden your *hearts* as in the rebellion, on the day of testing in the wilderness, where your fathers put me to the test and saw my works for forty years. Therefore, I was provoked with that generation, and said, 'They always go astray in their *heart*; they have not known my ways.' As I swore in my wrath, 'They shall not enter my rest.'" Take care, brothers, lest there be in any of you an evil, unbelieving *heart*, leading you to fall away from the living God. But exhort one another every day, as long as it is called "today," that none of you may be hardened by the deceitfulness of sin (Heb 3:7–13).

It is imperative that we hear how God speaks to us in our tough situations, and that we know his ways. Remember, we need good theology to know God and good training to follow God—especially when the going gets tough. If we permit our hearts to go astray and become sinful and unbelieving, we harden our hearts by willful rebellion. Look at rebellion in the world. Look at it in your own life or in your family. What causes it?

22. Ibid., 16.

Is it not hard hearts—sinful, defiant, and deceived? The result is unrest! There is a corporate way to help us watch our hearts, so we do not have to tough it out alone, "But encourage one another daily, as long as it is called "Today," so that none of you may be hardened by sin's deceitfulness" (Heb 3:13). And finally:

> And since we have a great priest over the house of God, let us draw near with a *true heart* in full assurance of faith, with our *hearts* sprinkled clean from an evil conscience and our bodies washed with pure water. Let us hold fast the confession of our hope without wavering, for he who promised is faithful (Heb 10:21–23).

Third, guard and guide your heart with God's word. Practice and pray this text: "How can a young man keep his way pure? By guarding it according to your word. With my *whole heart,* I seek you; let me not wander from your commandments! I have stored up your word *in my heart*, that I might not sin against you" (Ps 119:9–11). To keep your way, your course of life pure, you must guard it. Keep watch over it with God's word (*debar*). This is God's dynamic speech-word as the sum of what he has spoken, particularly as a word or command for action.

This passage especially applies to young adults who face constant moral pressure. This echoes Proverbs 4:23, which advises us to guard our hearts. Let us pray, like the Psalmist, with our whole heart—with singular focus—that God would not let us wander, swerve, or turn astray from his commandments like an ignorant lost sheep or an intoxicated fool. Saturated with prayer, we must deliberately store up—hide, conceal, treasure—God's word (*imrah*) in our hearts that we might not sin against him. In this verse, the Hebrew for God's *word* refers to the content of what God *says*. This includes Scripture, but it also includes any way in which God might speak to us. What God says comes to us in his word, written or otherwise. Scripture is not merely a record of what God *spoke*, but also of what God *speaks*. Many of us store up what our parents spoke to us as children and continue to hear them speak those words to us today.

In countless churches, we have extensive dimness in Bible literacy and ignorance about how to hear God's voice. Many Christians do not seem to value and do not know how to read, listen to, or store up God's word and what he says to them in their hearts. This refers to more than mere Bible memorization. To *store up* means to conceal, treasure, and stockpile God's word. Lovers store up in their hearts what they say to each other, where they can treasure and recall those words repeatedly. Women are especially prone to save letters or remember words from their loved ones. Those who live the devout life do the same with God's words.

Have you heard of "method actors?" These actors internalize their scripts and create in themselves the thoughts and feelings of their characters to enable lifelike performances. What could happen if you adopted a similar approach to real live performances of your Christian life? As I have, let us say you selected the final "script" of Colossians to internalize and live out, and to use as a source through which you will hear God personally speak to you. You slowly read and ingest your *script*-ure portion for each scene of your day. As you head out, you closely monitor your heart so it does not get distracted as you also store up what the Scripture says and pray that God, like a director, helps you stay in character. You think about specific verses and passages and themes of Scripture. Almost intuitively, with improvisation in the moment, you let it direct your heart and open a wavelength to hear God speak to you. As you go about your day, you recall the word and hear God say to you: "Therefore, as you received Christ Jesus the Lord, so walk in him" (Col 2:6). Invite Jesus into this important meeting today. Pause and consider his rule in your thoughts. Listen before you speak. Abide in him! Perhaps later that day, your co-workers draw you into a heated conversation of personal attacks, slander, and four-letter words about your boss. You feel they have a plausible case, but stored in your heart from your reading that day was: "You must put them all away: anger, wrath, malice, slander, and obscene talk from your mouth" (Col 3:8). Be vigilant in God's word to guard and guide your heart.

For good Pietist preaching, preachers should also aim at the heart of the hearers, not simply at the head, without flashy displays of academic information and rhetoric. Spener exhorts:

> The pulpit is not the place for an ostentatious display of one's skill. It is rather the place to preach the Word of the Lord plainly but powerfully . . . Our whole Christian religion consists of the inner man or the new man, whose soul is faith and whose expressions are the fruits of life, and all sermons should be aimed at this . . . and presented in such a way that faith, and hence the inner man, may ever be strengthened . . . It is not enough that we hear the Word with our outward ear, but must let it penetrate to our heart, so that we may hear the Holy Spirit speak there . . . Since the real power of Christianity consists of this, it would be proper if sermons, on the whole, were pointed in such a direction.[23]

23. Spener, *Pia Desideria*, 116–17.

The evangelical church largely falters in spiritual and missional vitality and discipleship, and pastors feel that the most critical elements of discipleship are matters of the heart rather than of structure. Let us rediscover and release that initial Pietist impulse that swells in devotion to heart religion. For enduring spiritual renewal, let us regularly pray: "Create in me a clean heart, O God, and renew a right spirit within me" (Ps 51:10).

John Wesley translated a wonderful hymn composed by the great Christ-centered Nikolaus von Zinzendorf. Pray or sing it today:

1 O thou to whose all-searching sight
The darkness shineth as the light,
Search, prove my heart; it pants for thee;
Oh, burst these bands and set it free!

2 Wash out its stains, refine its dross,
Nail my affections to the Cross;
Hallow each thought; let all within
Be clean, as thou, my Lord, art clean!

3 If in this darksome wild I stray,
Be thou my light, be thou my way;
No foes, no violence I fear,
No fraud, while thou, my God, art near.

4 Savior, where'er thy steps I see,
Dauntless, untired, I follow thee!
Oh, let thy hand support me still,
And lead me to thy holy hill!

5 When rising floods my soul o'erflow,
When sinks my heart in waves of woe,
Jesus, thy timely aid impart,
And raise my head, and cheer my heart.

6 If rough and thorny be the way,
My strength proportion to my day;
Till toil, and grief, and pain shall cease,
Where all is calm, and joy, and peace.

FOR REFLECTION AND PRACTICE

1. When you ponder David's charge to his son Solomon to serve God with wholehearted devotion (1 Chr 28:9), what comes to mind, what does this mean? How would you rate your own depth of devotion to a Pietist understanding of heart religion?
2. What is required for a biblical renovation of the heart? Describe the idea of *theologia cordis*.
3. Describe and develop some key ways you plan to implement or improve your life by the three suggested biblical practices that serve as a blueprint for heart renovation.

FOR PASTORS AND CHURCH LEADERS

1. Pastors and church leaders often resort to structural methods to incite renewal in their churches. How would you address the deeper issues of devotion to heart religion in your own life and leadership, and how would you seek to address this in your church context?
2. What plan or strategy do you have, or might you develop, to facilitate the renovation of the heart as a church-wide venture to stimulate spiritual renewal? How would you modify your preaching and teaching to address matters of the heart more than just more material for the head?

3

DEVOTION TO PURE DOCTRINE AND LIFE

"How can the truth of pure doctrine be upheld without a holy life?"[1]

(JOHANN ARNDT)

YEARS AGO, I SAT hushed and humbled in a graduate theology class at Dallas Theological Seminary, rattled with a jumble of anxiety and excitement. Dr. J. Lanier Burns, a genteel yet calculated man, launched our class into an excursion of enormous depth with a doctrinal study of the person and work of Jesus Christ—Christology. We explored the vast terrain of the second person of the Trinity. We probed specific biblical passages and surveyed assorted theological views—both miniscule and magnificent. Over time, I watched pure doctrine and life in action, incarnated, infused, in and through the head, heart, and hands of this remarkable theology professor. Like a true Reformed Pietist, Dr. Burns modeled the devout life.

Recently, I had coffee with a long-time friend and colleague. We discussed the condition of our conference, and our pastors—some of whom were angry and combative—and of our own lives. We mused on the dire necessity for today's church and culture to behold glorious theology that adorns godly pastors.

"Do you see a future for our movement?" he asked.

1. Arndt, *True Christianity*, 175.

I replied, "What makes a movement a movement is where things actually *move*. Think of the civil rights movement led by Martin Luther King Jr., or the Charismatic movement, or the Methodist or Moravian movements, or the Pietist movement. What do they have in common?"

"A unified vision with an unrelenting focus and energy for change," he replied.

I agreed. We also mused on the character of a seminary professor we knew.

"I don't know the future of this prof. Though his students seem to like him, among his colleagues he's prickly and contentious," my friend said.

"It's difficult to fuel a movement where pastors and professors lead lives that don't match their theology, when their conduct or character shackles the cause of Christ," I reflected.

ORTHODOX BELIEF AND BEHAVIOR

To plunge the depths of spiritual renewal, we need a snug alliance between pure doctrine and pure living. Olson and Winn state, "Pietism embraced and accepted *orthodox Protestant Christian doctrine, broadly defined*," though as an exception, some individual Pietists deviated from it.[2] The early Pietists, as dedicated Lutherans, maintained the grand doctrines of the Protestant Reformation. But these only mattered insofar as pastors, professors, and people lived them out through a practical faith, rather than merely assented to them as an abstract faith. John Weborg writes, "If in Orthodoxy doctrine was tested by Scripture, in Pietism life was tested."[3]

Spener and the early Pietists sought to connect an objective faith in justification with a subjective faith in sanctification. In justification, God declares a believer righteous through an intellectual faith. He removes your guilt. Like a legal verdict, salvation is received not achieved. It is the indicative—you believed God; you are righteous; God is *for* you. In sanctification, God works to transform a believer into righteousness through an inward faith. He removes your sin. Like a summons to action, salvation is spent not banked. It is the imperative—keep on believing God; continue to become righteous. God is *in* you. Dale W. Brown writes:

2. Olson and Winn, *Reclaiming Pietism*, 85.

3. Weborg, "Reborn to Renew."

> Pietism reiterated the motif that the reformation of doctrine, which had been initiated by Luther, must embody a new reformation of life. Pietism shifted the center of interest from maintenance of orthodox doctrine to the practice of piety, from the objective form to the subjective appropriation of doctrinal precepts and from the fact of salvation to the moral obligation of the saved . . . Instead of charging that Pietism developed no theology because of its emphasis on practice and life, it is more accurate to maintain that it fostered a different theology: namely, a theology of [Christian] experience, of regeneration, or of devotion.[4]

Spener offered a challenge for professors and students of theology. He wrote: "Since theology is a practical discipline, everything must be directed to the practice of faith and life . . . We show ourselves to be Christians and theologians by our godly faith, holy living, and love of God and neighbor rather than by our subtle and sophistical argumentation."[5] Professors were to be teachers and spiritual directors, and the seminary was to be a Pietist nursery that planted the seed of pure doctrine into the soil of life. Mere knowledge of Christian faith does not suffice. Demons have that! Spener wrote: "The people must have impressed upon them and must accustom themselves to believing that *it is by no means enough to have knowledge of the Christian faith, for Christianity consists rather of practice*."[6] The mark of Christian doctrine and discipleship was a practical rather than an intellectual love for God and neighbor.

A pastor sent me an email with some prayer requests. One was that I pray, "for his people to grasp the truth of Scripture and to be more than intellectual in their faith." Bam! As disciples, followers, pupils, and apprentices of Jesus our Rabbi and Teacher, we must learn how to live in him, and we "ought to walk in the same way in which he walked" (1 John 2:6). Pure Christian doctrine gives us the content of our faith, and shows us how Jesus walked (lived).

Paul advised Timothy the young pastor, to help him straighten warped church matters in Ephesus. He warned, "Watch your life and doctrine closely. Persevere in them, because if you do, you will save both yourself and your hearers" (1 Tim 4:16 NIV). The first two verbs are present tense: "Continually fix attention on yourself, and to the teaching. Continually persist in this, for by doing so, you will rescue both you and your hearers." Paul

4. Brown, *Understanding Pietism*, 57, 59.

5. Spener, *Pia Desideria*, 105, 112.

6. Ibid., 95.

wrote: "If you put these things before the brothers, you will be a good servant of Christ Jesus, being trained in the words of the faith and of the good doctrine that you have followed" (1 Tim 4:6). Donald Bloesch writes: "One cannot speak of the renewal of devotion without stressing the importance of theology. Devotion to Jesus Christ cannot long maintain itself apart from theological fidelity and integrity. A holy life divorced from sound doctrine soon becomes moralism. At the same time, correct doctrine apart from a holy life is nothing other than intellectualism."[7] For pastors and leaders, Paul advises, "Pay careful attention to yourselves and to all the flock, in which the Holy Spirit has made you overseers [elders], to care for [pastor] the church of God" (Acts 20:28). We must uphold a sacred and seamless congruence between our personal lives and our pastoral leadership.

Continue to keep a close watch on your life as you also continue to keep a close watch on your teaching (doctrine). As good servants (literally *deacons*), we are to follow the good doctrine, not just believe it. We should superimpose our life onto the template of pristine Christian doctrine and re-adjust it as needed to keep us aligned with high-definition clarity. Sound morals align with sound doctrine, which align with the gospel (1 Tim 1:10–11). And sound or healthy teaching aligns with godliness (piety): "If anyone teaches a different doctrine and does not agree with the *sound* words of our Lord Jesus Christ and the teaching that accords with godliness [*eusebeia*, piety], he is puffed up with conceit and understands nothing" (1 Tim 6:3–4). Sound or healthy words, teaching, and doctrine are vital for healthy congregational life, godliness, and faith (cf. 1 Tim 1:10; 6:3; 2 Tim 1:13; 4:3; Titus 1:9; 1:13; 2:1–2). Eugene Peterson remarks:

> The phrase "sound words" or "sound doctrine," as J.N.D. Kelly puts it, expresses [Paul's] conviction that a morally disordered life is, as it were, diseased and stands in need of treatment . . . whereas a life based on the teaching of the Gospel is clean and healthy. The Greek word for "sound" is *hygiein*, from which we get hygiene. The main thing that Timothy is to do in Ephesus in order to clean up the mess is to teach sound words, sound truth, healthy thinking and believing. Verbal hygiene. Healthy gospel.[8]

Johann Arndt asked: "Because Christ and faith are denied by an ungodly life and almost done away with, what will happen to his doctrine?"[9]

7. Bloesch, *The Crisis of Piety*, 3.

8. Dawn and Peterson, *The Unnecessary Pastor*, 131–32.

9. Arndt, *True Christianity*, 169.

Great question! I want healthy belief and behavior, don't you? In our conference, like other denominations, when we grant credentials to pastors, we require that they sign our statement of faith and code of ethics. We also ask them to read two books and develop a plan for their spiritual upkeep. Many evangelical churches invite people to become members. They usually require them to also sign a statement of faith and a membership covenant. In both cases the expectation is for people to believe and behave in noble ways. However, over time, we might witness defects of behavior connected to defects of belief. I have heard Hugh Halter say, "Whatever is not transformed is transmitted!"

Perhaps that successful businesswoman and astute Bible teacher with a charming personality who serves on several ministry teams, commited to marginalized people and social justice, turns out to be an overbearing and divisive driver who holds the pastor and church hostage through her dogmatic views and steely control. One look at her library reveals that her main diet of leadership philosophy is drawn from secular sources and Oprah-style spirituality, merged with a social gospel. Or that endearing pastor and captivating preacher with musical talent and warm wit, who grew the church from forty to four hundred, turns out to be an insecure, self-absorbed narcissist who knows theology, but does not know himself or God. One look at his track record reveals a trail of used, hurt, and discarded people who no longer serve his interests. His real view of "servant leadership" works itself out as style rather than as substance to persuade people to follow *his* vision for *his* church. Bad belief seeds bad behavior. Bad root breeds bad fruit.

How can some churchgoing people and pastors, who read their Bibles and pray, when overcome with calamity or consternation, choose to grab the bottle, watch soap operas, surf internet porn sites, drain their bank accounts, cash in their marriages for a one-night fling, or pop pills to end it all? Some cheap lie, some grinding pattern, some coping tool, or some dastardly philosophy, sent their soul to the "dark side of the force," which betrayed and blackened them. The drift to the edge is often subtle, like a tire low on air that gradually pulls the car to the right and into the ditch before we realize it. If we let the dog into the house, it is tough to get him out! We must re-calibrate the task of theology to serve as a tool for devotion. Puritan William Ames wrote: "Theology is the doctrine of living to God . . .

men live to God when they live in accord with the will of God, to the glory of God, and with God working in them."[10]

Depression and anger, suicidal thoughts, personality and eating disorders, control issues, and addictions of all brands, are not easily dislodged from people's lives. It is difficult for *me* to change! Sin plagues humanity and runs as deep and steep as the Grand Canyon. And yet, *we can no longer live as we once did because we are no longer the people we once were.* Peter shows the way: "Having purified your souls by your *obedience to the truth* for a sincere brotherly love, love one another earnestly *from a pure heart*, since you have been born again, not of perishable seed but of imperishable, through the living and abiding word of God" (1 Pet 1:22–23). That is doctrine and life Krazy-glued together. We secured permanently purified souls (perfect tense) by our obedience to pure doctrine (gospel truth). This sustains a pure life because we are permanently born again (perfect tense) by the living and abiding word of God. Orthodox belief must lead to orthodox behavior, and love is orthodox piety in action, with doctrine and devotion.

DOCTRINE AND DEVOTION

Peter Vogt writes: "In 1738 the poet Isaac Watts wrote a letter of recommendation to President Edward Holyoke of Harvard College: 'He is a Person of uncommon Zeal and Piety, & of an Evangelic Spirit.' The person in question was Nikolaus Ludwig von Zinzendorf, Imperial Count of the Holy Roman Empire and leader of the renewed Moravian Church, one of the most colorful and intriguing figures of eighteenth century Pietism."[11]

Zinzendorf was a descendant of Austrian nobility reared by his maternal grandmother who supported Lutheran Pietism. In 1722, He founded the *Herrnhut* colony on the East German border, which developed into a vibrant experimental Pietist community comprised of spiritual exiles and seekers from all over Germany. It flourished as an interdenominational center for spiritual renewal and global missions. What fuelled his passion and leadership was Christ-centered doctrine and devotion— "To know nothing except Jesus Christ and him crucified (1 Cor 2:2) summarizes the essence of the Christian faith. For Zinzendorf, Christology is thus not simply one area of Christian doctrine among others, it is the beginning and end of *all*

10. Ames, *The Marrow of Theology*, I.I.1.6.

11. Vogt, "Nikolaus Ludwig von Zinzendorf," 207.

theology."[12] He stressed one's personal relationship to Christ with an emotional as well as an intellectual side, branded as the "religion of the heart."

> Zinzendorf's influence is felt much wider than in the Moravian Church. His emphasis on the "religion of the heart" deeply influenced John Wesley. He is remembered today, as Karl Barth put it, as "perhaps the only genuine Christocentric of the modern age." Scholar George Forell put it more succinctly: Zinzendorf was "the noble Jesus freak."[13]

Christ-centered doctrine and devotion will fortify our ability to watch our life and doctrine and practice the devout life for spiritual renewal. When we view the vast panorama of both Old and New Testaments, Christ is an interpretive prism. Through him we can see the brilliant light of the Christian faith separated into its doctrinal colors.[14] All the grand doctrines of God, creation, the kingdom, humanity, the gospel, salvation, the Spirit, sanctification, the Scripture, the church, mission and discipleship, the end times, and so on, find ultimate expression in and through the person and work of the Lord Jesus Christ—Christology.

Over the centuries theology morphed into an academic science to discuss God and offer a systematic and rational explanation of the Bible, its "textbook." For example, "Jesus died for our sins" can lead to a meticulous harangue of why, how, and for who he died, and the meaning of sin, and whether he died as a substitute or on our behalf, along with a penchant to debate the theories of the atonement. Or, "Jesus is Lord" can lead to a deadpan analysis of the historical name *Jesus*, the cultural background of the term *Lord*, and whether this was simply the first Christian creed or a counter-cultural political statement against Rome.

The Pietists reacted to the task of scholastic theology in their day, which used Scripture as a source for Lutheran confessions and doctrine amid hair-splitting controversies. We should study the Christian faith with rigor and accuracy, but the task should be a quest for piety shaped by doctrine. I embrace the main contours of Pietism, but I also align with Donald Bloesch, who expresses his simultaneous indebtedness and break from Pietism. He writes:

12. Ibid., 211.

13. Galli and Olson, "Nikolaus von Zinzendorf."

14. See Ferguson, "Preaching Christ From the Old Testament."

> I am profoundly indebted to the movement of Pietism for its stress on life in unity with doctrine, on regeneration with justification, on the Spirit in unity with the Word, on costly discipleship over subscription to a creed, and on the "church within the church." My break with Pietism lies in my appreciation for creeds as well as for experience, my emphasis on the gospel before the law, and my contention that the theological has priority over the practical. What I call for is a marriage between Pietism and orthodoxy, a theology of Word and Spirit.[15]

He goes on to reflect, as I do: "In the earlier part of my theological journey, the emphasis was on faith seeking understanding (Anselm) . . . The later part of my spiritual journey has revolved around *faith in search of obedience* . . . a faith that is intent on exploring the ramifications of a lifelong commitment to Christ. It is not enough to believe in Jesus: we must follow him in faith and obedience and live out the implications of faith with the aid of the Holy Spirit."[16]

When I study Scripture and theology, I do so in an ambience of prayer and devotion to fortify my faith and service to Christ. All biblical roads eventually lead to Jesus Christ, the Way, the Truth, and the Life. We access God solely through him. It takes only one excursion through the book of Colossians to prove this point, and to grapple with the significance that "all things were created through him and for him. And he is before all things, and in him all things hold together. And he is the head of the body, the church" (Col 1:16–18). The greater our devotion to pure doctrine—which displays the radiant red, green, and blue hues of Christ's splendor—the greater will be our devotion to him in magnificent surrender and to a pure life.[17] When his impeccable love, grace, forgiveness, and holiness seize our hearts, we should also then crave to live our lives permeated by impeccable love, grace, forgiveness, and holiness. Regularly read good books on theology and the devotional life. As we study our Christian faith it will illumine our understanding of the world. C.S Lewis wrote, "I believe in Christianity as I believe that the Sun has risen not only because I see it but because by it I see everything else."[18]

15. Bloesch, *The Paradox of Holiness—Faith in Search of Obedience*, 55.
16. Ibid., 60–61.
17. See, Helland, *Magnificent Surrender.*
18. C.S. Lewis Institute, "Christianity Makes Sense of the World."

In addition, a renewed interest in the use of *catechism* (instruction) to learn and teach doctrine for devotion is something you might restore in your discipleship strategy. The chief practice in discipleship is learning (Matt 28:20). Marilyn Monroe mused, "I believe in everything, a little bit." In today's postmodern world, with its smorgasbord of Oprah-type options, people pick and choose to believe in everything—a little bit—if it works for them. Postmoderns feel that truth is relative and absolute truth is unobtainable. The church has an educational task to orient believers in Christian truth.

Spener leveraged *catechism*. To foster Pietist discipleship, he published *The Spiritual Priesthood*—seventy questions and answers based on Scripture whereby common Christians would understand the nature and responsibilities of their priestly service.[19] Spener also connected catechism to regeneration, baptism, and communion. Believers are immersed in the washing of regeneration and renewal of the Holy Spirit (Titus 3:5), and baptism portrays their new birth. He argued that Christians must return to and make constant use of their baptism as a lifelong renewing force with sincere repentance, "Accordingly, if your Baptism is to benefit you, it must remain in constant use throughout your life."[20] He also taught that communion—the Lord's Supper—strengthened believers in faith and nourished their souls in Christ. As with baptism, it is concerned with the inner man, "Nor is it enough to have received the Lord's Supper externally, but the inner man must truly be fed with that blessed food."[21]

Church leaders are responsible to teach and preach sound doctrine, the gospel, the faith, and the word as passed on, received, and believed by the church (1 Tim 6:3–4; 2 Tim 1:13–24; 2:14–15; 4:2–3; Titus 1:9; 2:1; Mark 16:15; 1 Thess 3:2; 1 Cor 15:1–8). Catechism or instruction in the faith, is "*the church's ministry of grounding and growing God's people in the gospel and its implications for doctrine, devotion, duty, and delight*."[22] A passionate and interactive use (not a mechanical use) of available historic and contemporary catechisms can increase Bible, theological, and gospel literacy in our churches. Few churches have a strategy to teach their children up through the adults the basics of the Christian faith and the storyline of the Bible. To learn the Apostles' Creed, the Ten Commandments, the Lord's

19. Spener, *Pietists: Selected Writings*, 50–64.

20. Spener, *Pia Desideria*, 66.

21. Ibid., 117.

22. Packer and Parrett, *Grounded in the Gospel*, 29.

Prayer, the gospel, the sacraments, and basic Christian doctrine is a lost historic practice in discipleship these days. We teach membership classes to orient people to a church. We offer Bible studies, book studies, sermons, Sunday school classes, seminars, and programs to nourish God's people.

What if we offered membership and discipleship instruction that included *catechesis* in Christian doctrine designed for devotion? Tim Keller offers a fifty-two-week *New City Catechism*[23] and John Piper offers a *Baptist Catechism* with commentary.[24] The *Westminster Shorter Catechism* is still in use (available in modern English).[25] The early Pietists disdained sterile loyalty to Lutheran confessions and catechism and lifeless mental assent to an intellectual faith. However, they did respect the place of confessions and catechism insofar as they agreed with Scripture. In wide use today is The *Book of Common Prayer* and its Catechism for Children. *The Book of Common Prayer (1979) Daily Office Lectionary* is available on Logos Bible Software. Let me offer some suggestions to enrich your devotion to pure doctrine and life.

First, read Scripture devotionally. Read with an alert mind to understand and with an open heart to respond. *Second*, read Scripture theologically and note what it communicates about God. As they surface, apply the great doctrines of the Christian faith to your attitudes and actions. Packer remarks, "Theology is for doxology and devotion—that is, the praise of God and the practice of godliness."[26] Finally, in the words of Pietist New Testament scholar, Johann Albrecht Bengel (1687–1752), "Apply yourself wholly to the text; apply the text wholly to yourself." Feed the virtues of your heart with God's word.

I crave to practice devotion to pure doctrine and life. What about you? As we plunge the depths of spiritual renewal, our inner beliefs and our outward behavior will display an impeccable match. Pietist Danish philosopher Søren Kierkegaard wrote, "As you have lived, so have you believed."

23. *New City Catechism.*

24. *A Baptist Catechism.*

25. *The Westminster Shorter Catechism in Modern English.*

26. Packer, *Concise Theology*, xii.

FOR REFLECTION AND PRACTICE

1. Read 1 Timothy 4:16 in three translations. Consult two good commentaries. How do you understand the meaning of this text? How can pure doctrine or Christian theology inform and shape your life and the life of your church?
2. How can you cultivate a Christ-centered theology and a Christ-driven life? How can you keep theology from falling into a cold intellectual and abstract academic discipline, and instead reflect on the great doctrines of orthodoxy and apply them to your piety, worship, prayer, discipleship, service, and mission?
3. Reflect on the quotes in this chapter by Johann Arndt, Nikolaus Ludwig von Zinzendorf, Karl Barth, and Søren Kierkegaard. How do they relate to the devout life?

FOR PASTORS AND CHURCH LEADERS

1. Consider how you can raise the level of theological literacy as a shaping resource in discipleship and membership in your church, using a catechism, an ongoing course in Applied Christian Theology, a leader's group commited to read and discuss different theology texts, and preaching more Christ-centered and applied doctrinal messages.
2. Read through the books of 1 and 2 Timothy and Titus to develop a philosophy of spiritual leadership that you will implement to raise your devotion to pure doctrine and life.
3. If you are involved in seminary or Bible college ministry, how can you integrate head and heart in your teaching content and style and in the types of assignments or curriculum you require? How can you integrate a Pietist vision of spiritual renewal into theological education?

4

DEVOTION TO CONTINUOUS CHRISTIAN CONVERSION

"The sum of Christianity is repentance, faith, and a new obedience."[1]

(Philipp Jakob Spener)

When people ask me what my background was, I answer with one word: *pagan*! I was darkness—a lightless cavern of seething sin. I grew up in a southern California non-Christian family where "Jesus Christ" was a swear word and "God damn" was a frustration mantra! As a pagan kid and teen, I never attended church or read the Bible—never. However, as an eighteen-year-old, on a crisp, clear, December winter night I stood at a location on Glendora Mountain Road that overlooks the city where I grew up. This was a familiar Friday night site where my high school friends and I would go to drink and do drugs. Only this Friday night was uncommon. I was there with Danny, a buddy I used to deal drugs with who had recently become a "Jesus freak." God arranged a divine appointment that would forever change my life.

I was about to peak on LSD when Danny told me about Jesus. Somehow the gospel pierced the darkness to convict me by the Spirit. I cannot remember the content of the conversation, only the impact. A magnetic

1. Spener, cited by Brown, *Understanding Pietism*, 61.

force tugged at my heart. I had to decide something, anything. I was lost and lonely—at rock bottom in my life. My mind rummaged through its files as it frantically looked for words to offer. I managed to mutter my very first prayer, a pungent prayer—a prayer of faith. This is what I blurted out to Jesus while Danny listened in: "OK Jesus, if you are real, I want to believe." My story paralleled the Corinthians:

> Do not be deceived: neither the sexually immoral, nor idolaters, nor adulterers, nor men who practice homosexuality, nor thieves, nor the greedy, nor drunkards, nor revilers, nor swindlers will inherit the kingdom of God. And such were some of you. But you were washed, you were sanctified, you were justified in the name of the Lord Jesus Christ and by the Spirit of our God (1 Cor 6:9–11).

On a brisk Saturday morning two weeks later, as I read the gospel of John, I felt an unspeakable joy well up inside me, infused with impeccable light. I now know it was the indwelling Spirit of adoption and the filling of the Holy Spirit. God altered me. He answered my Friday night prayer. Four years later a pastor dunked my tanned body and shoulder length hair into the icy waters of baptism in an inlet from the Pacific Ocean near Newport Beach, California. Jesus by the Spirit delivered me from darkness to light and plunged me into the depths of the devout life, washed, sanctified, and justified. I went from a pagan then to a pastor now!

CONTINUOUS CHRISTIAN CONVERSION

You may not be able to pinpoint a specific time or place where you placed your faith in Christ. Perhaps you grew up in the church, were baptized as an infant, attended catechism, and were confirmed. You participated in the life of the church. In a sense, you morphed into your faith and thus your conversion was unnoticeable. Or perhaps in a less liturgical context, you grew up with Christian parents, were dedicated, attended Sunday school and youth, and lived a Christian life with the instruction of your parents or peers. Perhaps you were later baptized to seal the faith you always had. Still others of you grew up in a Christian family or a non-Christian family or attended church, and yet never came to an active faith in Christ beyond a token assent that you believe in God and the Bible. Yet some of you, like me, grew up in a non-Christian family, never attended church, but encountered the gospel, believed, were baptized, and born again.

A central feature of Pietism is the doctrine of *new birth*. Dale Brown states, "The 'born again' figure of speech, which has remained popular in many strands of Protestantism, has strong roots in German Pietism."[2] Some writers equate the evangelical doctrine of rebirth—or regeneration—with conversion. But when we ask, "What is conversion, when does it occur, and how does it occur?" we discover the use of overlapping terms with elusive answers. For example, Olson and Winn identify the third hallmark of Pietism as *conversion, regeneration of the "inner person."* This is the *event* of inward, transforming experience of God, where it begins.[3] They equate conversion, regeneration, and salvation, but then Olson stipulates that repentance and conversion result in regeneration and a progressive amendment of life, known as sanctification.[4] So, repentance and conversion now result in regeneration as an *event*? Certainly, sanctification is a result. Richard Lovelace notes: "Birth is a passive experience and not the effect of action initiated by the one born . . . and regeneration or rebirth is a beachhead of sanctification in the soul, and that the conscious effects of regeneration are summed up in conversion, the response of turning toward God in repentant faith which accompanies the hearing of the gospel."[5]

Regeneration is a work of the Holy Spirit that exterminates sin and recreates new life in those believers once dead in sins (Eph 2:1). As a mechanic connects an alternator to a dead battery to generate it with new electrical life, so the messiah connects the Spirit to a dead soul to generate new spiritual life. This doctrine held a central place in Spener's doctrine of salvation. Dale Brown notes: "Pietists believed faith and works to be manifest together in living unity, so they spoke of justification and sanctification as bound together in perfect coordination, the forgiveness of sins and the creation of a new person belong together."[6] Sanctification then follows justification. However, "This coupling together of justification and sanctification created a real problem in the nomenclature of early Pietism . . . and that Spener often confused sanctification and regeneration and should have joined justification and regeneration."[7] The Pietists insisted that biblical faith is more than a mental assent to doctrine, an external faith; it is a

2. Ibid., 67.
3. Olson and Winn, *Reclaiming Pietism*, 91.
4. Ibid., 92–94. Also see, Olson, "Reclaiming Pietism."
5. Lovelace, *Dynamics of Spiritual Life*, 104, 106.
6. Brown, *Understanding Pietism*, 64.
7. Ibid., 65.

personal internal living faith that results in regeneration and sanctification. I do not want to split hairs, but let me clarify what I mean by devotion to continuous Christian conversion.

Conversion is not the same as salvation, regeneration, or sanctification, though they are related. Gordon T. Smith shows that evangelicals inherited the language, paradigms, and practices of the nineteenth century American revivalism of Finney and crusade evangelism. It tended to regard conversion and salvation as the same thing and saw them as an event. To be "converted" or "born again" was to be saved, in the past tense at a point in time. It was decisive and personal. It stressed human will and technique. Come forward to the altar and pray the sinner's prayer. Decide now to believe in Christ and become a convert. When you receive or "accept Jesus into your heart" you are saved or converted. If you accept Jesus as Lord and Savior you will be "born again." The mission of the church, then, is to "win souls" and secure "conversions" and baptisms. When we equate a past tense event with either regeneration or salvation we can sabotage the goal of conversion, which is *transformation* through the regenerate life expressed in progressive sanctification, "for conversion is the point of departure for the rest of our Christian life, the working out of the meaning of our conversion."[8] Salvation encompasses more than initial conversion and belief (cf. Phil 2:12).

The English term *conversion* is related to the Greek *epistrepho* and the Hebrew *shuv*, both of which mean to "turn" or "return," through a change in direction or course of action, often of sinners in relation to God, sometimes translated as "repent" (2 Chr 6:26; Hos 14:2; Acts 9:35; 11:21; 1 Thess 1:9). According to Grenz, "The Hebrew *naham*, which reflects the idea of displaying emotion, suggests the radical, heartfelt nature of repentance (Job 42:6)."[9] Conversion is also related to the Greek verb *metanoeo* and its noun *metanoia*, usually translated as "repent" and "repentance." Bloesch writes: "This term signifies not simply a change of mind (as in Classical Greek), but a change of heart. John Wesley was certainly true to the basic witness of Scripture when he defined conversion as 'a thorough change of heart and life from sin to holiness, a turning.'"[10] *Metanoeo* emphasizes a negative turning away from sin, while *epistrepho* is broader, and sometimes includes

8. Smith, *Transforming Conversion*, 1.

9. Grenz, *Theology for the Community of God*, 406.

10. Bloesch, *The Crisis of Piety*, 63.

faith and the entire conversion process and turning of the will to God.[11] Repentance involves the heart, mind, emotions, and will.

The call to repentance and thereby to salvation is a general call for all people to conversion. But this is only a beginning or an initiation, not an event. Neither our faith nor our baptism can save us. We cannot always capture conversion in one specific event, moment, or decision, as many converted people cannot point to such a time or experience. Francke's dramatic moment of conversion through an emotional "struggle of repentance" he called *Busskampf*, influenced later Pietism and evangelical conversion theology and "all the early Pietists affirmed the freedom of the human will to either accept or reject God's saving work in the heart."[12] This is a dilemma for people who grew up in the church or in Christian families. And some cannot point to what the Pietists called the "fruits of faith" as evidence of their conversion (Matt 7:16, 20; John 7:17; Gal 5:22; Rom 6:22). While the Pietists emphasized the *fruit* of faith—seeded by the inner life of regeneration—we must balance that with the *source* of faith—the Lord Jesus Christ and God's external work of justification. Repentance and faith are intertwined (Mark 1:15; Acts 20:21).

Both Puritans and Pietists held that conversion, preceded by justification, must follow with sanctification—growth in holiness. Conversion contains but is distinguished from rebirth or regeneration, which only results when God justifies the believer. Bloesch says: "Justification as divine acquittal is extrinsic to man, but the fruits of this justification are then applied to man by the Holy Spirit . . . The Spirit must seal justification in the hearts of people,"[13] which activates regeneration and salvation: "But when the goodness and loving kindness of God our Savior appeared, he saved us, not because of works done by us in righteousness, but according to his own mercy, by the washing of regeneration and renewal of the Holy Spirit, whom he poured out on us richly through Jesus Christ our Savior, so that being justified by his grace we might become heirs according to the hope of eternal life" (Titus 3:4–7).

Justification and regeneration, which confer salvation, are *God's part* through his initiative. Conversion is *our part* through our response to God's initiative by repentance and faith. Conversion is a beginning of the

11. Grenz, *Theology for the Community of God*, 407.

12. Olson and Winn, *Reclaiming Pietism*, 94.

13. Bloesch, *The Crisis of Piety*, 65.

salvation experience not the end.[14] The regenerate life is the justified life carried out through sanctification. *Continuous* Christian conversion is a lifelong process. The call of the gospel is to continuous Christian conversion, to discipleship—to follow Christ Jesus as Lord.

Mark describes conversion: "Now after John was arrested, Jesus came into Galilee, proclaiming the gospel of God, and saying, "The time is fulfilled, and the kingdom of God is at hand; *repent* and *believe* in the gospel" (Mark 1:14). The verbs are present tense: continue to repent and continue to believe in the gospel. This summons is for unbelievers *and* believers. Then, "Passing alongside the Sea of Galilee, he saw Simon and Andrew the brother of Simon casting a net into the sea, for they were fishermen. Jesus said to them, '*Follow* me, and I will make you become fishers of men.' And immediately they left their nets and *followed* him" (Mark 1:16). The goal of conversion is not to make decisions but to make disciples, who continually repent, believe, and follow Jesus. The devout life as Spener depicts it, is one of "repentance, faith, and a new obedience."

Continuous Christian conversion is central to the devout life, which fosters sanctification toward godliness (piety). Conversion involves a response of the heart to God's call and word regarding salvation through repentance, baptism, forgiveness of sins, reception of the Spirit, and fidelity to Christ Jesus as Lord. Both Stanly J. Grenz and Gordon T. Smith argue persuasively that incorporation into the church is also an aspect of corporate conversion, as water and Spirit baptism initiate believers into a new life in Christ and into a new community, the church.[15] Here is one biblical summary that shows a paradigm of conversion:

> "Let all the house of Israel therefore know for certain that God has made him both Lord and Christ, this Jesus whom you crucified." Now when they heard this they were cut to the heart, and said to Peter and the rest of the apostles, "Brothers, what shall we do?" And Peter said to them, "Repent and be baptized every one of you in the name of Jesus Christ for the forgiveness of your sins, and you will receive the gift of the Holy Spirit. For the promise is for you and for your children and for all who are far off, everyone whom the Lord our God calls to himself." And with many other words he bore witness and continued to exhort them, saying, "Save yourselves from this crooked generation." So those who received

14. See, Smith, *Beginning Well* and *Transforming Conversion*.

15. See Grenz, *Theology for the Community of God*, 423–40, and Smith, *Transforming Conversion*, 148–52, and *Beginning Well*, 179–206.

> his word were baptized, and there were added that day about three thousand souls (Acts 2:36–41).

The call to continuous Christian conversion is for all people, regardless of their spiritual history: whether you were baptized and confirmed, whether you grew up in the church or in a Christian family, whether you grew up as a pagan, or whether you have fallen away from grace. Spener writes: "Your God has indeed given you Baptism, and you may be baptized once. But he has made a covenant with you . . . This covenant must last through your whole life . . . Accordingly if your Baptism is to benefit you, it must remain in constant use throughout your life."[16] You may or may not be able to pinpoint the time or place of your initial conversion. Nevertheless, you are called to a deeper conversion. You do not need to decide whether to target unbelievers or believers in your mission as the call to continuous conversion and discipleship is for all people regardless of where they are in their spiritual journey. Donald Bloesch argues:

> Because Christians are still sinners, even they need to be converted. In the New Testament believers are called upon to repent and turn again to Christ (cf. Luke 17:3, 4; 22:32; Rev 2:5, 16, 21; 3:19). It is Christians who are urged to be renewed in mind and spirit and to put on the new nature (Eph 4:22–23; Rom 13:14) . . . We should perhaps say that the Christian stands in need not so much of reconversion as of deeper conversion. We are incorporated into Christ in the decision of faith, but we have not yet been brought into perfect obedience to Christ.[17]

Scot McKnight asserts that: "Conversion is a process, sometimes more sudden than others. At its core, conversion is a process of identity formation in which a person comes to see himself or herself in accordance with the gospel of Jesus Christ . . . and 'the hermeneutic of confessing Jesus as Lord.'"[18] Everyone's context of conversion is different. Though Lutheran Pietists lived with the confessions of their doctrine of infant baptism, they emphasized the necessity of confirming baptism with personal faith as an adult, which created tensions for later Pietists. The Radical Pietists adopted a believers-only baptism position, like Baptists and Anabaptists. Nevertheless, Gordon T. Smith offers a helpful perspective:

16. Spener, *Pia Desideria*, 66.
17. Bloesch, *The Crisis of Piety*, 72.
18. McKnight, *Turning to Jesus*, 4, 22.

> For many if not most, conversion to Christ actually begins with "conversion" to the church. Like any of the other elements of conversion, the communal can come first in a person's experience. We will increasingly find that this element of a Christian conversion comes early on in people's experience: a person first becomes a participant in the life of the community of faith and only then, as a loved member of the community, comes to Christian faith.[19]

THE SPIRITUAL PRACTICE OF REPENTANCE

Unique and central to the Pietists was the doctrine of the inner person, connected with the indwelling Christ and the *internal* application of Christian doctrines and sacraments. You can believe that Jesus is Savior and the Bible is God's word; you can be baptized, receive communion, and be confirmed; you can affirm the Apostle's Creed and the Westminster Confession. It will not matter if these do not transform your heart and life. Because true religion and the devout life is a matter of the heart, our hearts need renovation through regeneration energized by the life of continuous Christian conversion in sanctification through the indwelling Spirit.

Salvation is God's part. Conversion is our part. Repentance is key to conversion where we turn from sin and turn or return to God. Initial conversion is the launch of the devout life. This must lead to sanctification through surrender to Christ Jesus as Lord as his follower, with the goal of *transformation*. Continuous Christian conversion will transform the inner person life-long. Crucial to the devout life is inner repentance with external results:

> According to Arndt—and Spener and Francke followed him in this—the new or renewed inner person, the core of one's personality, the "heart," is brought about and into conformity with Jesus Christ through repentance and heartfelt trust in the Savior through the Word of God: "This is true repentance when the heart internally and through sorrow and regret is broken down, destroyed, laid low, and by faith and forgiveness of sins is made holy, consoled, purified, changed, and made better so that an external improvement in life follows."[20]

19. Smith, *Beginning Well*, 206.

20. Olson and Winn, *Reclaiming Pietism*, 92.

Ongoing repentance is imperative for spiritual renewal, as it does not permit us to anchor our conversion in a past experience nor in the rites of passage in a sacramental tradition. An incomplete evangelism goal might overlook a call to ongoing repentance, conversion, and discipleship. God's kindness leads to the gift of repentance (Acts 11:16–18; Rom 2:4). Calvin wrote, "The whole of conversion to God is understood under the term 're-pentance' . . . So, I think repentance may well be defined as a true conversion of our life to God, issuing from pure and heartfelt fear of him, and consisting in the mortification of our flesh and old man and the vivification of the Spirit."[21]

I attended a Sunday service in a small church to support a faithful pastor who had resigned and had only two weeks left. He failed to overcome complex issues of disunity, dysfunction, and stunted missional focus in this barren congregation. After the service, a long-standing, pent-up parishioner approached me with a friendly smile and launched a vicious assault on this pastor's leadership and the board's inaction with their financial issues. She also indicted another sister church for its alleged failure to help this church grow. This style of fierce blame is all too common in churches and denominations where irreverent slander, criticism, and bitterness stampede unbridled to defile many (Heb 12:15). What made this so stark was the pastor had just delivered a compelling Bible message that dealt with sin and repentance, followed by a chorus that we gently sang, "Create in me a clean heart, O God, and renew a right spirit within me!"

Richard Lovelace calls this "baptized depravity," and advises that "the minister aiming at renewal must work toward one in which the members are growing in sanctification and making progress at conquering sin in their lives."[22] The level of tolerated sin in our churches should dumfound us. A biting sense of guilt can linger in our hearts, laminated with bland indifference or ignorance, while moral and ethical vice affects us all. Church leaders tend to not instruct regenerate parishioners on the problem of indwelling sin and on how to practice repentance and conquer sin through a gradual detection and detonation process. Some tools that you might consider are *Freedom Session*, *Celebrate Recovery*, or *Freedom in Christ Ministries*.[23]

21. Calvin, *Institutes of the Christian Religion*, III, III, 5.

22. Lovelace, *Dynamics of Spiritual Life*, 212, 214.

23. Freedom Session, http://freedomsession.com; Celebrate Recovery, http://www.celebraterecovery.com; Freedom in Christ Ministries, http://www.freedominchrist.com.

Pietist August Francke understood conversion primarily as an *enduring change of the will*, and thus the experience of the reality of conversion is bound first to the depth of repentance, known in Lutheran Confessions as *contritio*. This is the remorseful struggle of a contrite sinner, a necessary struggle of the reborn for daily renewal, particularly drawn from Psalm 51. Also, for Francke, true repentance is the center of the theological curriculum.[24] Perhaps our Bible colleges and seminaries should equip students in repentance. To repent and believe is not a one-time event or experience that decisively destroys sin. Gordon T. Smith says, "John Wesley insisted that while faith and repentance are certainly needed in coming to Christ (the experience of justification and regeneration), 'repentance and faith are fully as necessary in order for our continuance and growth in grace.' He declared that though sin does not *reign* in the Christian believer, it nevertheless *remains* in the heart of the new Christian, thus necessitating ongoing repentance."[25]

Repentance should be a regular spiritual discipline on par with prayer, Bible reading, worship, silence, solitude, fasting, and service. Could it be that repentance and faith are the foundational spiritual practices without which none of the other practices will gain any traction or foster much spiritual fruit? We can worship God and study Scripture. We can pray and fast. We can have solitude and serve. But if we do not mortify sin through repentance and faith, by the word and the Spirit, nurtured in prayer, meditation, confession, and so on, permanent change will not occur in our lives. *We can no longer live as we once did, as we are no longer the people we once were*. Carefully read Arndt's insights into continuing repentance:

> True Christianity consists only in pure faith, and a holy life. Holiness of life, however, arises out of true repentance and regret and of the knowledge of oneself. As a result, a man learns to understand his wrongdoings daily and to improve daily. By faith, he becomes a participant of the righteousness and holiness of Christ (1 Cor 1:30) . . . Seven things move us to repentance: God's mercy, Christ's warmth, the warning of temporal punishment, temporal death, final judgment, eternal pain in hell, and the joy of eternal life.[26]

24. Lindberg, *The Pietist Theologians*, 107, 109.

25. Smith, *Transforming Conversion*, 134.

26. Arndt, *True Christianity*, 104, 204.

Confession

In continuous Christian conversion, we will practice the prayer of *Examen*, and seek forgiveness, cleansing, and spiritual renewal through confession (Ps 51:1–17; 66:18–19; 139:23–24; Luke 11:4; 1 John 1:9). Unconfessed sin and transgression burden and block free and harmonious fellowship and vitality with God and others. Again, it boils down to a theological and heart issue: "Whoever conceals his transgressions will not prosper, but he who confesses and forsakes them will obtain mercy. Blessed is the one who fears the Lord always, but whoever hardens his heart will fall into calamity" (Prov 28:13–14). Do you abhor evil and cling to what is good (Rom 12:9)? Careless habits, laziness, and lack of sense, can gradually allow intrusive nettles and thorns of sin to overtake the garden of our souls, and leave us destitute like an armed man (Prov 24:30–34). Pray this historic confession regularly:

> Most merciful God, we confess that we have sinned against you in thought, word and deed, by what we have done, and by what we have left undone. We have not loved you with our whole heart; we have not loved our neighbors as ourselves. We are truly sorry and we humbly repent. For the sake of your Son Jesus Christ, have mercy on us and forgive us; that we may delight in your will, and walk in your ways, to the glory of your Name. Amen.

Timothy Keller notes in John Stott's book, *Confess Your Sins: The Way of Reconciliation*, that many Christians routinely confess their sins. Yet most people do not find that their confessions change them. They repeatedly return to the same bad patterns. Stott argued that we must couple two things: *confess* and *forsake* our sins. When we confess—admit our wrongs, and forsake—disown those wrongs, we turn away (repent) from those wrongs and weaken our ability to do them again. He also notes how John Owen's little book *The Mortification of Sin* (available online) offers a remarkable range of doctrines to use on ourselves, to weaken sin's hold on us.[27]

For self-examination, Keller applies George Whitefield's four categories of the Christian life where he wrote, "God give me a deep humility, a well guided zeal, a burning love, and a single eye."[28] This prayer hangs on my office wall to remind me to examine how my humility, zeal, love, and

27. Keller, *Prayer*, 212, 216.

28. Ibid., 218; George Whitefield, cited in Arnold Dallimore, *George Whitefield: The Life and Times*, 140.

singular eye are faring. Confession of sin with repentance is both a private and a public spiritual discipline for conversion and renewal (1 John 1:9; James 5:16; Ezra 9–10; Neh 9–10; 2 Chr 34–35). Private sin may require a public admission before others. In some cases, the whole community is culpable. Confession might also require decisive actions of repentance and in some cases restitution with others (Luke 3:8–14; 19:8; Acts 19:18–19; Exod 22:2–14). Corporate confession held a vital place in Pietism with James 5:16 as a core text, "Therefore, confess your sins to one another and pray for one another that you may be healed." For example, "Like Spener, Zinzendorf saw confession as essential to Christian growth, and the communal life of the church as its proper place. It was for this purpose, especially, that bands were useful."[29] Have you ever viewed confession of sin and prayer as power sources for healing?

I often observe dramatic results when I facilitate public confession of sin in some of the men's small groups or prayer retreats that I conduct. I invite people to spend time in private silence and solitude with Scripture and confession, while they journal what they feel the Spirit brought to mind through his conviction. And then as appropriate, we return to share our personal assessments with one or two others of the same gender. Sadly, most churches lack the kind of genuine fellowship and spiritual formation for private and public confession for this to occur. Is your church in danger of God's chastisement or closure if he were to confront its sin and call it to repentance? He did that with most of the seven churches in Revelation 2–3. Confession and repentance are daily spiritual disciplines for me. What about you and your church?

Crucifixion

We cannot counsel people into wholeness. In continuous Christian conversion, we will also crucify our sin. Sin is a vicious taskmaster that only the cross and the Spirit can conquer. We must crucify the flesh with its passions and spike sin to the cross where its wretched stench belongs, where Christ defeated it (Rom 6:6; Gal 5:24; 6:14). Based on Romans 8:13, John Owen writes, "That the life, vigor, and comfort of our spiritual life depend much on our mortification of sin." And, "Every unmortified sin will certainly do two

29. Snyder, *Signs of the Spirit*, 149.

things: (1) it will *weaken* the soul, and deprive it of its vigor, (2) it will *darken* the soul, and deprive it of its comfort and peace."[30] Dallas Willard comments:

> I have inquired before many church and parachurch groups regarding their plan for putting to death or *mortifying* "whatever belongs to your earthly nature" or flesh (see for example, Colossians 3:5). I have *never once* had a positive response to this question. Indeed, mortifying or putting things to death doesn't seem to be the kind of thing today's Christians would be caught doing. Yet it's at the center of New Testament teaching.[31]

Do you have a plan to kill (mortify) sin? Does your church? The devout life requires that we must. At the root of Pietism are the first and third of Luther's *95 Theses*: (1) "When our Lord and Master, Jesus Christ, said 'Repent,' He called for the entire life of believers to be one of repentance . . . (3) Yet its meaning is not restricted to repentance in one's heart; for such repentance is null unless it produces outward signs in various mortifications of the flesh."

Arndt says: "This is the true knowledge of God in which repentance consists, in a change of mind and the renewal of the mind for the improvement of life . . . Understand now that true worship stands in the heart, in the knowledge of God, in true repentance by which the flesh is mortified and man is renewed to the image of God."[32] We must take drastic measures with such a hostile enemy, "*Put to death* therefore what is earthly in you" (Col 3:5) and "For if you live according to the flesh you will die, but *if by the Spirit* you *put to death* the deeds of the body, you will live" (Rom 8:13). Let us abstain from evil and pray that the "God of peace himself would sanctify us completely, that our whole spirit and soul and body be kept blameless" (1 Thess 5:23). A.B. Simpson erected his theology of sanctification on this verse. Let us also deal not just with the general but also with the specific details of our lives. Carlson and Lueken advise:

> Transformation happens in the specific details of our hearts and lives. There are so many unformed areas; we don't know where to start. Generalities are a good hiding place. "Jesus died for my sins" is less scandalous than "Jesus died for my out-of-control anger that severely damages the people I love most." "I'm a sinner" is easier to admit than "I'm a lustaholic." In generalities, no one is exposed,

30. Owen, *On the Mortification of Sin in Believers*, 22–23.

31. Willard, *The Great Omission*, 84.

32. Arndt, *True Christianity*, 116.

> but no one really grows. Real transformation happens in the unattractive details of our lives.[33]

The goal of confession and repentance is change. We must develop an aversion to specific sins as we come to know God and his character more, are enthralled with his colossal beauty and holiness, and seek to forsake our sins and please him. Psalms 32 and 51 are particularly helpful. Regularly review Paul's lists of sins that we must repent of and crucify, to initiate change in us, lest we incur God's judgment: sexual immorality, impurity, passion, evil desire, covetousness, anger, wrath, malice, slander, obscene talk, lying, idolatry, sorcery, enmity, strife, jealousy, fits of rage, rivalries, dissensions, divisions, envy, drunkenness, and orgies, and so forth (Col 3:5–9; Gal 5:19–21). In addition, "Men ought not to content themselves with a general repentance, but it is every man's duty to endeavor to repent of his particular sins, particularly."[34]

An old Cherokee told his grandson: "My son, there's a battle raging between two wolves inside us all. One is Evil. It is anger, jealousy, greed, resentment, inferiority, lies, and ego. The other is Good. It is joy, peace, love, hope, humility, kindness, empathy, and truth."

The boy thought for a moment, and then asked his grandfather: "Which wolf wins?"

The old Cherokee quietly replied: "The one you feed."

FOR REFLECTION AND PRACTICE

1. This chapter is central to an understanding of Pietism and crucial for the devout life. Reflect on Spener's opening quote, "The sum of Christianity is repentance, faith, and a new obedience." What are your thoughts about his statement?
2. How do you understand the idea of devotion to continuous Christian conversion? Have you ever thought of it being continuous and ongoing, rather than just as a decisive moment? Pray through this topic and ask for God's direction.
3. Develop a process where you will practice the discipline of repentance through confession and crucifixion. Read and pray through Psalms

33. Carlson and Lueken, *Renovation of the Church*, 123.

34. *Westminster Confession of Faith*, XV, V.

32, 51, and 66 to increase your biblical attitudes and actions. Regularly review Col 3:5–9 and Gal 5:19–21.

FOR PASTORS AND CHURCH LEADERS

1. Richard Lovelace states, "The minister aiming at renewal must work toward one in which the members are growing in sanctification and making progress at conquering sin in their lives." How can you develop a healthy and not legalistic process to address this in your church?
2. How can you develop healthy *corporate* confession and repentance, and ongoing conversion?

5

DEVOTION TO A TRANSFORMATIONAL USE OF SCRIPTURE

"Thought should be given to a more extensive use of the Word of God among us . . . The more at home the Word of God is among us, the more we shall bring about faith and its fruits."[1]

(Philipp Jakob Spener)

My aim is to help pastors, church leaders, Christians, and churches thrive. The odds are against them. Sin and Satan are hefty opponents; coupled with the allure of secular culture and the church's gravitational veer toward mission drift and stifling institutionalism. Problems and micro-management, personal agendas and needs, often drive churches more than Christ's cause and community. Churches and denominations can also lose their way in the hunger games of power and control, bankrupted by deficits in spiritual formation and spiritual warfare. Add bad teaching, bad character, and bad blood into the fusion, and you will likely experience snarled results like those depicted in 1 and 2 Timothy and Titus. I wish these disorders were not so in our churches. How can we proclaim the gospel if we do not live by it (Phil 1:27)? There are multiple causes for the dysfunctions, but in my opinion, the root is a famine of God's word among us. We do not always

1. Spener, *Pia Desideria*, 87.

"live by the Book." Like the Puritans, the Pietists led a "back to the Bible" movement to reform church life, not just church doctrine. Spener's first prescription to cure the corrupt conditions in the church forms the charter of the devout life: "Thought should be given to a *more extensive use of the Word of God among us* . . . The more at home the word of God is among us, the more we shall bring about faith and its fruits." To plunge the depths of spiritual renewal, we must practice devotion to a *transformational* use of Scripture among us.

How well do you and your church read, know, preach, teach, and apply the Bible in transformational ways? Is it extensive and at home? How lively and luscious is your faith and its fruits? Widespread Bible illiteracy litters our social landscape, with many churches having scant strategies to equip people in how to read, know, interpret, and apply the Bible. Research in the United States and Canada should provoke our response to the challenge.

In the United States:

1. 56 percent of Americans view the Bible as God's word, yet only 37 percent read it once per week or more, and 57 percent of those use it as a transformational text applied to their lives.
2. 80 percent of American adults believe American values and morals are declining—but perceptions about the reasons for the decline have shifted over time. Compared to 2013, people are more likely to blame declining morals on movies, music, and TV rather than on a lack of Bible reading. And while half of all adults would say the Bible has too little influence on society, only 30 percent of Millennials believe this.[2]

In Canada:

1. Most Canadians, including Christians, read the Bible either seldom or never, and Bible reading and church attendance are both in decline. Only 14 percent of Canadian Christians read the Bible at least once per week.
2. 64 percent of Canadians and 60 percent of Canadian Christians agree that the scriptures of all the major world religions teach essentially the same things.

2. *Barna Update*, "The State of the Bible: 6 Trends for 2014."

3. 21 percent of Christians reflect on the meaning of the Bible for their lives at least a few times per week.[3]

THE TRANSFORMATIONAL USE OF SCRIPTURE

Just as King Josiah restored the law to Israel and incited renewal, we must restore the Bible to the church. The devout life will restore a transformational use of Scripture that addresses our inner person as we read the Bible for life not just for learning. The Pietists, in lock step with the Puritans and evangelical Protestantism, "exalted the supremacy of the Bible above all other external standards . . . and it was their exaltation of the Bible as the supreme authority over the claims of doctrinal interpreters and church symbols that the early Pietists differed most with their contemporaries."[4] The Bible was not a textbook from which to construct doctrine, creeds, or confessions, nor a source for academic sermons, theology, or study—confined to professional scholars and clergy. Spener argued that preachers and scholars could acquire the knowledge and letter of the Scriptures and assent to true doctrine, and yet be unacquainted with true biblical faith.

Francke "called for Christians to believe what Scripture teaches, do what Scripture commands, and hope what Scripture promises. His approach to Scripture was to ask how we ought to believe, live, and hope."[5] He distinguished the outer letter (husk) and the inner witness (kernel) of the word, the latter often obscured in orthodoxy. The letter is dead apart from the illumination of the Spirit upon both the text and the inner life of the believer. For Spener, the Bible contains an outer word (the printed page) and an inner word (the understanding given by the Holy Spirit). "The Word of God is that which shows, impresses, and brings the mind of Christ into our hearts."[6] When illuminated by the Holy Spirit in the hearts of regenerate believers, it was a source of spiritual formation and hearing God's voice. Michael Hardin writes:

> The Pietists insisted upon Bible study as the means of spiritual formation; indeed, one may say that the goal of Bible study for the Pietists was spiritual formation, but this is not a gnostic spiritual

3. *Canadian Bible Engagement Study*, "Are Canadians Done with the Bible?"
4. Brown, *Understanding Pietism*, 46–47.
5. Clifton-Soderstrom, *Angels, Worms, and Bogeys*, 20.
6. Stein, *Philipp Jakob Spener*, 310.

> formation in which the human mind plays no role. On the contrary, the Pietists insisted upon good historical and critical work in the Scriptures and among them Bengel was a pioneer in critical research . . . The word-Spirit dialectic allowed the Pietist forbearers to study Scripture, "to do their homework," and then to listen patiently to the voice of God as he spoke to them through the text they had so diligently studied.[7]

To place the Bible into the hands of common people as a spiritual resource for a devout life and to discuss it in small groups called conventicles was trademark Pietism. These types of groups sowed the seeds for later evangelical renewal and revival and unleashed the force of God's word through the spiritual priesthood of common workaday believers, as it also unshackled itself from institutional church life. Someone quizzed British Baptist preacher Charles Spurgeon how he defended the Bible. "Very easy," he replied, "I defend the Bible the same way I defend a lion. I simply let it out of its cage!"[8]

We have unlimited Bibles and study materials unsurpassed in human history, available through print, online, smart phones, and software. The Bible, "outlives, outlifts, outloves, outreaches, outranks, and outruns all other books."[9] We also have access to more Bible colleges and seminaries, conferences and seminars, study groups, television and radio programs, and churches that offer Bible based content than ever. You would think that we would excel at world-class levels of spiritual formation, mission, and church health. But we can be like some spoiled celebrities with enormous fortunes, who squander or invest them unwisely through reckless and unsatisfied living and fail to realize how much they have. We must apply what we already know. Paul exhorts, "Only let us live up to what we have already attained" (Phil 3:16 NIV). A diligent use of God's word will reform us. Spener remarks:

> The diligent use of the Word of God, which consists not only of listening to sermons but also of reading, meditation, and discussing (Ps 1:2), must be the chief means for reforming something . . . The Word of God remains the seed from which all that is good in us must grow. If we succeed in getting the people to seek eagerly and diligently in the book of life for their joy, their spiritual life

7. Hardin, "The Authority of Scripture," 9.
8. As quoted by McLean and Bird, *Unleashing the Word*, 27.
9. A. Z. Conrad, quoted by Guthrie, *Read the Bible for Life*, 4.

> will be wonderfully strengthened and they will become altogether different people.[10]

I spent an afternoon retreat with a winsome group of church leaders and their new pastor. The church and its finances had shrunk in size due to defective leadership from the previous pastor. A remnant of dedicated people continued to rebuild a wounded congregation. I led them in a devotional that included Colossians 4:2, Acts 2:42, and Acts 6:4. I encouraged them to cultivate a hardy devotion to divine revelation that matched what T. F. Torrance wrote concerning theologian Karl Barth: "For Barth, true Biblicism meant accustoming himself to breathe the air of divine revelation . . . and to indwell its message in such a way that the truth of divine revelation became built into the very walls of his mind."[11]

It was the worship leader, of all people, who told us how his life had changed in the past few months. He grew up in a Christian family and attended church all his life. He married his wife twenty years ago at the age of nineteen, and was now the father of four children. Yet he stated that he had never really read the Bible that much for himself. The new pastor had challenged these leaders and the congregation to practice "faith in action" and to get serious and intentional about discipleship, Bible reading, prayer, holiness, worship, and gospel witness. This worship leader mentioned how he had recently read Matthew 1–5 and began to read through the Gospel of John. While his wife dabbed her tearful eyes as she listened, he recounted how he had experienced newfound joy and inner transformation as he now read the Bible and prayed daily, and how he wanted to be one with Jesus as Jesus declared that he was one with the Father. We then prayed. The Spirit's presence charged the atmosphere with sacred warmth.

WORDS AND THE WORD, THE SPIRIT AND THE SCRIPTURES

All words have potential for exponential influence. Words shape worlds. My dad crooned, "Mark my words," which meant, "Remember what I said as it'll come true or will be important!" Often, to my chagrin, he was right! In elementary school we would chant, "Sticks and stones will break my bones but words will never hurt me!" Who truly believes that? We might

10. Spener, *Pia Desideria*, 91.

11. Torrance, *Karl Barth: Biblical and Theological Theologian*, 117–18.

say of a good person, "He keeps his word." Which means, "He's reliable and does what he declares." Horace wrote, "The pen is the tongue of the mind," and Edward G. Bulwer-Lytton penned, "The pen is mightier than the sword." Place a microphone before a famous politician, celebrity, or elite athlete and people will hang on their every word. God's word contains transformational words.

Like the Pietists, let us believe that God communicated his words through the Bible to mankind in order to "edify, console, encourage, warn, reprimand, and help the church and its members as well as lead men and women to God by bringing about repentance and change."[12] Their goal of Bible study was to determine the external, historical-grammatical objective meaning of the text, and the internal, spiritual subjective meaning of that text for application—only made possible by the inner witness of the Holy Spirit through a regenerate heart. August Hermann Francke and Johann Albrecht Bengel influenced later methods of hermeneutics, and Bengel also was a Pietist pioneer in textual criticism. As a serious exegete, Francke published *Guide to the Reading and Study of the Holy Scriptures* (1694) and *Christ the Sum and Substance of All the Holy Scriptures, in the Old and New Testament* (1732). He believed that true piety assisted Bible understanding, which must also affect a Christian's will. Bengel published *Gnomon of the New Testament* (1742), a commentary on the New Testament reflecting twenty years of careful Pietist biblical exegesis. John Wesley consulted it for his commentaries.

Francke took Bible study further than Spener, particularly through his leadership at the University of Halle in Germany—a Pietist center for theological education and missionary training. He valued the original languages and taught students to study the Bible at two levels: (1) *the Letter*—the grammatical, historical, and analytical, and (2) *the Spirit*—expository, doctrinal, inferential, and practical.[13] This was "contemplative exegesis" to determine: the (1) *literal* sense and absorb that into the heart for the (2) *transformational* sense, through the practices of prayer, meditation, and struggle, or *oratio*, *meditatio*, and *tenatio*. According to Olson and Winn:

> For most if not all the early Pietists, the main point of Scripture is to be found not in its literal, historical sense but in its ability to give life. One scholar has described Francke's approach to the interpretation of Scripture as a 'hermeneutics under the sign of

12. Brown, *Understanding Pietism*, 48.

13. Francke, *Guide to the Reading and Study of the Holy Scriptures*, 1–2.

> rebirth.' Thus, Francke and others differentiated between 'living knowledge' and 'theoretical knowledge' of God . . . The main purpose of Scripture, according to the Pietists, is not to *inform* but to *transform*.[14]

Currently, there is interest in a Christ-centered and gospel-centered approach to biblical interpretation and preaching. Francke himself appealed for a christological approach to biblical interpretation, in which he termed Jesus as the "Soul of Scripture." He wrote: "Since Jesus is the very Soul of Scripture, and the Way by which we have access to the Father, he who, in Doctrinal Reading, does not fix his eyes on Him, must read in vain. Truth and Life are attainable only through this Way. To know Christ and the Doctrines concerning Christ, only in theory, is not the Soul of Scripture; it is faith in him, and that imitation of him which flows from faith."[15]

An issue in church history especially between the Roman Catholic Church and the Protestant reformers concerned the location of authority and truth. What has final authority, the church or the Scriptures? For the Pietists, the Scriptures aided and applied by the Spirit, were the locus of authority over the institutional church. Rather than use the Scriptures to support the creeds and confessions of the church or as proof texts for church dogma, the Pietists used Scripture, and thus its careful exegesis, to articulate God's will. However, a radical Pietist or even a postmodern approach can undermine the role of the church as a Spirit-led community of interpreters who counterbalance the possibility of heresy, bad theology, or "prophetic revelations" that can emerge from subjective and private interpretations of individuals or groups who only find "what this text means to me/us" or "God said to me/us." This is where authority and truth are relative and confined within individuals. But early Pietists used conventicles, also called *colleges of piety*, as small groups of people who gathered outside formal worship services with clergy to discuss the Sunday sermon, read the Bible, and pray. This was a Pietist innovation, which saw these as *ecclesiola in ecclesia*—little church in the church. Michael Hardin notes:

> Pietists were known as the *ecclesiola in ecclesia* that is a group within the church who studied Scripture. This observation is important for the *Pietist never studies Scripture in isolation but only in communion and dialogue with other brothers and sisters*. The Pietist is not a receiver of revelations; he or she is bound to the

14. Olson and Winn, *Reclaiming Pietism*, 98.

15. Francke, *Guide to the Reading and Study of the Holy Scriptures*, 105.

> community of faith where common rules of interpretation allow for dialogue, observation, and change.[16]

Of course, these Bible study groups threatened the institutional church and other clergy then, as they can today. The early Pietists also pioneered an implementation of the spiritual priesthood of all believers and placed the Scripture at the center of church life. Spener appealed for "scriptural study and illumination, but that did not refer primarily to private devotional reading but rather to reading and discussing in the cell group or in the presence of the community."[17] In his tractate on the spiritual priesthood, Spener wrote, "But how shall they occupy themselves with the Word of God? They shall use it for *themselves* and *among or with* others."[18]

The Scriptures were the center of authority because the Holy Spirit inspired and illuminated them as God's eternal word to mankind. Pietists were pioneers in the applied doctrine of illumination, where they "alluded frequently to the 'internal testimony of the Spirit', believing it is the Holy Spirit who enables the dead letter of the sacred writings to become a living power within us and which enlightens the mind of the believer in understanding. Spener spoke of 'true faith, which is awakened through the Word of God by the illumination, witness, and sealing of the Holy Spirit.'"[19] The Scripture inspired by the Spirit (2 Tim 3:16) carries spiritual seed that must be enlivened by the illumination of the Spirit in our minds and hearts (1 Cor 2:6–16; 2 Cor 3:14–17; 1 John 5:7,11; Luke 24:45) as the Canon within the community of faith.[20] Like a true Pietist, pray Psalm 119:34, "Give me understanding, that I may keep your law and observe it with my whole heart." Robert Webber offers initial counsel in how to practice spiritual reading: "As you read the Scriptures that lead you into a walk with the Spirit, open your heart and mind to the voice of God met in the words and images of Scripture. Take time to reflect, to ruminate, to chew on what you hear: Have a good walk and allow yourself to be formed more deeply by your companion, the Holy Spirit."[21]

While I pastored a church in Vernon, British Columbia I led a men's group that met weekly from 7:00 am—8:00 am. For a year, we read daily

16. Hardin, "The Authority of Scripture," 10.

17. Olson and Winn, *Reclaiming Pietism*, 176.

18. Spener, "The Spiritual Priesthood," in *Pietists: Selected Readings*, 54.

19. Brown, *Understanding Pietism*, 49.

20. See Grenz, *Theology for the Community of God*, 381–91.

21. Webber, *The Divine Embrace*, 210.

selections in the Old and New Testaments from a one-year Bible and recorded our reflections in our journals. We adopted Wayne Cordeiro's structure of S.O.A.P.: *S*cripture-*O*bservation-*A*pplication-*P*rayer. We read the same passages at home daily. Then on the Wednesday morning of our meeting, we would read the passage for that day and quietly journal. Then each of us would share our journal reflections with the others and then pray. It was a deep experience where we practiced devotional reading and prayer. The transformational use of Scripture helped us experience God, where the room was often thick with his presence. We enjoyed tears and laughter, sacred prayer, and awe-struck silence from the observations and prayers we read from our journals. We enjoyed vibrant community.

Over time, we desired to open the group to others. One day, one of the men felt compelled to offer a ride to a man he saw walking on the side of the road on his way into town. They met a few days later for coffee. This man needed a place to stay, so the men's group member offered him the small guesthouse on his property. He invited him to our men's group, where he began to share his life and story. We loved and accepted him, and he eventually gave his heart to Christ. Six months later he asked me to baptize him! So, one Wednesday morning our men's group met down at a local lake at 7 am to witness his baptism. Afterward, our spiritually charged men's group went for breakfast to celebrate our journeys into Jesus as a *college of piety*.

PRINCIPLES FOR THE TRANSFORMATIONAL USE OF SCRIPTURE

- Like a God-appointed king, *read* Scripture all the days of your life to learn the fear of the Lord and to keep all his words and statutes and do them (Deut 17:19).
- *Pray* for God's gracious dealings with you that will enable you to live and obey his word (Ps 119:17).
- To be a true disciple, *abide* in Jesus's word, and you will know the truth that will set you free (John 8:31).
- Pastors and church leaders should *devote* themselves to the public reading of Scripture, to exhortation, and to teaching (1 Tim 4:13).

- Pastors and church leaders must *preach* the word; be ready in and out of season; and reprove, rebuke, and exhort, with complete patience and teaching (2 Tim 4:2).
- We must be *doers* of the word, and not hearers only, deceiving ourselves (Jas 1:22).

When I was a student at Dallas Seminary, Dr. Howard Hendricks lodged a compelling image in my mind. We can either be pipe or tree students of Scripture. A pipe is merely a conduit through which water flows from one end to the other. The water does not affect or change the pipe. A tree draws water into itself from underground to nourish itself and produce leaves and fruit. The water affects and changes the tree (Psalm 1). What are you, a pipe or a tree student of Scripture? Are you merely an information conduit of Scripture, or does Scripture transform you?

PRACTICES FOR A TRANSFORMATIONAL USE OF SCRIPTURE

I advise churches to equip their people in Bible literacy for church membership and for leadership positions, and to ask people to bring their Bibles to every church service and gathering (whether hard copies or in smart phone Bible apps). Many pastors preach topics from a sheet of paper, and do not even have a Bible with them on their pulpit! Most people just sit and listen with no Bible, or they merely read it projected from PowerPoint. Most do even less at home. You will not plunge the depths of spiritual renewal as a person or as a church if you do not devote yourself to a transformational reading of Scripture. Peterson remarks: "In this business of living the Christian life, ranking high among the most neglected aspects is one having to do with the reading of the Christian Scriptures. What is neglected is reading the Scriptures formatively, reading in order to live . . . that in order to read the Scriptures adequately and accurately, it is necessary to live them *as* we read them."[22]

Many pastors do not preach the actual text of Scripture itself nor in transformational ways. They preach their notes, outlines, and points, rather than preach the biblical text, God's word. Many simply read verses that they use as launching pads and quickly leave them behind as they blast on to excursions of their own ideas or Christian themes, or arrange them as proof

22. Peterson, *Eat This Book*, xi–xii.

texts for their pre-thought agendas. Or they showcase the excavations of their exegetical and historical detail and sprinkle them with quotes, illustrations, and human-centered applications, rather than Christ-centered theology according to the original author's words and purpose. Or they preach character studies from narratives, but fail to keep them God-centered. Authority then becomes human-centered, jailed in the preacher's style, rather than set wild and free from the Scripture itself. Topical or character studies often become moralistic burdens placed on people to live better like Joseph or to lead better like Paul. Abraham Kuruvilla remarks: "The goal of preaching is not merely to explicate the informational content of the chosen text but to expound the text in such a way that its transformational implications are brought home to the listeners. Of course, life change is not a one-time phenomenon, accomplished instantaneously; rather it involves a lifetime of gradual and progressive realignment to the will of God in Scripture."[23]

The Bible passage itself should drive all studies and sermons according to the author's purpose in context. How many times have you listened to a great sermon *on* a great passage only to leave the service feeling muddled as you concluded, "Everything the preacher said was true; the only problem is that what he said wasn't *in* the passage!" A message is in the text not outside it. Preachers need to point to and expound the text. Show them the basis of your words. *The sermon is in the text*! We should align our application with the author's purpose. Each author had an *agenda* where he sought to *do* something with the text in the lives of his hearers and readers. Johann Albrecht Bengel advised, "It is the special office of every interpretation to exhibit adequately the force and significance of the words, which the text contains, so as to express everything, which the author intended, and to introduce nothing, which he did not intend."[24]

We should also restore the public reading of Scripture, and learn to do it with skill and equip teams of Scripture readers.[25] Paul commands, "*Devote* yourself to the public reading of Scripture, to exhortation, to teaching" (1 Tim 4:13). This present tense verb means, "pay attention to, apply oneself to" a continuous public reading of Scripture. Fred Craddock remarks, "For all the noises ministers make about the centrality of the Bible in the church, the public reading of Scripture in many places does not support

23. Kuruvilla, *A Vision for Preaching*, 93.

24. Bengel, "Gnomon of the New Testament," 259.

25. See Arthurs, *Devote Yourself to the Public Reading of Scripture.*

that conviction."[26] The Spirit speaks through his word, and we must learn to hear it audibly once again. In your quiet time, read the Scripture out loud to hear the word. Listen to the Bible in digital audio formats such as the *YouVersion* app.

In *Pia Desideria*, Spener cites 2 Timothy 3:16 and notes that because all Scripture is inspired by God and profitable for teaching, reproof, correction, and training in righteousness, "accordingly *all* Scripture, without exception, should be known by the congregation if we are all to receive the necessary benefit."[27] He notes that this cannot occur if we only rely on weekly sermons on appointed lessons that comprise only a small fraction of the whole counsel of God.

1. Diligently read the Scripture, especially the New Testament, and have every father, or another person in the family, read from the Bible daily. Encourage people to read privately at home, and to read the Scripture book by book in public services without further comment.
2. Re-introduce apostolic kinds of church meetings such as those described in 1 Corinthians 14:26–40. This could be where there is a communal reading, exposition, and discussion of Bible passages, applied to the edification of the whole gathering, to enhance doctrine and piety. Songs can also be introduced according to Colossians 3:16.
3. It is not enough that we hear the Word with our outward ear, but we must let it penetrate to our heart, so that we may hear the Holy Spirit speak there—that is, with vibrant emotion and comfort feel the sealing of the Spirit (Eph 1:14; 4:30) and the power of the Word.[28]

In 2016, our district of churches read the New Testament in a year together, one chapter per day, Monday to Friday. You might use these practices that I developed called ***PROP.***

P ray

- Pick a quiet spot. Turn off all social media. Quiet yourself in solitude (Ps 46:10). Relax your body and thoughts. With open hands, pray the prayer of relinquishment (Mark 14:36). *Place yourself in the presence of God.*

26. Craddock, *Preaching*, 210.
27. Spener, *Pia Desideria*, 88.
28. Ibid., 88–90, 117.

- Pray for the Spirit's *illumination*. Open your heart to the Lord and offer thanksgiving, confession, and repentance (Ps 100; 32; 66:16–18). Literally pray Psalm 139:23–24.

> The first means to proper Bible reading is heartfelt prayer (Ps 119). Where the Spirit does not open the Scripture, the Scripture is not understood even though it is read. We must turn ourselves to prayer, so that his Spirit may prepare our hearts for the knowledge of the truth and open them as they did that of Lydia (Acts 16:14), so that he might open to us the Scripture and its understanding (Luke 24:32; 45). We are to pray during our reading and often lift up our souls anew to God that he might open to us one door after another into his Word. We are to close off our reading with prayer so that the Holy Spirit might hallow what we read and seal it not only in our thoughts but impress itself into our soul that we might hold the Word in a good heart and bring forth fruit in patience (Luke 8:15). Prayer, if it is to be heard by God, must come out of the heart pleasing to God for God hears those who fear him and do his will (John 9:31). The prayer, which is given in reading, must come from such a heart, which stands in true repentance.[29]

R ead

- Read the text slowly and attentively *out loud*; reflect on it with your heart. Note what an author is *doing* with the text to accomplish his purpose. Enter the text, imagine the scene.

O bserve

- Observe the *text*: key terms, mood, and *main point*.
- Observe the *theology*: what it says about God, Jesus Christ, and the Holy Spirit.

P ractice

> All knowledge of God and his will does not exist in mere knowing but must come forth in practice and action. There must continually be a holy intention to put into practice that which one comes to know as the divine will in one's reading. The person who comes to his reading with this intention and endeavors to rapidly and willingly do what he comes to understand will not only in his soul

29. Spener, "From the Necessary and Useful Reading of the Holy Scriptures," 71–73.

> be more and more convinced that what he reads is divine truth, but such truth will then truly enlighten his heart.[30]

- Practice and *personalize* the text-theology for life: truths to believe, attitudes to develop, examples to follow, sins to kill, actions to take, commands to obey, promises to hold.
- Listen for God's voice as you mediate on the text and theology for your life. *Pray*. Be attentive to any thoughts that emerge, impressions, a strong sense, or illumination, or tug on your heart of a verse or verses, or a sense of the "witness of the Spirit," a picture, your imagination being stirred, or a compelling action you feel you need to take.

> Because the Holy Scripture is a book directed to all times and to all men, one ought to read it, to direct it continually to the reader himself, and to attend in it how our God speaks not only generally or only to those to whom the words were immediately directed, but to each person who reads these words.[31]

Consider the words of Anglican Bishop Jeremy Taylor, who helped catapult John Wesley toward the devout life with his profound book *Holy Living*. He advises:

> When the word of God is read or preached to you, be sure you be of a ready heart and mind, free from worldly cares and thoughts, diligent to hear, careful to mark, studious to remember, and desirous to practice all that is commanded, and to live according to it; do not hear for any other end but to become better in your life, and to be instructed in every good work, and to increase in the love and service of God.[32]

May you "*devote* yourselves to the *apostle's teaching* and the fellowship, to the breaking of bread and the prayers" (Acts 2:42), and "*devote* yourselves to prayer and to the *ministry of the word*" (Acts 6:4). The ministry of the word is the entire pattern of proclaiming the gospel message as contained in the whole counsel of Scripture. May a transformational use of God's word, matched with tenacious prayer, be at home in your personal and family life, in your small groups, board meetings, staff meetings, congregational and committee meetings, and in your classrooms. Let John Wesley's devotion stir you to sustained action:

30. Ibid., 73.
31. Ibid., 75.
32. Taylor, *Holy Living*, 246.

> In the year 1729, I began not only to read, but to study the Bible, the only standard of truth, and the only model of pure religion. Hence, I saw, in a clearer and clearer light, the indispensable necessity of having "the mind which was in Christ," and of "walking as Christ also walked;" even of having, not some part only, but all the mind which was in him; and of walking as he walked, not only in many or in most respects, but in all things. And this was the light, wherein at this time I generally considered religion, as a uniform following of Christ, an entire inward and outward conformity to our Master.[33]

FOR REFLECTION AND PRACTICE

1. Over a twenty-two-day period, read and pray through each section of Psalm 119 out loud and then silently, according to the structure set out by the twenty-two letters of the Hebrew alphabet. Practice PROP. Then resolve to live into each section of the Psalm each day.
2. Read Matthew 13:1–23, and spend at least three thirty-minute sessions with the passage. Observe the text, theology, and life as you listen to the Lord and contemplate it. Then recall it during each day and resolve to live it into the passage each day. Pray and then enter the passage as you read it three times out loud. Read the context before and after this account. If you have a study Bible, look up parallel passages and comments on the verses.

FOR PASTORS AND CHURCH LEADERS

1. Pray and think through Spener's proposal in how to correct the conditions in the church: "Thought should be given to a *more extensive use of the Word of God among us* . . . The more at home the Word of God is among us, the more we shall bring about faith and its fruits."
2. Consider how you will raise the level of *Bible literacy* in your church (adult, youth, and children) or denomination. Plan:

33. Wesley, *A Plain Account of Christian Perfection*, 3.

- How you will teach people how to read, interpret, and apply the Bible in a transformational way for themselves, and have them bring their own Bibles to all church gatherings.
- How you might develop a Bible reading and prayer plan in your church or denomination.
- How you might learn and teach others to learn how to practice the public reading of Scripture with skill and passion.
- How you will *preach the text* more effectively with the author's purpose, and emphasize Christ-centered rather than human-centered exposition, focusing less on your own ideas, outline, and agenda. Remember, the sermon is in the text.

6

DEVOTION TO HEART-FELT PRAYER

"Just as prayer is the cardinal evidence of faith, so prayerlessness is the salient hallmark of unbelief . . . Prayer is faith in action."[1]

(DONALD BLOESCH)

I HAVE A VIVID memory where my mother had me recite my first childhood prayer for bedtime comfort: "Now I lay me down to sleep. I pray the Lord my soul to keep. If I should die before I wake, I pray the Lord my soul to take." As a little boy, that prayer gripped my heart with fear not comfort! We may feel that our adult prayers are as inferior as childhood ones. Since then, I have learned to express better prayers, and I have learned vastly more about prayer. I am now *devoted* to prayer (Acts 6:4; Col 4:2). John Wesley challenges, "The neglect of prayer is a grand hindrance to holiness." Charles Spurgeon muses, "The condition of the church may be very accurately gauged by its prayer meetings. If God be near a church, it must pray. And if he be not there, one of the first tokens of His absence will be a slothfulness in prayer." Richard Lovelace describes a widespread and ghastly condition in the church:

> In much of the church's life, both in Evangelical and non-Evangelical circles, the place of prayer has become limited and almost vestigial [a trace, functionless]. The proportion of horizontal

1. Bloesch, *The Struggle of Prayer*, 132.

> communication that goes on in the church (in planning, arguing and expounding) is overwhelmingly greater than that which is vertical (in worship, thanksgiving, confession and intercession). Critically important committee meetings are begun and ended with formulary prayers, which are ritual obligations and not genuine expressions of dependence—when problems and arguments ensue, they are seldom resolved by further prayer but are wrangled out on the battlefield of human discourse. The old mid-week prayer meetings for revival have vanished from the programs of most churches or have been transformed into Bible studies ending with minimal prayer . . . *Deficiency in prayer both reflects and reinforces inattention toward God.*[2]

You can have a prayer life. But do you have a life of prayer? Richard Foster declares, "All who have walked with God have viewed prayer as the main business of their lives."[3] Jesus said, "My house shall be called a house of prayer" (Matt 21:13; cf. Isa 56:7). He did not say that it would be a house of preaching or of worship, but a house of prayer. Is your church a habitation of prayer? Fred Hartley offers a compelling challenge: "When Jesus built his church, he built a praying church. *What kind of church are you building*? When Jesus made disciples, he made praying disciples. *What kind of disciples are you making*?"[4] Resident prayer is the oxygen of spiritual renewal. Without it we suffocate. Sparse prayer nets sparse disciplemaking.

PROBLEMS OF PRAYER

We say we believe in prayer. But largely there is rampant *prayerlessness* in our churches and in the lives of pastors. The busyness and demands of ministry itself roadblocks a life of prayer for pastors. Do an honest evaluation. How much quantity and quality prayer is planned for and practiced in your weekend services, small groups, courses, board and committee meetings, staff and faculty meetings, annual general meetings, denominational meetings, and in your private life and leadership? Do you have regular times of carefully planned and dynamic corporate prayer gatherings? No revivals or church renewal occur without planned, prevailing prayer. Daniel Butts of the American National Prayer Committee suggests, "The reason most

2. Lovelace, *Dynamics of Spiritual Life*, 153.
3. Foster, *Celebration of Discipline*, 34.
4. Hartley, *Living in the Upper Room*, 10.

people do not attend prayer meetings at their church is that they have been to prayer meetings at their church." Books on leadership and church life tend to jam the shelves of pastors more than books on prayer and spiritual formation. When I typed the word *prayer* in Google it yielded 357 million hits! It is a topic of global interest, and yet the curriculum of most seminaries and Bible colleges contain glaring shortages of required courses on personal prayer and intercession, on how to lead effective prayer meetings, and on how to hear God's voice and practice discernment, confession and repentance, and worship. Prayerless churches are powerless churches. Jesus Christ was a man devoted to prayer (Luke 5:16; 6:12). What about us? So:

> Prayer should be the breath of our breathing, the thought of our thinking, the soul of our feeling, and the life of our living, the sound of our hearing, the growth of our growing. Prayer in its magnitude is length without end, width without bounds, height without top, and depth without bottom. It is illimitable in its breadth, exhaustless in height, fathomless in depths and infinite in extension.[5]

Ponder Richard Lovelace's statement, "Deficiency in prayer both *reflects* and *reinforces* inattention toward God."[6] God is always there, but like a practical atheist, we can live as if he is not. The core issue is theological. Jewish theologian Abraham Herschel remarked, "The issue of prayer is not prayer; the issue of prayer is God."[7] Wow! If God exists, then that spot lights everything about prayer, and then piety. It is like a leader's meeting I mediated that deadlocked into a comatose wrangle about the structure and ministry of their church. The lead pastor sat there while not once in three hours did the other leaders ask him what he thought, nor what God thought either! Zero prayer—only heartless waffle that floundered by dreadful inattention to God! Many churches suffer from spiritual paralysis because they are prayerless. Eugene Peterson likens this to pastors who treat prayer as cut flower words that serve as table decorations with artificial beauty, uprooted from the soil of God's word. Pastors pray in ceremonial and decorative ways, where prayer starts things, but devolves into adolescent secularism, as everyone then becomes free to go their own way without thinking about

5. Bounds, citing Homer W. Hodge, in *The Possibilities of Prayer*, Kindle edition, 6831.

6. Lovelace, *Dynamics of Spiritual Life*, 153.

7. Herschel, *Man's Quest for Meaning*, 87.

God anymore, and can now get to the important things that require their attention.[8]

Of course, we offer routine prayer to God at our church services, at meal times, in our devotions, and as we open and close our meetings. But do we engage in cosmic combat with continuous, strenuous prayer, like "Epaphras, a servant of Christ Jesus, who always *wrestles in prayer* for you, that you may stand firm in all the will of God, mature and fully assured" (Col 4:12 NIV)? We moan about life's clutter and clatter. We are frenetic, weary, and preoccupied. We have strenuous jobs. We feel overwhelmed with all the unfinished jobs around the house. Our center is overrun with intrusive disappointments and losses. We plan to pray—someday, when we can "get it together." We are too busy to pray. Then we read a book, hear a sermon, or attend a seminar on prayer and resolve to finally become prayer warriors or launch prayer meetings—that then stall in mid-air and crash. We ask God, but we do not receive our expected replies. We sulk in disheartened defeat. We evacuate to patterns of inattention to God and succumb to self-effort. Regardless, Paul's exhortation should blast through the commotion of our problems of prayer, "Devote yourselves to prayer, being watchful and thankful" (Col 4:2 NIV).

DEVOTION TO PRAYER

To plunge the depths of spiritual renewal we must surpass casual prayer or callous prayerlessness. Paul commands, "Rejoice always, pray without ceasing, give thanks in all circumstances; for this is the will of God in Christ Jesus for you" (1 Thess 5:16–18). All three commands are present tense. As we play them like constant background music, they sustain us in God's will. John Wesley remarks, "God's command to 'pray without ceasing' is founded on the necessity we have of his grace to preserve the life of God in the soul, which can no more subsist one moment without it, than the body can without air."[9] Is it any wonder that our lives and our churches can stagnate and suffocate? Tim Keller writes, "Prayer is so great that wherever you look in the Bible, it is there. Why? Everywhere God is, prayer is. Since God is everywhere and infinitely great, prayer must be all-pervasive in our lives."[10] Andrew Murray, who was influenced by radical Pietist Johann

8. Peterson, *Working the Angles*, 44–47.

9. Wesley, *A Plain Account of Christian Perfection*, 61.

10. Keller, *Prayer*, 28.

Christoph Blumhardt, pastoral leader of a regional revival in Möttlingen (northeast of Stuttgart) in 1845–47, wrote, "The connection between the prayer life and the Spirit life is close and indissolvable."[11] Jesus prayed in a certain place, and when he finished, a disciple said, "Lord, teach us to pray, as John taught his disciples" (Luke 11:1).

Prayer is muscular, exercised faith in action. John Calvin holds that, "Prayer is the chief exercise of faith." To cultivate the devout life, we must believe that "prayer is the gymnasium of the soul" (Samuel Zwemer). Feel the tone in: "Do not be slothful in zeal, be fervent in spirit, serving the Lord. Rejoice in hope, be patient in tribulation, be *constant in prayer*" (Rom 12:11–12). Capture the cadence of: "And they *devoted* themselves to the apostle's teaching and the fellowship, to the breaking of bread and the *prayers*" (Acts 2:42). Embrace the resolve of: "But we will *devote ourselves to prayer* and to the ministry of the word (Acts 6:4). This is a team and an individual effort. And again, heed the appeal in: "*Devote yourselves to prayer*, being watchful and thankful" (Col 4:2 NIV). The Greek verb translated as *constant* and *devote* is the same in each instance and means, "to persist in, hold fast to, be strong toward." The present tense in Romans 12:12, Acts 2:42 and Colossians 4:2 suggests continual, obstinate, staunch, prayer.

I define prayer as "communion and communication with God." The English word *prayer* comes from the Latin root *precarius*, related to the word *precarious*. Biblical prayer is a precarious, risky practice—a weapon in the arsenal of spiritual wallop—when we "pray at all times in the Spirit, with all prayer and supplication" (Eph 6:18). It is not a method for self-improvement, shopping list requests, therapy, emotionally healthy spirituality, self-fulfillment, prosperity, an inner journey, or absorption into God. Prayer is the soul's operating system that coordinates all of life and leadership. It is the wavelength to hear the eternal harmonies of heaven. Charles Spurgeon wrote that prayer is "the slender nerve that moves the muscles of omnipotence."[12] If Jesus prayed and the Holy Spirit prays (Rom 8:26–27), should we not pray?

I try for at least an hour every morning, in quietness, to read Scripture, journal, pray, and read devotional material. Like a gyroscope, I start and stay centered in prayer and Christ. I seek to pray without ceasing all day, as I drive, enter meetings, chat with people, and prepare for any teaching or preaching for which I am scheduled. I send up "Nehemiah now"

11. Murray, *The Prayer Life*, 46.

12. Spurgeon, *Twelve Sermons on Prayer*, 31.

instant prayers during crucial conversations like when he prayed *to the God of heaven* while in the Persian king's presence (Neh 2:1–5). If Jesus would withdraw to desolate places and pray (Luke 5:16), I can do no less. He withdrew and prayed to the Father as a regular, prolonged, ongoing practice. When James references Elijah and announces, "The prayer of a righteous person is powerful and effective" (James 5:16 NIV), I gain atomic level energy and resolve to be a righteous man of God! Spener writes, "We must discuss hindrances to prayer. (1) The chief of these is a godless life. (2) Among such hindrances as well is far too much distraction in worldly activities."[13] Once when I was discouraged and distracted, I asked a woman of prayer to pray for me before I was to teach a Christian theology class at a Bible college. She sought the Lord and he placed the following verse into her mind for me: "Build yourself up in your most holy faith and pray in the Holy Spirit" (Jude 20). Wow, this gave me Eiffel tower vision to continuously "*build myself up*" in my most "*holy* faith" of Christian doctrine, and to continuously pray in the zone of the *Holy* Spirit—all present tense ongoing practices. The essence of prayer is supplication or petition.

PIETISM AND PRAYER

The Pietists placed five-star value on prayer from the heart more as conversation with God than as formal religion. Lifeless liturgical prayers read or prayed without piety or passion sabotage the devout life. The Pietists liberated prayer from the fixed externals of church ritual and planted it into the spontaneous and personal interiors of the Christian heart. There is still a valuable place for well-presented written prayers, whether Anglican, Lutheran, Puritan, or biblical, when infused with the warmth of piety, devotion, and the Spirit. Johann Arndt wrote:

> Prayer is conversation with God, a piece of the inner, spiritual, heavenly life, the characteristic and mark of a faithful Christian's heart, a continual movement of the Holy Spirit since he is a Spirit of grace and of prayer (Zech 12:10), a work of divine healing . . . Prayer occurs in secret, in a little chamber, in the heart, in all places, in all occupations, or openly in the congregation in the confession of faith to the honor of the holy Name of God and in thanksgiving for all blessings.[14]

13. Spener, "God-Pleasing Prayer," 90–92.
14. Arndt, *True Christianity*, 244.

Spener also expressed a Pietist sentiment: "Nor is it enough to pray outwardly with our mouth, but true prayer, and the best prayer, occurs in the inner man, and it either breaks forth in words or remains in the soul, yet God will find and hit upon it. Nor again, is it enough to worship God in an external temple, but the inner man worships God best in his own temple, whether or not he is in an external temple at the same time."[15]

The key to the devout life—to fruitful discipleship and effective prayer—is the Pietist doctrine of the inner life fed only by union with Christ. Pietist literature is replete with phrases such as "the indwelling Christ," "the inner meaning of doctrines and sacraments," "the inner person," and "inward or personal Christianity." We have union with Christ and are one with God the Father and Jesus as they are one. Key texts are: John 17:22; Galatians 2:20; 2 Corinthians 13:5; and 1 John 2:14. We live "in" Christ—a new place with a new pattern of life. Study John 15:1–11. The key is to abide, remain, stay, dwell, or reside in Christ. Francke stressed prayer: "Prayer is both the root and salt of all divine activities. Prayer may not be distant from anything one does and in prayer arises all union with the dear God . . . There is no better way to achieve a foretaste of eternal life than for one to humble oneself before God and truly pray, to remain constant in prayer, and to walk continually with the dear God."[16] Francke also exhorted ministers to "inculcate, with great plainness and seriousness, the necessity of prayer" in the minds of people, who are greatly ignorant concerning the duty of prayer.[17]

Union with Christ offers a grounded mysticism for prayer and the devout life. The two streams of biblical faith and mysticism converged in Pietism to produce what Timothy Keller called (citing Scottish theologian John Murray) an "*intelligent* mysticism—an encounter with God that involves not only the affections of the heart but also the convictions of the mind"—a synergy of truth and doctrine with spiritual power and experience—an experiential theology.[18] The mystical dimension of church Pietism does not view prayer as wordless absorption into God, as in radical Pietism or Quietism. Biblical or prophetic prayer requires communication and speech. The goal of prayer is not an impersonal union *in* God but a

15. Spener, *Pia Desideria*, 117.

16. Francke, "The Foretaste of Eternal Life," 153.

17. Francke, "A Letter to a Friend Concerning the Most Useful Way of Preaching," 121.

18. Keller, *Prayer*, 16–17.

personal communion *with* God. Donald Bloesch writes: "The Pietists, like the Reformers, conceived of prayer in terms of a dialogue between the living God and the regenerated sinner, though among the so-called radical Pietists mystical themes resurfaced, such as the loss of self in union with God. The goal of Pietism was the service of God in ministry to the world as opposed to be taken up in the grandeur and glory of God"[19] Arndt expressed Pietist themes with the basis and aids for prayer:

> The basis of our prayer is God's grace in Christ. The grace makes us alive . . . Prayer makes us heavenly, ignites us in the love of God, and protects against sins and misfortune. The second basis for prayer is God's gracious presence. This ought to stir us up at all times and places to speak to God. A third basis of prayer is God's truth. Moses and David were heard in prayer. A fourth basis of prayer is God's eternal Word. It is a great consolation that faith and prayer have an eternal foundation over which the gates of hell cannot conquer. The power and fruits of prayer are uncountable.[20]
>
> Since our flesh and blood are weak, there are three strong aids for our prayer: (1) The prayers of our own Intercessor and eternal High Priest (Heb 5:7), (2) The Holy Spirit who helps our weakness and himself intercedes for us with sighs too deep for words (Rom 8:26), (3) The holy Christian Church which prays for all true members of Christ (Eph 6:18).[21]

PRACTICES OF PRAYER

We can view prayer in three directions or movements: *upward*, *inward*, and *outward*. Prayer is trinitarian. We pray into each person of the Godhead. We pray *upward* to the Father in adoration, praise, thanksgiving, and lament. We pray *inward* to the Son in confession, repentance, submission, and communion. We pray *outward* through the Holy Spirit in intercession, supplication, empowerment, and mission for the needs of others and for witness in the world, and "that supplications, prayers, intercessions, and thanksgivings be made for all people" (1 Tim 2:1). We can ask with bold, confident, freedom of speech (*parresia*) in prayer before God (1 John 3:21–22; 5:14–15). Let us explore key practices of prayer.

19. Bloesch, *Spirituality Old and New*, 22.
20. Arndt, *True Christianity*, 212.
21. Ibid., 244–45.

Private Prayer

You will never plunge the depths of spiritual renewal if you fail to practice private prayer. You must plan, not just wish to pray. You must view prayer as a potent power source that operates quietly, though mightily, like a particle of uranium planted in the soil of your soul. Jesus beckons us to enter our private chamber, shut the door, and pray to our Father in secret, and he will reward us (Matt 6:6). We wait for his reply. Eugene Peterson tweeted, "Waiting in prayer is a disciplined refusal to act before God acts."[22] We have direct access to God anytime, anywhere. He is closer than our breath. As with Elijah, his voice blows more in the whisper than in the wind. As with Samuel, he quietly calls our name. We must forge our way through the clamor of our harried lives to that royal residence of solitude in the interior palace of private prayer. Pietist leader Spener offers initial practices for heart-felt private prayer:

1. Prayer must occur from a repented heart.
2. Prayer must occur in faith.
3. Prayer must occur with great humility on our part and with a heart inclined to great reverence toward God.
4. Prayer must occur with reflection, that is, with zealous concern and thought toward that concerning which we pray.
5. Prayer must occur with zeal and true desire for that for which we pray.
6. Prayer must occur with fitting modesty and discretion.
7. Prayer must occur in a fitting order.
8. Prayer must occur out of a heartfelt love for one's neighbor.
9. Prayer must be continual and unceasing.
10. The last thing necessary for prayer is that we give it in thanksgiving.[23]

Daniel Henderson exhorts us to move beyond "grocery list," need-focused prayer to worship-based, God-focused prayer that seeks God's face before God's hand.[24] Check the prayers of Jesus and Paul. They provide superb content for God-focused prayer. In our petitions, we must abide in

22. Peterson, Twitter@PetersonDaily, August 1, 2015.

23. Spener, "God-Pleasing Prayer," 90–91.

24. See, Henderson, *Transforming Prayer*, and *6:4 Fellowship*, http://www.64fellowship.com.

Jesus and ask in his name, for God's glory. Donald Bloesch then suggests: "Following our petitions, we should then look forward in anticipation to God's answer: 'Morning by morning I lay my requests before you and wait in expectation' (Ps 5:3). Dialogue should occur not just at the beginning, but also throughout our prayer. We should take time to pause in prayer so that we can hear God's response and receive further guidance from his Spirit."[25]

Prayer and Hearing God

The Bible supplies an avalanche of evidence that God not only spoke, but also continues to speak to individuals and to groups from all contexts, and that scores of people in the Bible clearly heard God communicate. He speaks in creation, the conscience, the heart, mind, and emotions, through visions, dreams, prophecy, words of knowledge, symbolic signs, miracles, audible voice, angels, visitations, worship, Scripture, Jesus Christ, the Holy Spirit, preaching and teaching, people, the church, the still small voice, the inner witness of the Spirit, impressions, prayer, and other ways.[26] To hear a certain radio station, we must tune into the right frequency. To hear the voice of Jesus, we must do the same. He does not confine his voice to the Bible, as some teach. We have a personal relationship with God, not with a book. We must recognize the Lord's voice as his sheep. He is our Good Shepherd. He declares, "The sheep *hear* his voice, and he calls his own sheep by name and leads them out. When he has brought out all his own, he goes before them, and the sheep *follow* him, for they *know his voice* (John 10:3–4).

All the main verbs: "hear, calls, leads, goes, follow, know," are present tense and signify continuous, ongoing experiences. Jesus communicates directly to his sheep *in accordance* with the Bible. Read the book of Acts. God's voice came in many ways—dreams, visions, prophecy, audibly, angels, the Holy Spirit, preaching, and so forth. There are at least thirty-two different examples where God spoke directly and immediately to individuals or groups of people in a book of twenty-eight chapters (not counting Acts 2:17–21). This is an average of more than once per chapter.[27] Did God confine to a written book, authored over a fifteen-hundred-year time frame,

25. Bloesch, *The Struggle of Prayer*, 62–63.

26. See, Willard, *Hearing God*; Blackaby, *Hearing God's Voice*; Smith, *The Voice of Jesus*; and Deere, *Surprised by the Voice of God*.

27. Anderson, "How Did God Speak in the Book of Acts?"

all that he had to say? What if you cannot read or you do not have access to the Bible? Most of God's people in history could not read and had no Bibles. Many people in the Bible could hear God's voice. Jesus said, "He who has ears to hear, let him hear" (Mark 4:9). Can God guide and speak to you, or is he mute? E. Stanley Jones remarked: "Does God guide? Strange if he didn't. The Psalmist asks: 'He that planted the ear, shall he not hear? He that formed the eyes, shall he not see?' (Ps 94:9). And I ask, 'He that made the tongue and gave us power to communicate with one another, shall he not speak and communicate with us?' I do not believe that God our Father is a dumb, non-communicative impersonality."[28] We need divine revelation, God's prophetic word to guide us, lest we run wild, "When people do not accept divine guidance, they run wild" (Prov 29:18 NLT).

However, I am nervous with so-called "listening prayer," if by that is meant self-directed, subjective, or gnostic ways to hear God's voice. There are too many misguided people and self-proclaimed prophets who announce, "God told me," but did not hear God speak at all. However, if prayer is genuine communication and communion with God, it must include listening, otherwise it is merely one-way talking, a monologue. The Pietist view of the outer word of God illuminated by the inner witness of the Holy Spirit leads to greater freedom with greater risk when we seek to hear God's voice in a two-way conversation, a dialogue. Donald Bloesch writes:

> Prayer is the core of spirituality . . . Prayer presupposes a two-way conversation. It is indeed the conversation of the heart with God (Luther). Yet we cannot enter into dialogue until we listen to what God says. As Christoph Blumhardt put it, "God can well hear the sighs of everyone, even the foolish; yet, in reality, only those can *pray* who *listen* to God." Biblical prayer consists of stillness as well as struggle.[29]

That we are made in God's image implies that we can speak and hear because God speaks and hears. We are oral beings before we are literary beings. We learn to speak and hear before we learn to read. For many, whether in private or public settings, prayer is often a one-way telephone call where *we* talk to God, and as soon as we are finished, we hang up. Relationship implies two-way communication. It requires that each party not only speaks, but also listens and responds. God's word is his creative,

28. Jones, *A Song of Ascents*, 188.

29. Bloesch, *Spirituality Old and New*, 133.

dynamic, action-speech. God does what God says. God's word existed before the authors of Scripture wrote anything down. The Bible as God's word locates its center and finality in Jesus Christ, who is the Word of God. But the Bible and Jesus do not merge into one entity called "the Word." Jesus reveals all who God is as the Word.

In Greek, two terms translated as "word" in English are *logos* and *rhema. Logos* refers to that which is spoken—thought, message, content, speech, or the documents produced. It is the root for the word *logic. Rhema* refers to active speaking, utterance, the spoken word, or an event. It is the root for the word *rhetoric.* As the "word of God," *logos* can refer to God's speech, the gospel message, the Scripture, and to Jesus Christ. All the recorded *rhema* words became part of the permanent written Scripture of *logos* as the word of God. Acts 10:44 uses both. Literally, it reads, "While Peter was still saying these words [*rhemata*], the Spirit fell on everyone hearing the word [*logos*]." Peter spoke and they heard the word. The two terms overlap. But it seems to me they also each have their own distinct ranges of meaning. *Rhema* as far as I can tell, never refers to the written word in the New Testament. It mainly refers to the word as spoken or proclaimed (often as the gospel). I could be wrong (and I am not a Greek scholar), but I do not think they are synonymous. However, the Septuagint does translate the Hebrew *debar* (word) with both *logos* and *rhema.*

Jesus "upholds the universe by the word [*rhema*] of his power" (Heb 1:3), and "by faith we understand that the universe was created by the word [*rhema*] of God" (Heb 11:3). Christ created and upholds the universe by the force of his *spoken* command. The universe "heard and obeys"! The word *rhema* is associated closely with the mouth and heart (a Pietist theme), and the spoken character of God's word or message. "But what does it say? 'The *word* [*rhema*] is near you, in your mouth and in your heart" (that is, the *word* [*rhema*] of faith that we proclaim); because, if you confess with your mouth that Jesus is Lord and believe in your heart that God raised him from the dead, you will be saved. For with the heart one believes and is justified, and with the mouth one confesses and is saved" (Rom 10:8–10). Richard Foster comments:

> The Holy Spirit moves among his people in the Prayer of the Heart. Perhaps the most common way of all is through special revelatory impressions and words that the Spirit imparts to the individual. This is often called a *rhema*, Greek meaning simply "word." When Jesus observed that we live not by bread alone but by every word

> that comes from the mouth of God, he used the word *rhema* (Matt 4:4). Likewise, when Paul spoke of the sword of the Spirit, which is the word of God, he used the word *rhema*.[30]

The *logos* as God's fixed word, sets the boundaries to hear God's dynamic *rhema* word. Faith does not come by reading, it comes by *hearing* God's word spoken or preached by a voice, "So faith comes from hearing, and hearing through the word [*rhema*] of Christ" (Rom 10:17). God's word is more than a book that you read. What God says is his word. A book neither created nor sustains the heavens (Ps 33:6; Heb 1:3; 2 Pet 3:5, 7); we were not born again through a book (1 Pet 1:23); a book cannot dwell richly inside you (Col 3:16); and Jesus is not a book (John 1:1). God's word is his dynamic declaration in what he *says* through Christ by the Spirit.

Jesus announced, "Man shall not live by bread alone, but by every *word* [rhema] that *comes* from the mouth of God" (Matt 4:4). This word is not the *logos* word, but the spoken *rhema* word. The verb *comes* (or proceeds) is present tense. We shall live on whatever God speaks. John uses the plural *rhemata* in John 15:7, "If you abide in me, and my *words* [*rhemata*] abide in you, ask whatever you wish, and it will be done for you." Have you ever read the Bible, listened to a sermon, or been in prayer, where you felt that "God clearly spoke" to you? What was that? I suggest it was God's *rhema* to you, not some charismatic "word-faith" revelation. Foster says:

> When reading the Bible, people commonly experience a special "word in the Bible," in which a particular passage seems to apply to an individual situation in a new way . . . This "quickening of the Word" encourages us that God is near and deeply interested in the particular circumstances of our lives. A special *rhema* also comes to us frequently from other people, in which divine revelation from God is applied to our lives.[31]

Jesus says, "It is the Spirit who gives life; the flesh is no help at all. The *words* [*rhemata*] that I have *spoken* to you are spirit and life" (John 6:63). The Spirit gives life (present tense) matched with the spoken words of Jesus, which are spirit and life. God speaks to you personally through *rhema*. The impact you will feel is spirit and life. Bloesch writes: "Christian prayer entails both external and internal relations. It's both an external act of communication and an inner act of communion. In the act of prayer, we

30. Foster, *Prayer*, 137.

31. Ibid.

are related to the God who stands outside and above us but who also, by his Spirit, dwells within us."[32] The receptive soil of your soul is the condition for lush spiritual acoustics, so "who has ears to hear let him hear" (Matt 13:1–23). Jesus speaks through the inner witness of the Spirit grounded in the written witness of the Scripture. In spiritual discernment and decision-making, we practice paying attention to his presence and leading. We must cultivate openness with an active response in a posture of humility.[33]

Samuel, who realized from Eli that God was speaking to him, said: "Speak, Lord, for your servant is listening" or hears (1 Sam 3:10). And for Elijah, God was not in the wind, the earthquake, and the fire, but in a "still small voice" or whisper (1 Kgs 19:11–13). God communicates by the inner illumination and witness of the Spirit who speaks through the word (*logos*) and words (*rhema*), in a "still small voice." God's word is God speaking. Dallas Willard writes:

> The Word of God, when no further qualification is added, is God speaking, God communicating. When God speaks, he expresses his mind, his character, and his purposes. Thus, he is always present with his word. All expressions of his mind are "words" of God. This is true whether the specific instrumentality is external to the human mind—as in natural phenomena (Ps 19:1–4), other human beings, the incarnate Christ (Logos), or the Bible—or internal to the human mind—as in thoughts, intents, and feelings.[34]

As indicated from the present tense, the Spirit will continually guide us into truth (John 16:13), or place a "check" or caution in us where something is not right or true. We have an inner teacher and anointing that abides in us, who teaches us so we continue to abide in him (1 John 2:20, 27). We must learn to recognize his often-quiet voice and listen, but "unfortunately," as Dallas Willard says, "this gentle low-key word may easily be overlooked or disregarded."[35]

However, when we pray, sometimes God does not particularly "say" anything to us. We hear the sounds of silence. We may need to wait on him, sit in silence, and practice the presence of God. According to Jeremy Taylor, this is a key to prayer and devotion. Ponder his words: "The benefits of this consideration and exercise being universal upon all the parts of piety, I shall

32. Bloesch, *The Struggle of Prayer*, 98.

33. See, Smith, *The Voice of Jesus.*

34. Willard, *Hearing God*, 159.

35. Ibid.,116.

less need to specify any particulars; but yet, most properly, this exercise of considering the Divine presence is an excellent help to prayer, producing in us reverence and awfulness to the Divine Majesty of God, and actual devotion to our offices."[36]

Often, evangelicals do not have a grid for genuine prophecy, dreams, visions, revelations, and the personal *rhema* voice of God. They consign his voice to Scripture, circumstances, and inner peace (which seems subjective to me). Would you trust a pastor or a board who seek to hear God only in these ways? The Pietists taught that we should hear God in Scripture with the illumination of the Spirit. But they did not go far enough. I have had God speak to me in unmistakable ways by his *rhema* voice through prophecy, impressions, spontaneous thoughts, and "leadings." And you?

Where do you begin? Create quiet space to listen. Read Scripture and pray. Scripture and the Spirit speak in stereo. Listen for the voice of Jesus to speak in and alongside Scripture. Spener writes: "Because the Holy Scripture is a book directed to all times and to all men, one ought to read it to direct it continually to the reader himself and to attend in it how our God speaks not only generally or only to those to whom the words were immediately directed, but to each person who reads these words."[37] Ask God questions, wait, and listen carefully for his replies. He may speak directly without or indirectly within. David *inquired* of the Lord and the Lord spoke to him directly (2 Sam 5:19, 23). God spoke indirectly to Nehemiah's heart (Neh 7:5). Scripture assures us that God guides (Ps 32:8) and that the Holy Spirit speaks (Acts 13:23).

By trial and error, we learn to detect God's voice. It is like a mother who detects her child's cry in the clamor of other children, or like a dog that knows its master's voice, or like a musician who plays by ear and knows how to distinguish between familiar notes. Just as a child learns language through immersion, let us immerse ourselves in God's word for the language of prayer. Through training and experience, we as sheep will not follow strangers for we do not know the voice of strangers but only that of our Shepherd who knows us and calls us by name (John 10:3–5). Listen to God as a lifestyle. God says, "This is my beloved Son; *listen* [continuously] to him" (Mark 9:7). To listen contains the idea of to *obey*. Dallas Willard offers principles:

36. Taylor, *Holy Living and Dying*, 25–26.

37. Spener, "The Necessary and Useful Reading of the Holy Scriptures," 75.

- Meditate constantly on God's principles for life as set forth in the Scriptures.
- Pay close attention to what is happening in your life for God's communication in your mind and heart.
- Pray and speak to God constantly and specifically about all matters that concern you.
- Listen carefully and deliberately for God, paying close attention to what you hear.[38]

Public Prayer

When we add praying alone to praying with others, with unity and God's direction, the results can be exponential. The birth of the church occurred in a prayer gathering not in a preaching service. It started with a medium sized group of ordinary men and women, and grew to a larger gathering of about one hundred and twenty. They practiced united, persistent, prayer for ten days. The Spirit then broke out on the Day of Pentecost (Acts 2:1). Luke records: "All these with one accord [one mind/impulse] were *devoting themselves to prayer*, together with the women and Mary the mother of Jesus, and his brothers. In those days, Peter stood up among the brothers—the company of persons was in all about 120" (Acts 1:14–15). Again, we see this same word used here as in Acts 2:42; 6:4; Rom 12:12, Col 4:2. Acts mentions prayer thirty-one times and appears in twenty of its twenty-eight chapters.[39] Most of it is corporate prayer. The success of public prayer depends largely on pastors and church leaders, who fuse listening prayer and discussion for discernment where "it seemed good to the Holy Spirit and to us" (Acts 15:28). If you are a pastor or a leader who facilitates public prayer gatherings, let me offer three ideas.

First, if you do not devote yourself to prayer as a leader (Acts 6:4), you will not lead your people to this either, and you will not have a church that can call itself a "house of prayer for all nations." You will put your priorities into care, conflict, and communication. Your practices follow your values. You must resolve that prayer will glow at the summit of spiritual importance as much as preaching, worship, and teaching do. Things will happen when you pray that will not happen if you do not pray.

38. Willard, *Hearing God*, 277–78.

39. Fernando, *Acts*, 74.

Second, design your services, small groups, or whatever gatherings of people you have, to contain all types of public prayer (Eph 6:18; 1 Tim 2:1). If you have a ninety-minute worship service, plan twenty-five minutes for music and liturgy, twenty minutes for prayer, and thirty minutes for preaching. Mix them around. Allot five minutes for announcements at the start or end of the service with PowerPoint bulletins, and only things that pertain to the whole church. Five minutes remain for other matters such as dismissing the children. Focus your weekend gatherings around worship, word, and prayer. With small groups, add community and mission. Prepare for times of prayer; do not just wing it on the spot with a "pastoral prayer" or only open and close your meetings with prayer, or solely for prayer requests. Prepare for prayer just as you do for preaching or worship, and place prayer into each weekend service and mid-week gathering. To cultivate a culture of prayer in your church, the lead pastor must lead the corporate prayer gatherings. It cannot be delegated to someone else, though others should contribute. All key leaders should also participate.

Third, hold at least one well planned and promoted ninety-minute prayer gathering or summit per month where you expect all your key leaders, staff, children, youth, and young adults to *participate*. Use my ***GPS*** template for structure and direction (God-focused; Participatory; and Scripture-fed and Spirit-led):

God-focused—the main key to dynamic public prayer is to focus on and experience God. Too many prayer times are hollow, pale, and human-centered. Many so-called worship songs are also human-centered Christian tunes, not intended for congregational worship and lacking theological depth and a God focus. If we mainly sing and pray about ourselves, is it any wonder there is a lack of awe and wonder? We must move from a self-orientation to a God-orientation or we will likely not experience God, even though he desires to reveal himself to us. We tend to have an elementary view of prayer in which we often pray merely to ask God for things or ask him to do things for us. There is an appropriate place for that. But God-focused worship fuels the furnace of Spirit-infused prayer and praise, thanksgiving, confession, lament, petition, supplication, and intercession, as we first seek God's priorities and purposes. Most Psalms and biblical prayers, even though often framed within human need, are God-focused— "Holy is *your* name. May *your* kingdom come and *your* will be done on earth as it is in heaven!"

Do not start with or focus on "prayer requests" that become me-centered shopping lists, usually prefaced by too much talk. Focus on themes and pray them through. Select music and Scripture that support the themes. Keep the pace moving with focus. Ensure there is movement *upward* and *outward* in prayer—not just *inward*. Here are some ways to establish God-focused public prayer that will open the channels for God's presence.

- Prayers in response to the Holy Spirit's leading rather than following a specific agenda.
- Prayers that flow from Scripture and focus more on God's ability instead of our needs.
- Prayers to advance his kingdom rather than our desires.
- Worship and prayer mingled together with thanksgiving and praise.
- Pray-ers listening to one another and prayers that are connected.[40]

Participatory—another key for dynamic public prayer is to *involve* everyone. People need to participate, not just sit and spectate. First Corinthians 14 is an example of a public prayer and worship gathering with varieties of participation that is Spirit-led and God-focused, with decency and order. There are music, teaching, prayer, thanksgiving, revelation, tongues, interpretation, and prophecy, designed to edify the church and glorify God. I do not advocate that churches must become charismatic or Pentecostal, but that public prayer gatherings should involve everyone in a variety of practices, charged with God's presence and supernatural outcomes. But dynamic public prayer requires planning and attention to flow. A role of gifted leaders is to equip God's people in ministry for maturity (Eph 4:11–16), where people should receive prayer training. Everyone should bring a Bible, a notebook or journal, with an expectant heart to pray and experience God. Invite children and youth to participate too.

Plan ways for people to read and pray Scripture or use liturgies like the *Book of Common Prayer* or Matthew Henry's *Method for Prayer*, take notes or journal their insights, draw, sing, confess, be silent, praise, intercede, wait on God, listen for God's voice, share what they feel the Lord may be saying, pray for others (especially for healing and direction; provide vials of oil for anointing in prayer), pray alone, pray in small groups and as a large group, intercede for the community and its civil servants, the country,

40. Fuqua, *United and Ignited*, Kindle edition, 9.6.

the nations, share answers to specific prayers, sit, stand, walk, kneel, briefly share requests. And pray outward for mission. Finally:

> It is important to remember that the intercessory prayer of many humble people nurtured in the churches of evangelical Pietism has been responsible for the great missionary outreach of Protestantism. While the Reformers stressed intercessory prayer, it was directed more to the reform of the church than the conversion of the world to Jesus Christ. Not until the advent of Pietism and Puritanism in the seventeenth century did foreign missions begin to flower within Protestantism.[41]

Scripture-fed and Spirit-led—a final key for dynamic public prayer is to pray the passages and themes of Scripture endowed with the leading and unction of the Spirit. Because the Spirit inspired the Scriptures, "When therefore the believer uses the word of God as the guide to determine both the spirit and the dialect of his prayer, he is inverting the process of divine revelation and using the channel of God's approach to him as the channel of his approach to God."[42] Furthermore, everyone's level of Bible literacy and devotion to prayer will rise, especially when they experience God's electrifying presence, voice, and answers to prayer first-hand. They will encounter Scripture as alive and active, throbbing with heart-stirring and mind-bending theology adorned with colossal, elegant, and at times chilling truths.

> Biblical saints often used the language and themes of Scripture to interpret and express their experience. At least thirteen occasions in the Old Testament later prophets learned from Moses how to praise God (Num 14:18; 2 Chr 30:9; Neh 9:17,31; Ps 103:8; 111:4; 112:4; 116:5; 145:9; Joel 2:13; Jonah 4:2; etc.). Mary drew upon the Song of Hannah (Luke 1:46–55, cf., 1 Sam 2:1–10); Solomon at the dedication of the temple incorporated Ps 132:8,9; (2 Chr 6:40–42); Jesus on the cross used the words of Psalms 22:1 and 31:5 (Matt 27:46, Luke 23:46); and the early church cited Psalms 146 and 2 (Acts 4:24–30). In each case the language of Scripture provided the language for prayer.[43]

41. Bloesch, *The Struggle of Prayer*, 89.

42. Pierson, *George Muller of Bristol and His Witness to a Prayer-Hearing God*, Kindle edition,1608.

43. Johnson and Duncan, "Recommendations for Improving Public Prayer."

Pietist Reformed Baptist pastor John Piper remarks: "I have seen that those whose prayers are most saturated with Scripture are generally most fervent and most effective in prayer. And where the mind isn't brimming with the Bible, the heart is not generally brimming with prayer."[44] Look up the actual prayers in the Old and New Testaments, and use those passages to shape the content and focus of your prayers. Ensure that your public prayer is *Scripture-fed.*

Also ensure that your public prayer is *Spirit-led.* Practice the robust present tense appeal of Jude, "But you, beloved, building yourselves up in your most holy faith [Scripture-fed] and *praying in the Holy Spirit* [Spirit-led], keep yourselves in the love of God, waiting for the mercy of our Lord Jesus Christ that leads to eternal life" (Jude 20–21). Our holy faith runs parallel—like train tracks connected by railroad ties—with the Holy Spirit toward a common goal: to keep us in God's love. Peter Davids interprets verse 20:

> What this shows is that praying in the Spirit is in line with the usual sense of doing something in the Spirit (Mark 12:36, prophecy produced by the Spirit; Acts 19:21, travel directed by the Spirit; Rom 14:17, joy produced by the Spirit; 1 Cor 12:3, speech controlled by the Spirit; Eph 5:18, controlled by alcohol versus controlled by the Spirit), which means that it refers to prayer *controlled* or *guided* by the Spirit.[45]

The Spirit as God's wind, fire, and water will inspire, radiate, and irrigate your corporate prayer. Endeavor to "take the sword of the Spirit, the word of God [Scripture-fed] and pray at all times in the Spirit, with all prayer and supplication" [Spirit-led] (Eph 6:17–18). Let's hoist our spiritual sails to navigate the open seas of God's will with the Spirit's intercession: "Likewise the Spirit helps us in our weakness. For we do not know what to pray as we ought, but the Spirit himself intercedes for us with groanings too deep for words. And he who searches hearts knows what is the mind of the Spirit, because the Spirit intercedes for the saints according to the will of God" (Rom 8:26–27).

Have you experienced times of public prayer where the atmosphere was charged with God's electric presence? Or have you noticed occasions where the unction and authority of the prayers mysteriously beamed forth with laser clarity and propulsion? Scripture-fed and Spirit-led public prayer

44. Piper, "How to Pray for a Desolate Church."

45. Davids, *The Letters of 2 Peter and Jude*, 94–95.

will transform your prayer gatherings and your church. Design times of silence and listening, read Scripture, keep prayers short and focused, and pray in missional ways (Luke 10:2; Col 4:2–6). At almost every strategic advance of the Spirit's missional action in Acts, Luke mentions public prayer (e.g., Acts 1:14, 24; 4:23–31; 6:1–7; 8:14–17; 13:2–3).

PREACHING AND PRAYER

I love to preach and prepare. However, as pastors, we often *prepare too much, preach too long, and pray too little*, with unremarkable results in our sermons. Prayer is underrated and preparation is overrated. Many pastors are devoted to preparation and preaching but not devoted to prayer. They rely on preparation and presentation. We must devote ourselves to the public reading of Scripture, to exhortation, and to teaching (1 Tim 4:13), and devote ourselves to prayer and to the ministry of the word (Acts 6:4). We should preach the word, yes, but powered by prayer in the Spirit. Few resources on homiletics and preaching spend significant time on the necessity of prayer in the preparation and delivery of sermons. I have decided to balance my preparation with more time in prayer and less time in study and trust God with the results. Keen study and right handling of Scripture is vital (2 Tim 2:15) but we must not neglect closet time in prayer. Spener concludes his last proposal to correct conditions in the church with the great need for revived preachers: "May many preachers be revived thereby to preach the heart of Christianity after this model with simplicity and power. May it also be a means for some further reform of the wretched condition of our church which we deplored so heartily above."[46]

Evangelist D. L. Moody proclaimed, "The best way to revive the church is to build a fire in the pulpit."[47] We need pastors who will preach with fire, prayer, and holy affections, with messages saturated with Scripture not just based on Scripture. We need preaching with heat in the heart and light in the mind, just as John the Baptist was "a burning and shining light" (John 5:35).[48] Jonathan Edwards, Pietist-Puritan pastor and American theologian, and leader in the First great awakening in the New England American colonies in the 1730s–1740s wrote, "Ministers, in order to be burning and

46. Spener, *Pia Desideria*, 122.

47. Sweeting, *Great Quotes and Illustrations*, 219.

48. Much of this paragraph is adapted from Piper, *The Supremacy of God in Preaching*, 86–102.

shining lights, should walk closely with God, and keep near to Christ; that they might ever be enlightened and enkindled by him. And they should be much in seeking God, and conversing with him by prayer."[49] John Piper writes, "Good preaching is born of good praying. And it will come forth with the power that caused the Great Awakening when it is delivered under the mighty prayer-wrought influence of the Holy Spirit."[50]

It was said of Charles Finney, nineteenth century revivalist preacher, "When he opened his mouth, he was aiming a gun. When he spoke, bombardment began." He preached with prayer-drenched *unction.* Unction gives insight, grasp, and projecting power as it permeates revealed truth with God's energy and sharp potency. Unction is spiritual anointing that enters a fourth dimension, beyond skill in communication and rhetoric. E. M. Bounds affirms,

> The character of our praying will determine the character of our preaching. Light praying will make light preaching. Prayer makes preaching strong, gives it unction, and makes it stick . . . The preacher must be pre-eminently a man of prayer. No learning can make up for the failure to pray. No earnestness, no diligence, no study, no gifts will supply its lack . . . This unction comes to the preacher not in the study but in the closet. Prayer, in the preacher's life, in the preacher's study, in the preacher's pulpit, must be conspicuous and an all-impregnating force and an all-coloring ingredient . . . The little estimate we put on prayer is evident from the little time we give it.[51]

How could John Wesley preach up to fifteen times per week, and report these kinds of results in his journal: "After preaching to an earnest congregation at Coleford, I met the Society. They contained themselves pretty well during the exhortation, but when I began to pray the flame broke out: many cried aloud; many sunk to the ground; many trembled exceedingly; but all seemed to be quite athirst for God, and penetrated by the presence of his power."[52] How could Peter on the Day of Pentecost give an extemporaneous summary of the Old Testament that led to Christ which cornered his audience and cut to their heart where they begged, "Brothers, what must we

49. Cited by Piper, *The Supremacy of God in Preaching*, 101.

50. Ibid.,102.

51. Bounds, *Power Through Prayer*, 32, 35, 38, 92.

52. As written by Wesley in his *Journal* (September 8, 1784), from Wesley, *The Works of John Wesley*, 288.

do?" (Acts 2:37). Only by the *unction* or anointing of a Spirit emblazoned preacher! Paul was the same. He wrote, "My speech and my message were not in plausible words of wisdom, but in demonstration of the Spirit and of power, so that your faith might not rest in the wisdom of men but in the power of God" (1 Cor 2:4–5).

Pastors must preach the word (2 Tim 4:2) as an act of *worship*, not as a presentation of exegetical ideas, with God's glory as the goal. George Whitefield was a bombastic preacher and contemporary of Wesley and Edwards and a revival leader in the first great awakening. In 1735, he recorded in his diary: "My mind being now more open and enlarged, I began to read the Holy Scriptures upon my knees, laying aside all other books and praying over, if possible, every line and word. This proved meat indeed and drink indeed to my soul. I daily received fresh life, light and power from above."[53] Devotion to heart-felt private and public prayer, hearing God's voice, and anointed preaching, will plunge you into the depths of spiritual renewal. Dive in!

FOR REFLECTION AND PRACTICE

1. Reflect on Richard Lovelace's quote at the start of this chapter. What are your thoughts? Study Acts 2:42; 6:4; Col 4:2 and 1 Thess 5:17. What would it take for you to devote yourself to unceasing prayer, and what changes must you make to overcome problems of prayer?
2. Reflect on what Jesus taught on prayer: Matt 5:44; 6:5–9; 7:7–8; 9:38; 17:21; 18:19; 21:22; 24:20, 42; 25:13; 26:41; Mark 9:29; 11:24–25; 13:18, 33–37; 14:38; Luke 6:28; 10:2; 11:2, 9–10; 18:1; 21:36; John 14:13–14; 15:7, 16; 16:23–26. Develop a plan to pray accordingly.
3. Describe the difference between the word of God as *logos* and as *rhema* and how you can increase your ability to hear God's voice. Do a concordance search and draw lessons from all the texts in Luke-Acts that refer to prayer and to the Holy Spirit.

53. *George Whitefield's Journals*, 60.

FOR PASTORS AND CHURCH LEADERS

1. Evaluate the quantity and quality of prayer in your life and in the life of your church. What changes do you need to make and what strategies will raise the level of all types of prayer?
2. How might you use the *G.P.S.* model? What changes can you make for Sunday services, in leader's meetings, and in your preparation and delivery of sermons to include more prayer?
3. How will you practice better prayer in your leadership to hear God's voice for direction and discernment particularly when you need to "inquire" of the Lord on a regular basis, and how will you learn to pray "in Jesus' name" up front? Study John 14:13–14; 15:16. Develop a policy and practice as a pastor and church leaders to always inquire of the Lord for discernment and direction in life and leadership.
    - Isaiah 8:19, "Should not a people *inquire* of their God?" Also see, 1 Chr 14:10–17.
    - Jeremiah 10:21, "The shepherds are senseless and do not *inquire* of the Lord."
    - Psalm 34:4, "I *sought* the Lord, and he answered me."

7

DEVOTION TO THE SPIRITUAL PRIESTHOOD

"Nobody can read Luther's writings with some care without observing how earnestly he advocated this spiritual priesthood, according to which not only ministers but all Christians are made priests by their Savior, are anointed by the Holy Spirit, and are dedicated to perform spiritual-priestly acts."[1]

(Philipp Jakob Spener)

On Halloween Day, October 31, 1517 a massive theological tsunami slammed the shores of the Holy Roman Catholic Church. One of its German monks, professor Martin Luther—gripped by a fresh understanding of salvation by faith and grieved by the abusive corruption of the papacy—launched a new movement within Christendom, later called the Protestant Reformation. On that day, he particularly protested the sale of indulgences as he nailed his *95 Theses* to the Wittenberg castle church door in Germany. Eventually, a revolutionary doctrine emerged with the Reformation phrase, *the priesthood of all believers*. It challenged the hierarchical and exclusive medieval church, which was a "vast ecclesiastical corporation through which salvation was offered to man. The inexorable corporation was

1. Spener, *Pia Desideria*, 92.

everything, the individual was nothing."[2] While Luther did not use this exact phrase, he recognized that in the teaching of the New Testament, especially 1 Peter 2:9, all regenerate baptized believers were priests and spiritual in God's sight. Though Luther and the Reformers taught the priesthood of all believers in the sixteenth century, it never really gained substantial traction, other than with the Anabaptists. In fact, after the 1520s the spiritual priesthood largely disappeared from Lutheran discussions and did not even appear in Lutheran church confessions.[3]

A century and half later, Pietism, and eventually evangelicalism, reclaimed and partially activated the doctrine. As another feature of the devout life and common among church renewal movements, we need to reactivate the practice of the spiritual priesthood of all believers in our churches today. It has the potential to unleash the church according to the gifts and callings of ordinary people who serve on mission together along with ordained clergy as the people of God, temple of the Holy Spirit, and body of Christ. The early Pietists pioneered its practice where it became a major feature for the expression of Pietist and later evangelical spiritual renewal. Spener elevated lay ministry alongside ordained ministry and gave it a central place in Pietist reform and ecclesiology (doctrine of the church). Olson and Winn comment: "A major thrust of Spener's ministry was to elevate the laity to a new spiritual position—not to replace ordained ministry as a teaching office, but to equip non-ordained Christians to study the Bible, pray, and engage in devotional practices without having to have clergy present. This infuriated many of his critics in the official churches."[4]

What comes to your mind with the words *priest* or *priesthood*? A man or group of men who wear black shirts with white reversed collars, who preside over the Eucharist, or a man with a gray beard wearing a long vestment and an oblong headdress, who swings incense balls and chants prayers, or a special order of Catholic, Anglican, or Lutheran clergy who received a call to ordained ministry? What about a twenty-two-year-old political science university student in London who recently gave her heart to Jesus Christ, or a fifty-six-year-old executive who works in the oil and gas industry in Alberta, Canada, or a sixty-seven-year-old retired and widowed schoolteacher in Perth, Australia, or a fourteen-year-old, blind

2. Eastwood, *The Priesthood of All Believers*, 217.

3. Strom, "The Common Priesthood and the Pietist Challenge for Ministry and Laity," 44.

4. Olson and Winn, *Reclaiming Pietism*, 105–06.

Chinese girl, in your hometown? Can you see yourself as a spiritual priest at work, in your community, and in your church? Note the conversation between Eliza Doolittle and Colonel Pickering in *My Fair Lady*:

> "You see, Mrs. Higgins, apart from the things one can pick up, the difference between a lady and a flower girl is not how she behaves, but how she is treated. I shall always be a common flower girl to Professor Higgins, because he always treats me like a common flower girl, and always will. But I know that I shall always be a lady to Colonel Pickering, because he always treats me like a lady, and always will."[5]

Many Christians do not see themselves as members of a spiritual priesthood. What, me a priest they muse? No way! I am not ordained or do not have a seminary degree. I am not a pastor nor do I preach. I am just a flower girl. They may have Catholic or Anglican backgrounds. They are *just* lay people. Could it be that many Christians do not act or feel like priests of Jesus precisely because clergy treat them like common *laity*? The spiritual priesthood of all believers, when practiced, can remove a hierarchical dualism between ordained clergy and non-ordained Christians, specialized professionals and amateurs. It can dismantle notions of spiritual aristocracy within the church. It can favor a missional adventure for workaday Christians who have direct access to God and who mediate God to their communities from an equal place of privilege and responsibility as clergy. All Christians are *missionaries* and *ministers*.

Unfortunately, churches that apply the doctrine merely to church polity through so-called congregational government fail to capture its core theological intent, which is spiritual and missional not institutional or political. It has little to do with democracy at church business meetings where a majority vote supposedly determines God's will for a congregation and yet may produce very unspiritual results. Granted, all believers have immediate access to God and can hear directly from him; pastors should consult people in a decision-making process; and discernment in community is a safeguard when a group seeks God's guidance. But the church is a spiritual priesthood—a *corporate* identity and function for priestly service.

The key texts that directly support the doctrine are: 1 Peter 2:4–12; Revelation 1:6; 5:10; and 20:6. In 1 Peter 2:4–12, Peter makes inescapable allusions to Israel and applies them directly to the church as God's spiritual house, holy and royal priesthood, chosen race, holy nation, and a people

5. *My Fair Lady*, Los Angeles: Warner Brothers, 1964.

for his own possession and mercy (Isa 43:20–21; Exod 19:5–6; 23:22; Hos 2:23). He assembled this set of Old Testament texts that directly refer to the *corporate* church of God carried forward from Israel. Theologians and Luther tend to focus on 1 Peter 2:9. But the fuller context bears the most fruit for the devout life, primarily directed to the corporate nature and function of the missional church as a people more than as individuals. In fact, no individual in the New Testament is ever called a *priest*. The term is always used in a corporate or plural sense and the responsibilities of the priesthood are never confined to a special clergy class. It's a holy and royal priesthood of *all* believers not of *each* believer.[6]

> As you come to him, the living Stone—rejected by men but chosen by God and precious to him—you also, like living stones, are being built into a spiritual house to be a holy priesthood, offering spiritual sacrifices acceptable to God through Jesus Christ . . . But you are a chosen race, a royal priesthood, a holy nation, a people for his own possession, that you may proclaim the excellencies of him who called you out of darkness into his marvelous light. Once you were not a people, but now you are God's people; once you had not received mercy, but now you have received mercy. Beloved, I urge you as sojourners and exiles to abstain from the passions of the flesh, which wage war against your soul. Keep your conduct among the Gentiles honorable, so that when they speak against you as evildoers, they may see your good deeds and glorify God on the day of visitation (1 Pet 2:4–5, 9–12).

This passage identifies the vocation of this holy and royal priesthood and holy nation: to be vice-rulers of God who practice worship and mission supported by observable holiness of calling, character, and good deeds in the world. Priests are set apart for holy worship and missional service for God—to proclaim the excellencies (or praises) of his redemptive work. The church as a holy and royal priesthood is to offer spiritual sacrifices and to proclaim or report the wonders of who God is and what he has accomplished. This involves both worship and evangelism for the spread of the gospel. The purpose clause, "that you may proclaim the excellencies of him who called you out of darkness into his marvelous light" refers to conversion-based mission. Conversion is often depicted as a sinner's transfer from darkness to light (Acts 26:18; 2 Cor 4:6; Col 1:13; 1 Thess 5:5). A missional spirituality of *sacramental* conduct and good deeds that glorify

6. See, Bennett, *Metaphors of Ministry*, 104.

God showcases the spiritual priesthood: "Keep your conduct among the Gentiles honorable, so that when they speak against you as evildoers, they may see your good deeds and glorify God on the day of visitation" (1 Pet 2:12; Matt 5:14–16). Paul viewed his ministry as a priestly service in the gospel to reach Gentiles and offer them as a sacrifice, "to be a minister of Christ Jesus to the Gentiles in the priestly service of the gospel of God, so that the offering of the Gentiles may be acceptable, sanctified by the Holy Spirit" (Rom 15:16). The Holy Spirit erects the church to be a priestly missional bridge.

The title *Pontifex* comes from the Latin meaning "bridge-builder." A priest—a pontiff—is a holy person who serves as a bridge from God to people. A priest serves as a mediator—a go between God and people in the context of worship—who offers sacrifices to God for people and offers instruction from God to people. Ordinary people, not just ordained people, constitute the spiritual priesthood. They are marked by holiness and set apart for sacred service as a community just as Old Testament Israel was as a nation, who also ordained specific priests. It is rare to see the priesthood of all believers practiced today even though touted by Baptists, Anabaptists, and other groups. Specialized professionals tend to dominate contemporary ministry models.

The two-tiered paradigm of most churches and denominations today perpetuates the Old Testament and medieval institutional model of priests and people, clergy and laity, ordained and ordinary. There is scant evidence in the New Testament for the concept of ordination as we see it today. The English term *clergy* is derived from the Greek *kleros*, which means, "lot" or "inheritance," a share or allotted portion (Acts 1:26; Col 1:12; Acts 26:18). In the New Testament, it never referred to distinct religious specialists concerned with ministry. The English term *laity* is derived from the Greek *laos*, which basically means, "people" or a "people group," and in 1 Peter 2:10 it refers to God's people as Christians. Greg Ogden notes,

> The distinction between clergy and laity did not become full blown until the fourth century, when the church adopted a secular model. In the Greco-Ronan world, the Greek word *kleros* referred to municipal administrators and *laos* to those who were ruled. As the gulf between these two grew, the *kleros* in the church became associated with the sacred, the *laos* with the secular. Since the lives of the *laos* were consumed with temporal affairs, they were perceived to be on the low rung of the saintly ladder. By the twelfth

> century, the partition between the clergy and laity was fixed with two kinds of Christians.[7]

Our mental models of ministry are not easily altered when elite importance is placed on the education and expertise of professional pastors and clergy today, and where lay people are called *volunteers*! The New Testament identifies leaders and people as slaves and servants not volunteers! A bottleneck or logjam for spiritual renewal in the church today is to pay lip service to the doctrine of the spiritual priesthood. Pastors are servant-shepherds called to lead, teach, equip, care for, and serve *among* the people of God as members of the *laos* themselves. Peter calls pastors-elders to, "shepherd the flock of God that is *among* you" (1 Pet 5:2). When we maintain the dominance of a clergy monarchy model of ministry we perpetuate Christendom. Pastors should not be a separate class of superstars or specialists who do not trust the Holy Spirit with God's people, the so-called laity. Lay people often do not trust themselves either while they become "spectators, critics, and recipients of pastoral care, free to go about their own business because the pastor is taking care of the business of the kingdom."[8]

PIETISM AND THE SPIRITUAL PRIESTHOOD

As I wrote above, the doctrine of the spiritual priesthood of all believers was a major feature of early Pietist spiritual renewal, through which many crucial Pietist practices were expressed. The Moravians seemed to apply the doctrine better than the German Pietists. Unfortunately, it waned as time progressed. The Pietists did not wish to reduce the authority and role of ordained clergy nor altogether replace them as the church still needed their guidance and supervision, as those called to vocational Christian ministry. This is a valid perspective for today as well. Spener also included women as members of the spiritual priesthood with some limitations in their public (though not in private) teaching roles. I place gold medal value on women in ministry. Spener was careful to refer to the priesthood as "spiritual" to frame the estate in which all Christians operate as derived from their identification with Jesus Christ their great High Priest. He preserved the distinction between laity and clergy but made them interdependent, and

7. Ogden, *Unfinished Business*, 89–90.

8. Lovelace, *Dynamics of Spiritual Life*, 224.

interestingly, "there are also clear sociological aspects, which underscores that the clergy—who were known colloquially as 'the spirituals'—have no monopoly on spiritual matters."[9]

Spener's first proposal to correct the corrupt conditions in the church was, "Thought should be given to a more extensive use of the Word of God among us." His second proposal, "which is altogether compatible with the first, is *the establishment and diligent exercise of the spiritual priesthood*."[10] He explains:

> Nobody can read Luther's writings with some care without observing how he earnestly advocated this spiritual priesthood, according to which not only ministers but all Christians are made priests by their Savior, are anointed by the Holy Spirit and are dedicated to perform spiritual-priestly acts. Peter was not addressing preachers alone when he wrote, "You are a chosen race, a royal priesthood, a holy nation, God's own people, that you may declare the wonderful deeds of him who called you out of darkness into his marvelous light" (1 Pet 2:9).[11]

All Christians are ordained to the order of Melchizedek. The devout life will include devotion to the spiritual priesthood because God's holy people, the *laos*, are Christ's body in the world to mediate God's presence and purposes in the gospel centered in Jesus Christ, empowered by the Spirit. Ordinary Christians comprise 95 percent of the global church, which ranks as the largest voluntary, religious agency on the planet. Nevertheless, paid clergy fill an important though overrated role. Unhappily, Spener targets clergy:

> Indeed, it was by a special trick of the cursed devil that things were brought to such a pass in the papacy that all these spiritual functions were assigned solely to the clergy and the rest of the Christians were excluded from them . . . The consequence has been that the so-called laity has been made slothful in those things that ought to concern it. No damage will be done to the ministry by a proper use of this priesthood. In fact, one of the principal reasons why the ministry cannot accomplish all that it ought is that it is too weak without the help of the universal priesthood. One man

9. Strom, "The Common Priesthood and the Pietist Challenge for Ministry and Laity," 49.

10. Spener, *Pia Desideria*, 92.

11. Ibid.

> is incapable of doing all that is necessary for the edification of the many persons who are generally entrusted to his pastoral care.[12]

Spener raised a perennial issue that continues to plague pastoral ministry and churches today like a flu epidemic—a clergy dominated role in Christianity and church life held in overprized esteem by both clergy and parishioners alike! A man once offered to pay me $10.00 per hour to meet each week as his pastor to teach him how to study the Bible. I agreed to meet with him but said, "Give the money to the food bank. You need to learn how to serve Jesus and what the Bible teaches, and learn to help others." His reply, "That's easy for you to say, you get paid to serve Jesus!" The unbiblical view in too many churches is that "we pay the pastor to do the ministry and to care for church members." But one key biblical role of pastors and teachers is to "equip the saints (Christians) for *their ministry* (Eph 4:11–12).

I know many pastors who burn out or paddle in the deep end like an anxious dog with the water level just below its nose as they try to *do* all the ministry themselves—preach, teach, counsel, care, lead worship, attend committee meetings, visit, administrate, attend anniversary and birthday parties, evangelize, marry, bury, taxi people around, and then banish any time left for their own personal and family life. In some situations, co-dependency enslaves them while their flawed theology betrays them. Some burn out or bail out. I also know many parishioners who appear on Sundays for their weekly feed of worship and preaching and then leave the church when the pastor doesn't meet their needs. Spener remarked, "One man is incapable of doing all that is necessary for the edification of the many persons who are generally entrusted to his pastoral care."[13] In 1677 Spener published a tract entitled "The Spiritual Priesthood," a sort of catechism, where he sets forth seventy questions with biblical answers. For example:

> 5. How do Christians become priests? As in the Old Testament priests were not elected, but were born to the office, so also the new birth in Baptism give us the divine adoption as sons and the spiritual priesthood connected with it (Jas 1:18).
>
> 11. Does not the name "priest" belong only to ministers? No. Ministers, according to their office, are not properly priests, nor are they so called anywhere in the New Testament, but they are

12. Ibid., 94–95.

13. Ibid., 94.

servants of Christ, stewards of the mysteries of God, bishops, elders, servants of the Gospel, of the Word, and so forth. Rather, the name "priest" is a general name for all Christians and applies to ministers not otherwise than to other Christians (1 Cor 4:1, 3:5; 1 Tim 3:1, 2, 5:17; Eph 3:7; Acts 26:16; Luke 1:2).

13. What are the offices of a spiritual priest? They are manifold. But we can divide them into three chief offices: (1) The office of *sacrifice*; (2) of *praying* and *blessing*; and (3) of the *divine Word*. The first two are always called *priestly offices*; the last is also called a *prophetic office*.[14]

PRACTICING THE PRIESTHOOD

Colleges of Piety

A key way Pietism expressed the spiritual priesthood was through a revolutionary innovation of small group gatherings called *collegia pietatis*—colleges of piety—also known as "conventicles." These were private gatherings of lay people that typically met in homes and elsewhere to cultivate holiness or piety, and fellowship, with a discussion of the Sunday sermon or other Bible texts. From 1670–1682, Spener hosted these meetings in his home on Sunday and Wednesday evenings. Conventicles included prayer, Bible and devotional readings, edifying discussions, and mutual support. They were considered as *ecclesiola in ecclesia*, "little church in the church" which at times became critical of clergy and godless church members. These small groups were to supplement not replace the regular worship services, but became contentious as they met outside of the institutional church structure and control, and some eventually separated from the State church altogether. Conventicles were a primary if not defining controversial feature of Pietism. The Pietists, Moravians, and Methodists shared similar structures where they implemented cell group ministries (conventicles, bands, classes, choirs) that generated expressions of the spiritual priesthood with lay leaders and people. Howard Snyder remarks: "The class meeting system tied together the widely scattered Methodist people and became the sustainer of the Methodist renewal over many decades. The movement was, in fact, rather a whole series of sporadic and often geographically localized revivals

14. Spener, "The Spiritual Priesthood," 51–52.

which were interconnected and spread by the society and class network than one continuous wave of revival which swept the country."[15]

Nowhere in the New Testament is the role of preacher, teacher, pastor, or one who presides over the Eucharist or baptism reserved for a professional or an ordained clergy class. Though it was a dominant Pietist model for Spener, his closest disciple August Hermann Francke did not promote conventicles or the spiritual priesthood at the University of Halle—the training center for Pietism. He promoted the importance of clergy piety and the conversion of the laity, one of the goals of preaching. Eventually, the doctrine receded and the State churches retreated to a clergy dominated church. It requires insistent focus to develop and sustain the spiritual priesthood. If you do not keep the tension of a rubber band that you pull in opposite directions taut, the default wants to return to its limp state. Pastors must help parishioners imagine what the Holy Spirit can do through them and bless their ideas when appropriate.

What pastors do, gifted people should also do, especially if they have the spiritual gifts and passion that match the responsibility. It is impossible for any pastor or pastoral staff to fulfill what numerous Christians gifted by the Holy Spirit in the New Testament widely shared for universal ministry. In many ways, most Christian service is lay ministry as the Holy Spirit gifts and empowers all Christians to serve. We must start with a bottom up, grass roots approach, and look to what God is doing in and through the so-called laity. The primary role of clergy and gifted leaders is to equip and support the saints for their ministry so the body is built up and grows in maturity as each member does its part in love (Eph 4:11–16). Let me offer six practices for the spiritual priesthood of ordinary as well as ordained people of God.

Sacrifice and Service

In question 14 Spener asked, "But what must spiritual priests sacrifice?" His answer, "First of all, *themselves* with all that they are, so that they may no longer desire to serve themselves, but him who has bought and redeemed them." In question 15 he asked, "How in particular must we offer our bodies and their members to God?" His answer, "By not using our bodies for sins, but *alone* for the glory and service of God." In question 16 he asked, "How shall we offer our souls to God?" His answer, "By letting them as well as our bodies to be holy *temples* and abodes of God . . . and by making an

15. Snyder, *Signs of the Spirit*, 224.

acceptable *sacrifice our spirits and souls in true repentance*."[16] God's people are a spiritual house (temple) and a spiritual priesthood called to offer spiritual sacrifices acceptable to God through Jesus Christ (1 Pet 2:5). They must offer themselves as a living spiritual sacrifice, holy and acceptable to God, which is their primary spiritual service and worship with transformed lives and renewed minds (Rom 12:1–2). This holy priesthood requires holy and spiritual people, who serve God with their lives and with their lips and their generosity, "Through him then let us continually offer up a sacrifice of praise to God, that is, the fruit of lips that acknowledge his name. Do not neglect to do good and to share what you have, for such sacrifices are pleasing to God" (Heb 13:15–16). Pastors must equip God's people in the devout life, in holiness of hearts and minds, and continuously call them to standards and service that are acceptable and pleasing to God. They must help them get out of the grandstands as spectators and onto the playing fields of sacrifice and service.

Worship and Sacraments

God's people must worship God and should never appear before him empty-handed (Exod 23:15), but offer themselves and their sacrifices of praise along with their time, talents, and treasure. Some people have the gifts and passion to also lead or serve in formal worship services as musicians, singers, artists, dancers, preachers, intercessors, Scripture readers, and liturgists. Pastors should see themselves as "worship choreographers and chief priests" who equip God's people to understand what worship is and how to worship God, and involve as many people as possible to plan and participate in the design and delivery of Spirit-led worship services. I always met weekly with a worship design team. I previously noted how 1 Corinthians 14 depicts the many ways that worship can work out in such gatherings. Pastors should also plan ways to equip and encourage worship leaders and teams in theological worship leading and not simply in musical leading.

For the Pietists, lay people could perform baptism but not administer the Eucharist. I think they can do both! Contrary to a Reformed perspective the Scriptures never assign "the word of God *rightly* proclaimed and the sacraments *rightly* administered" (baptism and Eucharist) to clergy, nor define the church in such terms. Rather, where you have a group of

16. Ibid., 52.

Christians who function like the family of God, the temple of the Holy Spirit, and the body of Christ—who practice the spiritual priesthood by the Spirit and the word—there you have a church. Pastors should equip God's people to understand what the sacraments mean and how to administer them. They should allow people to perform baptisms or administer the Lord's Supper in and outside of church services and involve parents, small group leaders, mentors, and others to participate as priests who baptize and teach disciples, and break bread together (Matt 28:19; Acts 2:41–42).

Prayer and Intercession

God's people are called to prayer and intercession, "First of all, then, I urge that supplications, prayers, intercessions, and thanksgivings be made for all people" (1 Tim 2:1). They must devote themselves to continual prayer (Acts 2:42; Col 4:2; 1 Thess 5:17) and to intercession where they make appeals to God on behalf of others. The Lord's primary role as high priest is one of continual intercession for his people (Heb 7:25). Prayer and intercession are primary practices for the spiritual priesthood of all believers. Pastors should equip and encourage God's people to understand the meaning, importance, and practice of prayer and intercession. They should incorporate prayer and intercession into all church services and ministries and involve many people to pray and intercede beyond the routine pastoral prayer, and become a house of prayer.

Teaching and Preaching

The Old Testament Levitical priests served as mediators between Israel and God where the priests officiated at the sanctuary, performed ritual sacrifices, and instructed Israel and the nations in the Torah, the Law. God made a covenant of life and peace with Levi and his tribe where they had an obligation to fear God, and serve as his instructors and messengers. We can learn from and adapt Malachi's description of the Levitical priesthood:

> So shall you know that I have sent this command to you, that my covenant with Levi may stand, says the Lord of hosts. My covenant with him was one of life and peace, and I gave them to him. It was a covenant of fear, and he feared me. He stood in awe of my name. True instruction was in his mouth, and no wrong was found on his lips. He walked with me in peace and uprightness, and he turned

> many from iniquity. For the lips of a priest should guard knowledge, and people should seek instruction from his mouth, for he is the messenger of the Lord of hosts (Mal 2:4–7).

God's people, not just clergy, are called to the ministry of the word, and must read, study, teach, and obey it (Ps 119; Acts 2:42; 2 Tim 2:15; 3:14–17; 4:2; Jas 1:22–25). They must also learn how to teach or share the word effectively, particularly in informal settings, and some will have the gifts and passion to proclaim the word in formal settings. Pastors should equip God's people in how to read, interpret, and apply the Bible and address the issue of Bible literacy and inspire the Pietist value on the transformational use of Scripture in all settings. Pastors should develop preaching and teaching teams and train gifted people in how to preach and teach Scripture and how to engage in the artful public reading of Scripture. The pastor who preaches all the time is a bottleneck for this aspect of the spiritual priesthood.

Care and Counseling

God's people are called to love and care for each other, and some will have spiritual gifts in the areas of exhortation, mercy, helps, and spiritual counseling. The notion of *pastoral* care and counseling can be another stranglehold which restricts the spiritual priesthood from the corporate practice of body life and the exercise of the "one another" passages in the New Testament. Pastors must care for the flock and develop care ministries, but they cannot provide all the care. They will burn out if they try. When each member does its part, the body builds itself up in love (Eph 4:16). Pastors must equip God's people in how to care and exercise their spiritual gifts. They should also develop and equip teams of gifted caregivers and counselors, and spiritual directors, some of whom might be small group leaders, deacons, elders, or others. Healing, mentoring, and counseling thrive in the warm incubator of love, care, and service, as God's people learn how to connect to the Holy Spirit and minister to each other as a spiritual priesthood.

Vocation and Mission

God calls people to both vocation and mission. People spend significant time each week in the workplace and community. The paradigm for many Christians, however, is to serve God on Sunday at church and then enter the real world on Monday, as they sometimes separate life into sacred and secular. Paul mentions numerous Christians with significant ministries in both the church and community (cf. Rom 16; Col 4). Os Hillman describes the dilemma,

> We have wrongly equated "ministry" to what takes place inside the four walls of the local church. We have failed to affirm the worker at IBM, the clerk at Wal-Mart, the nurse at the hospital or the sixth-grade teacher at the elementary school that the work they do five days a week is as important as any ministry they do within the four walls of their local church. In fact, surveys reveal that more than 90% of church members do not feel they are being equipped by the church to apply their biblical faith in their daily work life. As a result, they are ineffective for Christ at their places of employment.[17]

The spiritual priesthood includes *vocation* where God's people must listen to their "call," the voice of vocation,[18] and how God places them in the world to make a difference. Frederick Buechner writes, "The place God calls you to is the place where your deep gladness and the world's great hunger meet." People have natural bridges into the world to be priests on Christ's mission to spread the gospel and to be salt and light in their spheres of influence where God is at work too (John 5:17–19). Pastors should equip people in how to live out their faith in the workplace, community, and in their families. They must teach them that the spiritual priesthood, the church, gathers for ministry and scatters for mission in the world. What could happen if pastors ordained ordinary people, to work in various fields in the community according to their vocation, in daily mission?[19] Finally, "while many pastors try to use their own gifts and personalities as instruments of renewal, fixing the attention of their people on them, the clearest road to spiritual awakening in a congregation is to develop the independent relationship of each church member with the Holy Spirit, so that every parishioner is constantly looking beyond personalities and listening for the voice of God."[20]

The river of the Holy Spirit's power and presence will inundate God's people and pastors as they together practice devotion to the spiritual

17. Hillman, *The 9 to 5 Window*, 13.

18. The Latin root of vocation, *vocare*, means, "voice."

19. See, O'Connor, *Call to Commitment*, "Ordination to Daily Work," 101–107.

20. Lovelace, *Dynamics of Spiritual Life*, 223.

priesthood and plunge the depths of spiritual renewal. Jesus Christ will then flood like the Nile River into every area of the church, his body, with greater fullness, "as head over all things to the church, which is his body, the fullness of him who fills all in all" (Eph 1:22–23). As the church gathers and scatters as his holy and royal priesthood, devotion to Christian life in community will also activate the spiritual resources for every member ministry both in the church and mission in the world.

FOR REFLECTION AND PRACTICE

1. Read through 1 Peter 2:4–12 in three different translations and consult a good commentary or Study Bible. Note the key terms that depict the nature of the church. Also, note the key practices and how they relate. How would you describe the nature of the spiritual priesthood today in your context? How does it relate to the devout life?
2. Consider how you may proclaim the excellencies of him who called you out of darkness into his marvelous light, and what it means to be a sojourner and exile who abstains from the passions of the flesh, which wage war against your soul and keep your conduct among the Gentiles honorable.
3. Summarize the six practices of the spiritual priesthood. Which ones stand out to you the most and why? What changes do you need to make to apply some of them to yourself as a member of the spiritual priesthood?

FOR PASTORS AND CHURCH LEADERS

1. Many comments are made in this chapter about an ordained and non-ordained, clergy and laity, two-tiered paradigm and its implications concerning the *laos*—people of God—as the spiritual priesthood. What stands out to you and why? What do you agree with or don't agree with and why?
2. What changes in your philosophy of ministry and job descriptions might you consider that would align yourselves more closely with the doctrine of the spiritual priesthood of all believers? How would it facilitate spiritual renewal?

3. If you were to develop a strategic plan using the six practices of the priesthood as a template, how would you approach an equipping plan for these practices as pastors and church leaders over the next three years?

8

DEVOTION TO CHRISTIAN LIFE IN COMMUNITY

"There is no Christianity without community."

(Nikolaus Ludwig von Zinzendorf)

The Greek city-state, *polis*, had a remarkable way to call its citizens together when it needed a vote for some type of action. If, for example, another city-state marched against them for battle, a person would walk the streets and blow a horn to announce that all should gather in the amphitheater just outside of town. When the citizens of the city heard this, they would close their shops, head to the amphitheater to hear the news, and fulfill their civic duty with a cooperative response. However, some shop-owners refused to close as they hoped to take advantage of extra business while the competitor's businesses were closed. The Greeks referred to such persons as *idiotes*—idiots. This term referred to those, closed in their own worlds concerned only for themselves, ignored the greater public good of the community.[1]

Unfortunately, sometimes Christians and churches can close in on their own worlds and ignore the greater public good of the church as a community of love. Devotion to Christian life in community is vital for

1. Wilkins and Sanford, *Hidden Worldviews*, 30.

the devout life. This does not simply mean that you will make good Christian friends, or have so-called "fellowship" with coffee and cookies in small groups, or do mission with others in the Christian cause. These should all occur. But you need something nobler to plunge the depths of spiritual renewal. The New Testament portrays devotion to Christian life in community—*koinonia*—translated as *fellowship*. This means to share life in common association and interests—a common life in God's love. For example:

- And they *devoted* themselves to the apostles' teaching and *the fellowship*, to the breaking of bread and the prayers. And awe came upon every soul, and many wonders and signs were being done through the apostles. And all who believed were together and had all things *in common*" (Acts 2:42–44).
- Be *devoted* to one another in love. Honor one another above yourselves. Never be lacking in zeal, but keep your spiritual fervor, serving the Lord (Rom 12:10–11 NIV).

The Christian God Yahweh revealed in the Bible and in Jesus Christ is personal and *social* not impersonal and *solo* like Islam's God Allah depicted in the Koran. The Trinity as a divine community created human beings to live in community not in isolation, not as individuals, and not as idiots! You can become a mystic or a monk but at some point, you must live in relationship with others. The primary reason is because love is the basis of the Christian life and it takes more than one person for love to occur. We live and die as individuals but we love only in community. However, "One of the most common false views of Pietism is that it promotes spiritual individualism. It's true that there was the separatist and sometimes individualistic impulse that was especially evident in more radical forms; nevertheless, Pietists valued highly both the church and the Christian community outside the church."[2] Community is *communion*—common union. Pietist-Baptist scholar Stanly J. Grenz organized Christian theology around the theme of *Created for Community: Connecting Christian Belief with Christian Living*. Gordon T. Smith summarizes: "A Christian community is marked by worship, learning and witness, and all of these actions are tied up in the fellowship of the Spirit, which is the fellowship of mutual love. To be the church is to be a community of the mutual giving and receiving of

2. Olson and Winn, *Reclaiming Pietism*, 99.

Christ love."[3] Christian life in a community of love fuses with a common life in God's light. John reports:

> That which we have seen and heard we proclaim also to you, so that you too may have *fellowship* with us; and indeed our *fellowship* is with the Father and with his Son Jesus Christ. And we are writing these things so that our joy may be complete. This is the message we have heard from him and proclaim to you, that God is light, and in him is no darkness at all. If we say we have *fellowship* with him while we walk in darkness, we lie and do not practice the truth. But if we walk in the light, as he is in the light, we have *fellowship* with one another, and the blood of Jesus his Son cleanses us from all sin (1 John 1:3–7).

God's light radiates through us as we live as children of the light in fellowship (community), as his luminaries, whose love brightens a dark world (Matt 5:14; Eph 5:8; 1 John 2:9–10). I read somewhere that "the people who shine within don't need the spotlight!" Our piety is visible.

COLLEGES OF PIETY AND COMMUNITY

As I mentioned in previous chapters, a revolutionary Pietist innovation emerged where they used *conventicles*, or *collegia pietatis*—colleges of piety—also referred to as *ecclesiola in ecclesia*— "little church in the church." The transformational use of Scripture, prayer, and the exercise of the spiritual priesthood with brotherly love, generated enormous synergy expressed in these small groups. They unleashed the laity to practice Christian life in community. What we might take for granted today in small group ministry was controversial and central in Pietist church renewal. Importantly, the vital resource that governed Pietist Christian life in community was the word of God. This innovation defined Pietism: "The study of the word of God . . . in the home by individuals or in the family, in addition the communal reading of the Bible in special meetings of edification—this belongs essentially to Pietism, and this central reference to the Bible may not be dropped in answering the question, 'What is Pietism?'"[4] Spener mobilized and sought to "biblicize" the laity particularly through the *ecclesiola in ecclesia*,

3. Smith, *Called to Be Saints*, 128.

4. Wallmann, "Was ist Pietismus?," 4.

> The laity should have the opportunity to gather together with the clergy for common Bible Study. The people are not to be "objects" of sermons and pastoral activity, but "subjects" to be involved in practicing Christianity by means of meditative appropriation of the whole Bible. The laity were not just to be "catechized" but "biblicized." The formation of voluntary circles within the church, the *ecclesiola in ecclesia*, for the cultivation of the pious to complement public worship was epoch making in this regard. The *ecclesiola in ecclesia* was a new strategy for church reform.[5]

However, there is evidence that the initiative for the first Pietist conventicle did not necessarily originate with Spener but with two laymen in his church: Johannes Dieffenbach, a theology student, and Johann Shütz, a legal scholar (jurist).[6] And, Shütz also influenced a key feature of Spener's theology: while Orthodox Lutherans emphasized the role of *preaching* in the beginnings of faith, Spener followed Shütz in emphasizing the *reading of Scripture* as the key to the Spirit's work. It was through direct encounter with the Bible that seeking souls experienced the working of God's Spirit and came to faith.[7]

Mini-Churches

I love the concept of *colleges of piety*. These are more than just small groups, care groups, fellowship groups, or cell groups. In some ways, they might be closer to missional communities or to John Wesley's bands and societies I will discuss below. But if we desire to practice the devout life and plunge the depths of spiritual renewal from a Pietist posture, the word of God must serve as the core curriculum with the primary goal to cultivate piety that leads to holiness of heart and life, discipleship and mission. I wonder if too many small groups today fail to bear much fruit because the Bible is not the central curriculum and the goal is not to make disciples who practice Christian life in community for mission. There are many useful study and video materials out there today, but nothing will replace a *transformational* use of Scripture.

In every church where I pastored, I was the small groups, discipleship, and equipping pastor. I recruited group leaders and relentlessly worked

5. Lindberg, *Pietist Theologians*, 8.

6. Shantz, *An Introduction to German Pietism*, 77–78.

7. Ibid., 76.

to place people into groups. I taught seminars and organized small group leadership training, developed small group leader's manuals, and led many mixed and men's small groups. As I look back, the core of my theology and practice was to shape these small groups into lively *colleges of piety*—modern day conventicles that expressed the spiritual priesthood of all believers for Christian life in community.

In the first church where I served in the late 1980s, we called our small groups "mini-churches." As pastors, our philosophy of ministry was to decentralize the larger church ministry into smaller mini-churches or mini versions of the church. Essentially, they were conventicles. Weekly, people remarked they were off to "mini-church" and we called the leaders and assistants of those groups *mini-church lay pastors*. A key resource we used was an IVP book entitled *Good Things Happen in Small Groups*. We adopted its four main practices: *worship*, *nurture*, *community*, and *mission*. We applied early church life depicted in Acts 2:41–47 to fill in the detail of baptism, worship, word, prayer, fellowship, supernatural ministry, sharing of goods, communion, and evangelism.

We drew our philosophy of ministry from Frank Tillapaugh's, *Unleashing the Church* and Gene Getz's *Sharpening the Focus of the Church*. These resources launched us into practical applications of Christian life in community, which led to church renewal. We had anointed worship, preaching, teaching, prayer, evangelism, fellowship, and the exercise of spiritual gifts. We grew to one thousand in five years. We focused on the activation of the spiritual priesthood of all believers. Whether you gather in groups of three, ten, or twenty, practice Christian life in community. Do not just hold informational Bible studies, and then close with prayer, coffee and conversation. Repurpose your small groups as places to cultivate the devout life, as disciplemaking *colleges of piety* with *worship*, *nurture* (Scripture), *community*, and *mission*.

Moravians

Though they did not refer to them as an application of the spiritual priesthood, John Wesley's use of classes, bands, and societies, and Nikolaus Ludwig von Zinzendorf's experiment in Moravian Pietism at *Herrnhut*, actualized the doctrine with accompanying depths of spiritual renewal. Zinzendorf (1700–60) studied at the Universities of Halle and Wittenberg and was Spener's godson. In 1722, he permitted a small sect called the *Unitas Fratrum* (Unity of the Brethren) from Moravia near the Czech border to live on his estate in Berthelsdorf, Germany. This underground exiled church traced their origins to Czech reformer John Hus, who broke with the Roman Catholic Church and was burned at the stake in 1415. They established a new colony called *Herrnhut* ("the Lord's watch" based on Isa 62:1, 6–7) about one mile from Berthelsdorf. These Moravian Brethren were the remnant that under Zinzendorf united to renew the *Unitas Fratrum*. Between 1722 and 1726, three hundred Reformed, Separatist, Anabaptist, and Catholic refugees and spiritual seekers streamed to *Herrnhut*. It grew into a vibrant Pietist colony.

Zinzendorf believed that the divine life and pattern of the Trinity formed the basis and orientation toward Christian life in community. He held that Christian discipleship was not forged in the solitary life but in Christian *community*—what the New Testament refers to as *koinonia*—and brotherly love. He announced, "There is no Christianity without community."[8] The Moravians also reinstituted the love feast—a New Testament common meal joined with the observance of the Lord's Supper (cf. 1 Cor 10–11; Jude 12). The *Hernnhut* community became conflicted until Zinzendorf drafted and then ratified a rule of life called the "Brotherly Agreement" in a public ceremony on May 12, 1727. It stimulated community renewal during that summer. On August 13, 1727, during a communion service, *Herrnhut* experienced a "Moravian Pentecost." The Spirit moved their hearts with burning love towards the Lord and one another. The Spirit's power flowed, which included divine healing. The factions dissolved. Below are some of the forty-two rules that he drafted, which could apply to Christian community today:

> 2. Hernnhut, and its original old inhabitants must remain in a constant bond of love with all children of God belonging to the different religious persuasions—they must judge none, enter into no disputes with any, nor behave themselves unseemly toward any, but rather seek to maintain among themselves the pure evangelical doctrine, simplicity, and grace.
>
> 10. In general, we consider it an abominable practice for anyone to judge and condemn his neighbor rashly, and without clear and full evidence, and without previously using all the acknowledged and scriptural degrees of brotherly correction. Whoever, therefore, is

8. Cited by Vogt, *Pietist Theologians*, 215.

guilty of this unjustifiable proceeding subjects himself to well-merited censure.

13. Envy, suspicion, and unfounded prejudice against the brethren must be most carefully guarded against.

30. No one is to harbor anything in his mind against another, but rather immediately, and in a friendly and becoming manner, mention what may have offended him, without respect of persons. Complaints which have been purposely suffered to accumulate must not even be listened to, but quarrels, envy, and willful dissensions ought to be abominated by all, and those guilty of these things be looked upon as unbelievers.

36. The doctrine and example of Jesus and his apostles shall be the general and special rule of all our ministry and instruction.

37. Whosoever perseveres in an open course of levity and sin, though often before warned and admonished, shall be excluded from our brotherly fellowship, nor can he be readmitted till he has given sufficient proof of his being an altered character.[9]

Zinzendorf and the Moravians distributed Bible readings for each day of the year, called *Losungen* (Watchwords), still published today under the title of *Moravian Daily Texts* (like *Daily Bread*). As the oldest such guide in continuous use, The *Daily Texts* is a daily devotional guide published yearly since 1731. The first printed edition published in *Herrnhut*, quoted Lamentations 3:22–23, "The steadfast love of the Lord never ceases; his mercies never come to an end; they are new every morning." Each day the settlers at *Hernnhut* came together for morning and evening devotions to consciously situate their lives in the context of God's word. On May 3, 1728, during the evening service, Zinzendorf gave the congregation a "watchword" for the next day to accompany them through the whole day. The *Daily Texts* are available in print and online and read by millions in more than fifty languages around the globe.[10]

While I pastored in Kelowna, British Columbia, I led a men's group where six of us met weekly for one hour. We would discuss a chapter each week from Richard Foster and James Bryan Smith's *Devotional Classics: Selected Readings for Individuals & Groups*. Each of us would lead the discussion of a chapter we chose for the week, share our lives, and then

9. Nikolaus Ludwig, Count von Zinzendorf, *Pietists: Selected Writings*, 325–30.

10. This paragraph adapted from, "An Introduction to the Daily Texts," http://www.moravian.org/faith-a-congregations/an-introduction-to-the-daily-texts-2/.

pray for one another. We would then head to work. In true Pietist fashion, we lived what we learned and experienced spiritual renewal from both a transformational use of Scripture and devotional materials. We were like the Swedish *Läsare* (Readers) spiritual renewal movement in the eighteenth to nineteenth centuries. Influenced by Zinzendorf 's *Herrnhut* community, these Swedish Pietist lay people met as small cell groups in homes to read the Bible and devotional literature, and to pray. Revivals spread to many parts of Sweden, as did persecution, which launched Swedish migration to the United States and Canada. The Baptist General Conference, Evangelical Covenant Church, Evangelical Free Church, Bethel University and Seminary, and Bethlehem Baptist Church (John Piper), are heirs of these Swedish Pietists who read the Bible and prayed.[11]

Methodists

John Wesley sailed to Georgia in late 1735 as an Anglican missionary to evangelize the Indians in the new colony, where after two years he failed to convert any of them. On his way over, he observed the calm assurance of faith that Moravian passengers displayed when the ship encountered terrible storms at sea. As he returned to England in early 1738, Wesley questioned his own assurance of salvation. On May 24, 1738, he went unwillingly to a Moravian society meeting at Aldersgate Street in London. On this oft-cited occasion, when someone read Luther's preface to the Epistle to the Romans, at 8:45 pm Wesley felt his "heart strangely warmed" and trusted Christ alone for salvation with an assurance that Christ had removed his sins. Soon after, Wesley visited Pietist centers in Germany such as Halle and *Herrnhut* where he met Zinzendorf.

For Wesley, the devout life is "faith working in love" through holiness of heart and life— spiritual holiness toward God and social holiness toward people. Sondra Matthaei remarks, "In the Wesleyan tradition, a living faith is a gift from God and requires cultivation and nurture in a community of faith . . . [it is] Wesley's notion of 'communion in community' . . . John Wesley's emphasis on communion with God through a relational and repentant faith provides a needed counterbalance to contemporary preoccupation

11. See, *Baptist Pietist Clarion*, http://cas.bethel.edu/dept/history/Baptist_Pietist_Clarion_Issues/BPC_June_2007.pdf.

with individualism and autonomy."[12] He stated, "The Bible knows nothing of solitary religion." Note Charles Wesley's hymn *Communion*:

Father, Son, and Spirit, hear
Faith's effectual, fervent prayer!
Hear, and our petitions seal;
Let us now the answer feel.

Still our fellowship increase.
Knit us in the bond of peace,
Join our newborn spirits, join
Each to each, and all to thine!

Build us in one body up,
Called in one high calling's hope:
One the Spirit whom we claim
One the pure, baptismal flame.

One the faith and common Lord,
One the Father lives adored,
Over, through, and in us all,
God incomprehensible.

One with God, the source of bliss,
Ground of our communion this;
Life of all that live below,
Let thine emanations flow![13]

Most conversions, disciple making, and Christian life in community, came through a network of Methodist classes, bands, and societies. Steve Addison summarizes,

> The requirement for joining a Methodist class was "a desire to flee from the wrath to come." Most conversions took place in the classes rather than through the field preaching. The classes were also the disciplinary unit of the movement. Inquiry was made into the state of each member's soul, and unrepentant offenders were removed from the fellowship. Howard Snyder describes the classes as "house churches" meeting in the various neighborhoods where people lived. The class leaders (both men and women) were pastors and disciplers. All Methodists were class members. Those who were clearly converted moved on to join the "bands." While the major focus on the class was on conversion and discipline, the

12. Matthaei, *Making Disciples*, 55.

13. Cited by Matthaei, ibid., 56.

> focus of the band was on confession and pastoral care. The "societies" were composed of all class and band members within a local area.[14]

The bands were important in John Wesley's practice of piety and discipleship through Methodist "social holiness." I agree with him that growth in the Christian life occurs in community rather than in isolation. Wesley himself records a post conversion plunge into the depths of spiritual renewal he experienced at a Society meeting. In May 1738, shortly before the dawn of the English Evangelical Revival appeared in 1739, a group of four Moravians led by Peter Böhler established the Fetter Lane Society in London. It was largely an Anglican *college of piety* that met weekly. When Wesley returned from *Hernnhut* he attended this Society. On January 1, 1739, John and Charles Wesley and George Whitefield along with about sixty others held a watch night love feast service to usher in the New Year. John Wesley recounts:

> Mr. Hall, Hinching, Ingham, Whitefield, Hutching, and my brother Charles were present at our love feast in Fetter Lane with about 60 of our brethren. About three in the morning, as we were continuing instant in prayer, the power of God came mightily upon us insomuch that many cried out for exceeding joy and many fell to the ground. As soon as we were recovered a little from that awe and amazement at the presence of His majesty, we broke out with one voice, "We praise Thee, O God, we acknowledge Thee to be the Lord."[15]

The heart-centered spirituality and structure of Zinzendorf and the Moravians influenced him greatly, as did the spirituality of Thomas à Kempis, Jeremy Taylor, and William Law. The spark that ignited this spiritual renewal was devotion to Christian life in community. In community, we become people of the burning heart, as we gather together around the fireplace of God's presence for warmth. Dallas Willard describes it this way: "The fire of God kindles higher as the brands are heaped together and each is warmed by the other's flame. The members of the body must be in *contact* if they are to sustain and be sustained by each other. Christian redemption is not devised to be a solitary thing . . . The unity of the body rightly

14. Addison, *Movements That Change the World*, 57–58.

15. Telford, *The Life of John Wesley*, 394.

functioning is thus guaranteed by the people reciprocating in needs and ministries."[16]

When the going gets tough, our tendency is to withdraw. But God uses our spiritual and social relationships to refine and refuel us. True spirituality is not mystical and private; it is relational and public. If we are spiritual we will behave like it with others, in love. Spirituality is *social* not individual. Do you long for spiritual community? I do. I have plunged its depths. It can simultaneously make me cry and rejoice, hush and humble me. I have relished times of tangible connection with individuals and small groups where God's presence was so thick and the care and vulnerability were so authentic, that I experienced time warp and transcendent joy. The resplendent atmosphere of holiness took over. Spiritual community can enrich us at the deepest level of human experience. It is deeper than friendship. It is unhindered freedom. James Ryle depicts freedom as, "Nothing to fear, nothing to prove, nothing to hide, and nothing to lose." To foster spiritual community, we must abandon our dark drives to control, manipulate, talk incessantly, exclude, judge, and hide. Only when we meet each other at the level of our humanness, not at the level of our appearances, can authentic community occur. We must cultivate safe zones where we can "confess our sins to one another and pray for one another, that we may be healed" (Jas 5:16). The Pietists continued to value the role of confession for Christian life.

Todd Hunter offers a simple model that you might adapt today for a small conventicle or college of piety to foster Christian life in community—*Three Is Enough* groups or triads. It means: three friends or colleagues doing three activities. The TIE groups function in places of daily life—the workplace, school, retirement home or local coffee shop—*Three Is Enough* groups travel the inward journey of spiritual transformation and the outward journey of serving others. You meet weekly for sixty minutes (for breakfast, lunch, or evening coffee) with two other friends, colleagues, or others to grow in your Christian life.[17] In togetherness and connection you:

1. Pray for an alertness to the Spirit's guidance and pray for each other and for others.
2. Practice a transformational reading of Scripture and share your reflections together.

16. Willard, *The Spirit of the Disciplines*, 186–87.

17. Hunter, *Christianity Beyond Belief*, 157–58.

3. Serve others by being alert, by noticing others, as an expression of mission together.[18]

COMMITTEES TO COMMUNITIES

Over the years, I have either served on or led boards, committees, staff and leadership teams, small groups, ministry teams, and task forces in just about every configuration, size, and complexity imaginable, both secular and Christian. I would have to say, in many of the cases, the experiences were brain dead unsatisfying. I boil it down to one primary reason—spiritual community did not generate the life they needed. *Un*spiritual or *pseudo*-community eventually flattened the task-oriented tires through a steady leak of impersonal, loveless, lightless, management machinery. Yes, we must plan. Yes, we must discuss and decide. Yes, we must produce results. But all boards, teams, small groups, and committees are people, and all people crave relationship, love, listening, and community. To plunge the depths of spiritual renewal we must move from cold committees to warm communities soothed by God's love and light.

What marvelous results could occur if we moved from sterile committees to spiritual communities and altered the chemistry of our boards, teams, staff, and committees? What comes to mind when you think of boards, teams, staff, and committees? Do you think of impersonal and lengthy agendas, business, budgets, management, problems, politics, reports, and tasks, offered largely by people who do not always know each other, who meet in an office, basement, or boardroom, and sit on uncomfortable chairs and discuss items under the glare of fluorescent lights? There are exceptions, but my guess is that often, your experience was more like the stark stainless steel table and utility of an operating room than that of a soft sofa and warm living room. I work to cultivate environments of community where the group gathers around a Person, Jesus Christ through the Spirit, rather than simply around a task. Let us gather "in his name" (Matt 18:20).

In each meeting, I ensure that participants tell their stories and share from their lives, where we listen to each other without interrupting, and genuinely hear each other without competition. Stories and personal sharing help build community. Good coffee and refreshments also help to

18. Adapted, ibid.,159–60.

stimulate a tone of hospitality. I try to hold meetings in more comfortable and less formal surroundings, to create a more personal ethos. I also ensure that we pray for each other and seek God together. This is "worshipful work." I am not a big fan of paper reports, but rather of verbal updates, vision casting, dialogue and discussion in an atmosphere of prayer, conversation, and mission, rather than of impersonal business and management. I appreciate shorter agendas not packed with details of micro-management. I also keep in mind Patrick Lencioni's *Five Dysfunctions of a Team*, where he argues that if there is an absence of trust at the foundation of a team, board, or committee, the eventual results will be a fear of conflict, lack of commitment toward decisions, and then avoidance of accountability and inattention to results.[19]

Finally, and importantly, it is difficult to practice discernment and pursue God's will and make informed decisions apart from spiritual community. Each person on the board, team, staff, or committee must take responsibility to safeguard their own growth in transformational Bible reading, continuous conversion and repentance, prayer, mortification of sin, and hearing God's voice. This is the prerequisite to foster and maintain spiritual community and to place each person in a posture of openness to seek and hear from God with the others in corporate discernment and unity. Each person must contribute without hidden agendas or motives, with an attitude of dispassionate indifference, and be attentive to God's inner witness of the Spirit in their hearts and minds—a Pietist practice. The possibilities for spiritual church renewal become exponential when boards, staff, teams, and committees become leadership communities—bonded together in spiritual solidarity. Two good resources to consider in spiritual discernment are: Ruth Haley Barton, *Pursuing God's Will Together*, and Gordon T. Smith, *The Voice of Jesus*.

COMMUNICATION AND COMMUNITY

Essential to Christian life in community is loving and godly communication and conversation. We live in a world bombarded by deceptive, self-centered, and at times reckless and vicious words. The devout life will guard not only the heart but also the tongue (Ps 39:1), for out of the heart the tongue speaks, and an untamed tongue can spark a raging forest fire of insult and injury (Jas 3:1–12). The book of Proverbs has a great deal to

19. Lencioni, *The Five Dysfunctions of a Team*.

say about words and their direct relationship to a life of wisdom or folly. *Christian community requires Christian communication.* Our words communicate our inner attitudes, values, and thoughts. The Bible is clear that Christian life in community requires sanctified speech: "Let no corrupting talk come out of your mouths, but only such as is good for building up, as fits the occasion, that it may give grace to those who hear. And do not grieve the Holy Spirit of God, by whom you were sealed for the day of redemption. Let all bitterness and wrath and anger and clamor and slander be put away from you, along with all malice" (Eph 4:29–31); and "Let there be no filthiness nor foolish talk nor crude joking, which are out of place, but instead let there be thanksgiving" (Eph 5:4).

As we will discuss in the next chapter, the issue of heated controversy and disputes led to a core Pietist value of a peaceful spirit and godly conversation—much needed today. In 1689, Pietist leader August Hermann Francke wrote, "Rules for the Protection of Conscience and for Good Order in Conversation or in Society." Here are a few of his rules to ponder carefully:

> 4. Do not endeavor to speak too much. However, if God gives you the opportunity to speak, speak with reverence, good thought, gentleness, and insofar as you have certain knowledge with loving earnestness, with precise clear words, orderly and with good discretion.
>
> 6. See to it that your speech is not biting or sarcastic. Shun all abusive and useless words and manners of speech, which can bring about contention.
>
> 17. If someone begins to speak while you are speaking, be silent, for such a person wishes others to hear him. If you continue to speak, he will, of course, not understand you properly, for he is thinking on what he himself wishes to say.
>
> 19. If someone contradicts you, be well on your guard for this is a real opportunity for you to sin in society.[20]

Our churches are often plagued by impersonal and superficial dialogues of the deaf, of people so consumed by defensive self-interest with disinterest in and judgment of others, that we rarely meet as persons. Henri Nouwen suggests that true listening to one another is an act of hospitality. We become hosts who reach out to others and become healers. He writes:

20. Francke, "Rules for the Protection of Conscience and for Good Order in Conversation or in Society," 108–10.

> Therefore, healing means, first of all, the creation of an empty but friendly space where those who suffer can tell their story to someone who can listen with real attention . . . But listening is an art that must be developed, not a technique that can be applied as a monkey wrench to nuts and bolts. It needs the real presence of people to each other. It is indeed one of the highest forms of hospitality.[21]

Devotion to Christian life in community will dismantle the barriers that sin and self-interest erect, so that we will feel safe enough to allow people into the guarded interior of our hearts, let down our emotional drawbridges, and offer hospitality to each other. As we love and listen in community, we will nurture the devout life and plunge the depths of spiritual renewal.

FOR REFLECTION AND PRACTICE

1. What is your response to Zinzendorf's statement, "*There is no Christianity without community*?" How would you describe the nature of Christian community, translated as "fellowship" from the Greek *koinonia*? How would you practice Christian life in community?
2. What is the role of Christian communication for community? Reflect on Francke's ideas.

FOR PASTORS AND CHURCH LEADERS

1. Study the concept of spiritual community in the New Testament and compare it to Pietist practices. How can you raise the quality of spiritual community in your church?
2. How can you shape committees more into communities? How could you repurpose your small groups to function more like disciple-making colleges of piety? How can you cultivate more effective listening skills with God and others? For great benefit, read and discuss Adam S. McHugh, *The Listening Life: Embracing Attentiveness in a World of Distraction*.

21. Nouwen, *Reaching Out*, 95.

9

DEVOTION TO A PEACEFUL SPIRIT

"In essentials unity, in non-essentials liberty, in all things charity."

LAST YEAR WAS A hard-hitting one for me. Occasions of irate conflict and contempt charged my way. I received a dire call from a board member who informed me of a firestorm that ignited in his church over the senior pastor. Like a single thread pulled from a sweater that could unravel it, the trust level for this pastor started to unravel with some key people. A series of his actions, some naive, caused a few significant people to leave the church. Their reason: "We no longer respect or trust him." I had worked with this church to calm its foment. I had observed some of their leaders vent with hot-tempered agendas and calculated control. The core leaders would meet to discuss whether it was time for a church-wide pastoral evaluation or time for the pastor to go. They asked if I would come to assist and I replied that I would come if I could bring a couple of others with me. I knew that their firestorm could suck me in and burn me. Sadly, after many meetings, they forced the pastor to resign, which he gracefully did.

Another time, I returned from a lunch meeting with a pastor whose barriers toward me were palpable. When I inquired about our relationship he hurled a tirade of criticism against me about issues that occurred years ago and even with my predecessor. I listened, gulped down my pride, and tried to offer measured replies as he bombarded me with a personal assault tainted with malicious contempt. He misunderstood and judged me unfairly. Nevertheless, it ended well after I pleaded for forgiveness, which he granted. We hugged as we left, but my soul stung.

Lastly, I had to mediate a meeting between two ministry couples who were as far apart as the Grand Canyon in their emotions and in their perceptions of each other. Poor listening, faulty assumptions, and terse emails caused a chasm of misunderstanding, angst, and anger between them. The point is that the road to renewal will usually contain jagged rocks along the way! Job's words blare an apt reminder, "Man is born to trouble as the sparks fly upward" (Job 5:7).

Conflicts, and at times contempt, are inevitable brutal experiences for us all, as they were for many biblical characters. Look at Moses, David, Jesus, and Peter. Or observe Paul and Barnabas, Euodia and Syntyche. God opposes carnal conflict, but uses it to shape us. Not all conflicts originate from mistakes, poor judgment, or lack of God's favor. Some conflicts originate from contentious pride, control issues, and volatile disagreements. Others are conflicts energized by the spiritual warfare of ideas, spiritualities, and legalism, malicious feuds, entrenched sin, or demonic oppression. Demons and the devil can incite conflict. We do not locate the weapons of warfare in human arguments that we can solve with "conflict management." Conflicts can be spiritual in nature, and Satan can even set up shop in local churches (2 Cor 10:3–6; Eph 6:10–18; Col 2:16–23; Rev 2:8–29). We could suggest that possibly all conflicts that endanger or destroy peace and unity are in fact spiritual in nature, as the works of the flesh are enmity, strife, fits of anger, rivalries, dissensions, divisions, jealousy, and selfish ambition (Gal 5:20, Jas 3:16), while the primary fruit of the Spirit is love, joy, and *peace* (Gal 5:22). The mind set on the Spirit is life and *peace*, (Rom 8:6); and the kingdom of God is righteousness, *peace*, and joy in the Holy Spirit (Rom 14:17). So then, "Let us pursue what makes for *peace* and for mutual upbuilding" (Rom 14:19). The rule of peace comes through Jesus, the Prince of Peace (Isa. 9:6). A primary practice to plunge the depths of spiritual renewal is devotion to a peaceful spirit.

PIETISM AND A PEACEFUL SPIRIT

When you think of Pietism and the devout life, think of a *peaceful spirit*—that warm and unprovoked humility and grace that overcomes icy insults and injurious controversies. Imagine a pristine early morning Rocky Mountain lake, unruffled by wind or waves as it rests in spectacular glass-like calmness and tranquility. Imagine the Lord Jesus Christ, who when assaulted by the Sanhedrin, offered no defense but himself as a sacrifice to God for the sin of the world, and is now our peace who dismantled the dividing walls of hostility (Eph 2:14). Imagine a mob of irked pastors, theologians, or church leaders, who squabble and dispute their finicky positions, calmed by the meek and humble demeanor of a fellow pastor, theologian, or church leader. A true Pietist will model such gallant examples. Personalize Paul's advice, "If possible, so far as it depends on you, live peaceably with all" (Rom 12:18).

In *Pia Desideria*, Spener addressed controversies in the church and clergy of his day. He challenged the practice of vindictive lawsuits among church members and their "impiety, hypocrisy, injustice, frauds, unchastity, and other shameful acts, schisms, hatred, strife . . . and the sad breaking asunder of the bonds of holy, brotherly love."[1] His fourth proposal to correct conditions in the church was that, "*We must beware how we conduct ourselves in religious controversies* with unbelievers and heretics" so as to not offend them and to practice heartfelt love toward them.[2] And with fellow believers that, "We do not stake everything on argumentation, for the present disposition of men's minds, which are filled by as much fleshly as spiritual zeal, makes disputation fruitless."[3] Sometimes in our passion to defend the truth or stand by our principles, we ignite unnecessary flames of conflict and erect stonewall barriers between us. Remember, "A soft answers turns away wrath, but a harsh word stirs up anger" (Prov 15:1) and the Lord hates "one who sows discord among brothers" (Prov 6:19).

However, Spener affirmed that the defense of the truth is appropriate, but only in the way that Arndt expressed it in *True Christianity*, that "Purity of doctrine and of the Word of God is maintained not only by disputation and writing many books but also by true repentance and holiness of life."[4] Spener held that (1) not all disputation is useful and good, and (2) proper disputation is not the only means of maintaining the truth, but requires other means alongside it.[5] When it came to clergy and students of theology, he called for a reform of schools and universities to be "nurseries of

1. Spener, *Pia Desideria*, citing Dr. John George Dorsch, professor in Strasbourg and then in Rostock, 68.

2. Ibid., 97.

3. Ibid., 99.

4. Ibid.

5. Ibid., 100–101.

the church for all estates and as workshops of the Holy Spirit rather than as places of worldliness."[6] He also held that without piety, theological study is worthless and that "great care should be exercised to keep controversy within bounds. Unnecessary argumentation should rather be reduced than extended, and the whole of theology ought to be brought back to apostolic simplicity."[7] I agree wholeheartedly, don't you? Spener's proposals carry timeless biblical wisdom for the devout life if we seek to plunge the depths of spiritual renewal.

The Bible condemns carnal controversies, disputes, arguments, strife, dissension, and division. Jesus announced, "Blessed are the peacemakers, for they shall be called sons of God" (Matt 5:9). Paul declared, "God is not a God of confusion but of peace" (1 Cor 14:33), and advised, "Aim for restoration, comfort one another, agree with one another, live in peace; and the God of love and peace will be with you" (2 Cor 13:11). At one of my district board meetings we discussed the rampant problem of ungodly conflict in the church. We acknowledged that controversy and division are widespread blights on the church. One board member told us about a principle that his mentor offered him when they discussed the idea of being a peacekeeper or a peacemaker. He took it further; we should be *peace builders* not simply peacekeepers or peacemakers. Ken Rande writes, "God delights to breathe his grace through peacemakers and use them to dissipate anger, improve understanding, promote justice, and encourage repentance and reconciliation," and through the gospel, we must seek to glorify God, get the log out of our eye, gently restore, go and be reconciled.[8] I would add that we should be *peace maintainers* as well as peace builders and peacemakers, because we already possess the theological foundations for peace. Paul advises us to "eagerly maintain the unity of the Spirit in the bond of peace" (Eph 4:3) as we have "one body and one Spirit, one hope, one Lord, one faith, one baptism, and one God and Father of all" (Eph 4:4–6). "Peace," said Mother Teresa, "begins with a smile."

What is the tone in your church? What about in your staff, your board, faculty, committee, or conference? How is your emotional intelligence? Are you aware of how others experience you? Do you provoke argument or controversy? Do you welcome verbal contests where you can straighten out the views of others with whom you disagree? Are you dogmatic and forceful

6. Ibid., 103.

7. Ibid., 110.

8. Rande, *The Peace Maker*, 11–13.

in your opinions? Do you interrupt others when they talk? Do you challenge people's ideas in a way that backs them onto their heels? Do people view you as a person of peace or as someone who provokes disunity with a combative tone? From time to time, we all stimulate strong reactions from others, and it is OK to engage in respectful dialogue and disagreement. But if we stir the social pot with aggressive disputation and lead with a heavy hand that provokes toxic division, we need to repent and pray for sanctification at every level: "Now may the God of peace himself sanctify you completely, and may your whole spirit and soul and body be kept blameless at the coming of our Lord Jesus Christ. He who calls you is faithful; he will surely do it" (1 Thess 5:23–24). Do you see the direct connection between God's peace and sanctification? The presence of the Spirit will produce both peace and freedom (Gal 5:22; 2 Cor 3:17).

The roots of my denomination, the Baptist General Conference Canada (called *Converge* in the US), are with the Swedish Baptist Pietists who emigrated to the United States and Canada. A hallmark of those Pietists, still valued today, is what we call an *irenic spirit*—peaceful spirit. Bethel University and Seminary based in St. Paul, Minnesota—originally affiliated with the Baptist General Conference—identifies itself with Pietist values and practices. One of the core commitments of Swedish Baptist Pietism is an *irenic spirit*—speak truth in love, avoid harsh polemics, and reject irresponsible heresy hunting. Though they were Lutherans, Spener, Francke, and Zinzendorf all sought to practice a more inclusive and irenic Christian faith that respected other theological traditions, including Catholics and Reformed. They taught that the universal invisible church comprised all true believers and they sought to transcend dogmatic and punitive apologetics and arguments in Christian doctrine and church life. Rather, the devout life of godly piety through a peaceful and tolerant spirit should prevail. Though we do not know the exact source, the Pietists adopted the following motto: "*In essentials unity, in non-essentials liberty, in all things charity* [love]." What could happen in our churches and denominations if we adopted this? I do not know how many times in my travels I have heard leaders in my own conference refer to our need to practice an *irenic spirit* as they bemoan the mean-spirited tone of some meetings and emails that rouse disputes and disunity. When will we change?

Our dear Mennonite and Mennonite Brethren and the Anabaptist tradition can also point to Pietist influences in their approach to discipleship and spiritual formation, though they are more radical and political. They can teach us about peace and active non-violence, community, and self-surrender. Retaliation or revenge has no place in Anabaptist devotion. The way of Jesus, the path of discipleship which heads to the cross, disallows coercion, strife, war, and domination.

DISUNITY IN CHRIST

We value unity, and even teach and preach unity, so why is it so difficult to experience the unity that we have in Christ, about which Jesus prayed in John 17? Despite Jesus's prayer that all Christians may "be one," conflict and division are epidemic among churches and Christians. Church splits are as common as divorce. Unresolved feuds and resentment among fellow believers can simmer for decades. Christians find it difficult to handle conflict, and not all conflicts are equal. Some are subtle and others are blatant. Sometimes in the storms of conflict we are too soft and polite, and we flee instead of fight for peace. Prolonged unresolved conflict drains vital energy from people and congregations, and ingrained strife resists easy fixes. Often leaders and people will avoid conflict because it creates discomfort. Try to "speak the truth in love" to a defensive and brash person! The tendency is to appease or please difficult people and not tackle sin, disunity, and divisiveness head on with tough love. We can become passive aggressive and repress the tension, but our stomach churns and keeps track. We build walls instead of bridges. Our emotional distortion tends to bias our perceptions and interpretations of what we see and hear. At times, we believe that the Christian way is to simply show grace and let it go.

However, God's displeasure with division, disunity, and dissension is well documented in Scripture. Inflammatory competitiveness and criticism plagues many churches and denominations. Disunity in Christ will sack the quarterback of any church team. Pastors and church leaders have a biblical and spiritual mandate to foster and maintain as much unity and community in Christ as possible. However, Peter Steinke comments, "Leaders become pleasers. In return for their pleasing, they escape hostilities."[9] But they must confront things that are corrupt and manage the resulting fallout or friction that it will create.

Recently, I had a Skype conversation with a pastor of a large church in the United States. My friend, who served as the senior associate pastor for fifteen years, recounted how two years prior the senior pastor began to

9. Steinke, *Congregational Leadership in Anxious Times*, 121.

demonstrate toxic leadership patterns. The board asked him to take a sabbatical and trusted that when he came back matters would improve. They did not. Some very competent pastoral staff members had left, and a gnawing heaviness permeated the church culture. As the elder's board sought to determine the cause, the senior pastor sowed serious untruths about my friend and others. He blamed his fellow senior associate for the exodus and church problems, and called for the board members to resign so he could re-claim the church he founded. That did not happen either. As the truth came out, they discovered that he caused the exodus in the staff and tensions in the church. In the end, he resigned, left the church, and took about 150 people with him to plant another church in the same city. I call this a church "splant" as it is more like a nauseous split than a wholesome plant and "whatever is not transformed is transmitted." The DNA of that new church will carry the dysfunctional genes with it. My friend became the new senior pastor with a new board. It took two grinding years before he and the church could recover from such a devastating vacancy of peace and truth. Sadly, I have seen similar scenarios play out in other churches that suffer similar fates. Usually at the root are pride, control, carnal leadership, and a famine of truth, with an exodus of the Holy Spirit.

Christina Cleveland in her book, *Disunity in Christ*, seeks to help us uncover and heal the hidden forces that separate us. When we practice the devout life, we place our identity in Christ rather than in ourselves or in our group. We avoid the tendency to categorize, label, and judge others, and seek to operate free from our own narrow bias. We choose to overlook and forgive the offenses of others. We lead in humility and brokenness, through daily confession and repentance, and use language that does not instigate bad blood, but rather builds others up. We do not sweat the small stuff, we are attentive to our body language and tone of voice, and we practice good emotional intelligence. We seek to be the kind of people that Jesus affirms: "Blessed are the peacemakers for they shall be called sons of God" (Matt 5:9). We also use theology as discipleship where we live out the ministry of *reconciliation*—the theological foundation for devotion to an irenic spirit: "All this is from God, who reconciled us to himself through Christ and gave us the ministry of reconciliation: that God was reconciling the world to himself in Christ, not counting people's sins against them. And he has committed to us the message of reconciliation. We are therefore Christ's ambassadors, as though God were making his appeal through us. We implore you on Christ's behalf: Be reconciled to God" (2 Cor 5:18–21).

In his *Church Dogmatics*, book 4, Karl Barth treats reconciliation as a central doctrine of Christianity. Reconciliation refers to a change in relationship or attitude from enmity to peace—the termination of hostility in attitude or action. It is the restoration of a ruptured relationship. God in Christ initiated reconciliation to bring a hostile world into harmony with himself and offer his terms of peace through the Cross. This is gospel-centered ethics. This is not some uneasy truce or ceasefire that God arranges between him and sinners. He cannot overlook transgression, which is willful disobedient sin. Instead, he makes peace by the costly blood of Christ and grants forgiveness. What is significant is that Paul exhorts the Corinthians as Christians not as non-Christians to "be reconciled to God" (2 Cor 5:20). This required moral action for these Corinthian Christians. First and second Corinthians reveals that they had serious issues and discord with Paul, with each other, and therefore with God. David Garland comments:

> The fundamental problem behind the Corinthians' misunderstanding of Paul and their discord is that they are not fully reconciled to God. It explains why the values of the pagan society encircling them continue to make inroads and interfere with their obedience to God and why they are so easily beguiled by false apostles. Paul tells them to be reconciled to God because they have fallen short because of their bickering, sinful lifestyles, and participation with idols, all of which necessitate his frank reproof.[10]

Churches rarely practice the ministry of reconciliation internally with themselves and externally in the wider culture, even though God commissions us as ambassadors with the message and ministry of reconciliation. If we lack peace with each other as Christians, we are not reconciled with each other or with God either! If we harbor animosity toward others, we are not reconciled with God. Be reconciled with God! Paul is not interested in the *abstract doctrine* of reconciliation but in the *concrete task* of reconciliation.[11] Devotion to an irenic spirit of reconciliation will help us plunge the depths of spiritual renewal. Let us explore the anatomy of peace.

10. Garland, *2 Corinthians*, 299.

11. Ibid., 300.

THE ANATOMY OF PEACE

What follows is a real situation that I faced with a church. A long-standing woman leader in a local church had served over the years in women's ministries, the board, Sunday school, nominating committee, hospitality, and Bible studies. Her personality was so strong that few people were willing or able to address it. She had caused tension with the last three pastors, and would not accept any responsibility for her controlling and dominating ways. It appears she legitimately wanted to serve the Lord in her gifts and passion. A few people had tried to talk to her about how they experienced her as a bully. She appeared to respond—but then resorted to the same behaviors. She also had several other strong people in the church who were friends of hers. The ministry team and board felt she continued to be disrespectful to the pastor and used control and intimidation in the church to get her way. An elder was delegated to talk to her, but at the meeting he was too afraid to do anything, as he is very relational.

Over time, the other leaders felt they had to confront and ask her to step down from areas in the church where she served until she repented and changed. This occurred over a summer, and finally the elder left her a phone message to arrange an appointment at which he could deliver the news to her. She never responded to the message. A few weeks later he sent her an email that informed her of the "discipline." She took offense to the email, and to other emails she read between other ministry team leaders (on which she was accidentally copied). She felt they accused her of sin, and that she was being subjected to church discipline without due process. She sent a registered letter to the board, the pastor, and to me. She demanded a public apology or documented proof of her sins, or she would resort to legal action. Disunity in Christ! The board invited me in to mediate the situation. What would you do?

Before my initial meeting that included her, one of her invited friends, the pastor, board chair, and elder, I resolved to do three things: (1) pray, (2) disarm myself and suspend my personal bias and perceptions, and (3) come as a man of peace prepared to listen and offer support with a "non-anxious presence." Thomas à Kempis advised, "First, keep peace with yourself; then you will be able to bring peace to others."[12]

The first meeting was as tense as a horror film. Both parties sat on opposite sides of the ring, with perceptions and judgments hardened in

12. Thomas à Kempis, *The Imitation of Christ*, 45.

concrete, while the emotional temperature simmered like the Sahara Desert. It took two more meetings with just me, her, and the pastor, and several phone calls and email exchanges between her and the pastor and the other leaders before we crafted a place of mutual resolution and peace, through confession, apology, and forgiveness. Two critical resources aided my approach: (1) I practiced Paul's advice, "Let your reasonableness be known to everyone. The Lord is at hand; do not be anxious about anything, but in everything by prayer and supplication with thanksgiving let your requests be made known to God. And the peace of God, which surpasses all understanding, will guard your hearts and your minds in Christ Jesus" (Phil 4:5–7); (2) I applied the principles in a book entitled, *The Anatomy of Peace: Resolving the Heart of Conflict*. When people do not know one another very well and genuine Christian community is absent, the potential for misunderstanding and conflict rises. We might win the battle with others but lose the war—the war is inside *us*. James says, "What causes quarrels and what causes fights among you? Is it not this, that your passions are at war within you?" (Jas 4:1) The anatomy of peace starts with us, not with our "opponents."

Let me summarize key principles from *The Anatomy of Peace*. The premise is that we must treat others with love and choose to see them as people not as objects, as we first practice personal disarmament, and not be at war in our hearts towards others.

1. A fundamental change in us must occur if we are going to invite change in others. Very little changes through criticism and correction of what is wrong in others. The state of our heart, whether it is at war or at peace with another, is fundamental. Our way of being with others is of utmost importance. I can box myself in with perceptions that I am right, I am superior, I am entitled, and I am justified.

2. We tend to blame others, not take responsibility for our side of the conflict or tension, and treat people as objects rather than as people with real feelings, values, and views as strong as our own. Often conflicts are "collusions" where the parties are inviting the very things they are fighting against, where we begin to provoke in others the very comments and behaviors we are accusing them of. The conflict spreads as people talk and enlist others who begin to take sides.

3. No conflict is solved if all parties are convinced they are right. Resolution begins only when at least one party is humble enough to consider

how they might be wrong and begin to see the other person's point of view. We might be right in our position but wrong in our way of being toward others. Are we at war or at peace in our hearts? If we cannot end the violence within us, how can we end it outside of us?

4. When we are offended, or hurt, we can blame others, justify ourselves, dismiss them, and retreat to our position. We betray ourselves and go to war, which creates a new need in us to see others accusingly, and treat others with contempt. We then place ourselves in a superior position, which then begins to obscure the truth.
5. Unresolved and lingering resentment and grudges are subversive acts of war not peace with others. These do not disappear; the feelings are repressed or ignored. If we do not go to the person when we have issues, we bury the seed of conflict in our souls, and the prickly nettles that eventually surface will keep relationships distant and unspiritual.

Here are seven practices to cultivate devotion to a peaceful spirit:

1. Hold ourselves to the same standard that we demand of others.
2. When we betray ourselves, the faults of others can become inflated in our own hearts and minds. We can "horribilize" them. That is, we can make them out to be worse than they really are. The worse they are, the more justified we can feel. We must rebuild the relationship.
3. Surrender our own hearts to peace and disarmament first.
4. When we offend, or are offended, go to people privately first, soaked in prayer, and follow the process outlined in Matthew 18:15–17 and 5:23–24.
5. Apologize and forgive.
6. Agree on actions with a commitment for reconciliation and change.
7. Adopt John Wesley's view in which "peacemakers (Matt 5:9) love God and neighbor and 'utterly detest and abhor all strife and debate . . . forbearing one another in love; endeavouring to keep the unity of the Spirit in the bond of peace.'"[13] For all of us, "Let the peace of Christ rule in our hearts, to which we were called in one body" (Col 3:15).

13. Matthaei, *Making Disciples*, citing John Wesley, Sermon #23, "Upon Our Lord's Sermon on the Mount," 65.

Let me add two more vital practices. Jude declares that there will be scoffers in the last days, following their own ungodly desires and who cause divisions—worldly people, devoid of the Spirit (Jude 18–19). Wow, have you ever had ungodly, worldly people cause division in your church or conference? These people are *devoid of the Spirit*? What a grisly and hollow condition that is sure to suck carnal garbage into that vacuum. Jude goes on to exhort, "But you, beloved, building yourselves up in your most holy faith and praying in the Holy Spirit, keep yourselves in the love of God, waiting for the mercy of the Lord Jesus Christ that leads to eternal life" (Jude 20–21). When the Spirit is present, we will enjoy righteousness, peace, and joy, "so then let us pursue what makes for peace and for mutual upbuilding" (Rom 14:17, 19). Here are the practices: (1) keep yourself in God's love by continually edifying yourself with Scripture, the gospel, and Christian theology—your most holy faith—as you also continually pray in the Holy Spirit and wait for the second coming of Christ; (2) continually strive for peace and for what edifies one another. Peace is a result of righteousness (Isa. 32:17; 48:18; Ps 85:10; 119:165). God's character radiates peace (Rom 15:33; 2 Cor 13:11; Heb 13:20).

HARMONY AND HOLINESS

Let me offer a revolutionary verse for you to memorize as you deepen your devotion to a peaceful spirit. I never saw the relationship between the two halves of this verse before, where one present tense verb governs both objects. It is Hebrews 12:14, "Strive for peace with everyone, and for the holiness without which no one will see the Lord" (Heb 12:14 ESV). What Hebrews commands is that we must place peace with everyone at the forefront of an earnest, diligent, sustained chase, like a hunt, along with specific holiness in our conduct, character, and conversation, without which we will not see the Lord. It seems that the earnest pursuit of peace and holiness is a lost chase in our churches. Do we make every effort to *simultaneously* pursue peace and holiness? Jesus teaches, "Blessed are the pure in heart, for they shall see God" (Matt 5:8), and "Blessed are the peacemakers, for they shall be called sons of God" (Matt 5:9).

Devotion to a peaceful spirit requires that we strive for systemic spiritual reclamation efforts to achieve communal cleansing toward harmony and holiness—to replenish the toxic ponds of social, psychological, spiritual, and moral waste of bitterness and sexual immorality whose vile seepage eventually springs up to contaminate a church. God's grace offers an unlimited Niagara Fall's supply of pristine water. Hebrews advances the point, "See to it that no one fails to obtain the grace of God; that no 'root of bitterness' springs up and causes trouble, and by it many become defiled; that no one is sexually immoral or unholy like Esau, who sold his birthright for a single meal. For you know that afterward, when he desired to inherit the blessing, he was rejected, for he found no chance to repent, though he sought it with tears" (Heb 12:15–17).

People can make impulsive decisions with irrevocable consequences—a vow they made against their father; a murderous assault they hurled against a fellow Christian; a steamy one-night fling with another person's spouse. Like the fires of Mordor, a person ingrained with a root of bitterness will eventually erupt and cause fierce trouble, and defile many. Have you ever seen that occur? And then there are sexually immoral and unholy people, like the stubborn and self-serving Esau, who sold his birthright for a pot of stew, only to later regret his hasty, irrevocable actions. Have you ever seen that occur? Bitter and immoral people can ruin the harmony and holiness of a church. The only way out of this quagmire is to obtain the grace of God.

The life of holiness is the life of brilliant love, expressed in our love for God and neighbor. Harmonious relationships and holiness are joined. Neither is possible without the other. They are both *social*. You may think that a holy person is one who lives in solitude and isolation, detached from human contact. Can a holy person frequent Starbucks or attend a football game? Is holiness only the craft of church and clergy life? Holiness is the craft of human life in all its social aspects. When we kill our besetting sins, and live a righteous life in Christ, we mature in personal wholeness both in our inner spiritual life and in our outer social life. Jesus lived among people as a holy person, Spirit-empowered and social. He hung out with sinners and tax collectors, prostitutes and publicans, Galilean fishermen, and Samaritans. Scottish pastor Robert Murray M'Cheyne famously remarked, "My people's greatest need is my personal holiness." Andrew Bonar offered this report about him: "At Jedburgh, the impression left was chiefly that there had been among them a man of peculiar holiness. Some felt, not so much his words, as his presence and holy solemnity, as if one spoke to them who was standing in the presence of God; and to others his prayers appeared like the breathings of one already within the veil."[14]

14. Bonar, *The Biography of Robert Murray M'Cheyne*, Kindle edition, 2436.

When we strive for peace and holiness in a simultaneous pursuit, we will experience freedom from disputes and dissension and the sacred power and coordination of a holy life between God and people. If we are not strident peacemakers and peace maintainers we will dull the brilliance of holiness, as harmony and holiness gleam together. Paul also writes: "If possible, so far as it depends on you, live peaceably with all. Beloved, never avenge yourselves, but leave it to the wrath of God, for it is written, 'Vengeance is mine, I will repay,' says the Lord" (Rom 12:18–19). A sure-fire way to grieve the Holy Spirit and send him running for the hills is to permit corrupting talk, bitterness, wrath, anger, clamor, slander, and unforgiveness, to ransack your life or church. Read the following passage carefully, and note the key terms and tone:

> Let no corrupting talk come out of your mouths, but only such as is good for building up, as fits the occasion, that it may give grace to those who hear. And do not grieve the Holy Spirit of God, by whom you were sealed for the day of redemption. Let all bitterness and wrath and anger and clamor and slander be put away from you, along with all malice. Be kind to one another, tender-hearted, forgiving one another, as God in Christ forgave you (Eph 4:29–32).

As I worked on this chapter, I felt the inner conviction and pull of God's word and Spirit on my heart. At times, I have been combative or critical and have not always realized the weight of my words and their impact on people. What about you? I cannot afford to undermine my relationships with reckless words or ruinous ways. I must keep short accounts, be gracious and forgiving, quick to overlook an offense, and swift to cultivate an attitude of habitual humility, as I strive for peace and holiness. What about you? Peace and holiness are mingled in a sacred partnership that radiates fireside warmth and magnificent charm drawn from the depths of unrattled serenity that overcomes anxious competition and conflict, through a steadfast practice of the presence and fear of God. The only way to access that depth is to first loathe bitter jealousy and selfish ambition whose source is earthly, unspiritual, and yes demonic, which leads to disorder and vile practices. On the other side of the tracks is to love God's peaceable, gentle, reasonable, merciful, and meek wisdom, from above. It leads to a harvest of righteousness sown in peace by peacemakers. Wow! James writes:

> Who is wise and understanding among you? By his good conduct let him show his works in the meekness of wisdom. But if you have bitter jealousy and selfish ambition in your hearts, do not

> boast and be false to the truth. This is not the wisdom that comes down from above, but is earthly, unspiritual, demonic. For where jealousy and selfish ambition exist, there will be disorder and every vile practice. But the wisdom from above is first pure, then peaceable, gentle, open to reason, full of mercy and good fruits, impartial and sincere. And a harvest of righteousness is sown in peace by those who make peace (Jas 3:13–18).

Let me leave you with some thoughts to ponder as I conclude this chapter. Ponder the kind of person and church you want to see; whose goal is to make wise and winsome Jesus followers who exude impeccable devotion to an irenic spirit. Imagine yourself and your church as a community with moral excellence and pristine beauty, which transforms carnal conflict into peaceful consecration. Imagine a family of believers who chart the course of their thoughts with truth, adorned with noble virtue. Paul advises: "Finally, brothers, whatever is true, whatever is honorable, whatever is just, whatever is pure, whatever is lovely, whatever is commendable, if there is any excellence, if there is anything worthy of praise, think about these things. What you have learned and received and heard and seen in me—practice these things, and the God of *peace* will be with you" (Phil 4:8–9). God's peace resides in the shrine of Christian purity. May we "abstain from every form of evil" and "may the God of peace himself sanctify us completely, and may our whole spirit and soul and body be kept blameless at the coming of our Lord Jesus Christ" (1 Thess 5:22–23). Complete sanctification dwells in peace! When it does, we will then be better able to practice devotion to the gospel and mission.

FOR REFLECTION AND PRACTICE

1. Reflect on the Pietist motto, "*In essentials unity, in non-essentials liberty, in all things charity.*" How could you practice this in your attitudes and actions with others?
2. Reflect on key biblical passages, which appeal for unity and how to achieve it, which describe the root of conflict, and how harmony is directly related to holiness.

FOR PASTORS AND CHURCH LEADERS

1. How can you practice devotion to a peaceful spirit amid controversies? What are some practices offered by Spener and other Pietists who addressed this issue especially with Christian leaders?
2. Describe the Anatomy of Peace and practice it in your interactions with people, especially in situations of conflict.
3. Study the issue of disunity in the church and how to overcome it, especially in its theological basis. Study and practice the doctrine of reconciliation in its message and ministry, as you delineate its theological basis and principles, especially from 2 Corinthians 2:11–21.

10

DEVOTION TO THE GOSPEL AND MISSION

"It would be further useful, and it is highly necessary, that ministers should not only preach of the necessity of conversion, and instruct their hearers to depend on the grace of Christ for it, but also that they should, very frequently, in their sermons explain the nature and the whole progress of conversion, endeavoring thereby to lead their hearers into a true knowledge of the state of their souls, and showing them how they must repent of their sins, what they must do to be saved from their natural misery and, in short, how they may obtain the full salvation of the gospel, so that everyone may be able to give an answer to that most important question: What must I do that I may be a child of God and inherit eternal life?"[1]

(August Hermann Francke)

I taught a course on the book of Acts at a Bible College in Calgary. For four hours, each Tuesday night for five weeks, fourteen of us journeyed through its twenty-eight lively chapters of historical, theological, and missional narrative. Luke's account captivated us as we engaged in vigorous study, discussion, and prayer together. As I prepared at home and absorbed the classroom dynamics each week, I felt like a spiritual Incredible Hulk,

1. Francke, "A Letter to a Friend," 120.

ever bursting into superhuman dedication, strength, and resolve. Acts kindled my heart with an enlarged passion for the Lord Jesus Christ, the guidance, power, and filling of the Holy Spirit, the providence of God, and the clout of the cross-cultural gospel of the kingdom. It also incited a magnetic attraction in me for those godly first century believers who endured severe hardships, and whose character exuded the stately charm and fullness of the Spirit, wisdom, grace, faith, and power—Peter, James, Stephen, Philipp, Barnabas, and Paul.

In many ways, Acts is a Pietist manifesto that trumpets all the characteristics of the devout life, to plunge us into the depths of spiritual renewal. But we must end with the *goal* of spiritual renewal—*missional* renewal, which requires devotion to the gospel and mission. That is where Acts ends. Acts 2 begins with Peter and the disciples in Jerusalem after a ten-day prayer meeting. This began to fulfill what Jesus prophesied before his ascension: "But you will receive power when the Holy Spirit has come upon you, and you will be my witnesses in Jerusalem and in all Judea and Samaria, and to the end of the earth" (Acts 1:8). Acts 28 concludes with Paul in Rome under house arrest as he awaits his trial before Caesar. For two self-funded years, he "welcomed all who came to him, proclaiming the kingdom of God and teaching about the Lord Jesus Christ with all boldness and without hindrance" (Acts 28:30–31). In between, we see a missional church led and empowered by the Holy Spirit, fortified by a life of private and corporate prayer—mentioned throughout the narrative. Critical is that, "Prayer, as seen in the book of Acts, was not primarily therapeutic but transformational, then missional."[2] The devout life is a *Christ-centered* and *Spirit-empowered* life that integrates the spiritual and missional life—what I call a *missional spirituality*.[3]

MISSIONAL SPIRITUALITY

Missional spirituality is not primarily about self-improvement, "sin management," spiritual disciplines, personal devotional life, or even spiritual formation *for our own sake*. The devout life cannot become a retreat where we withdraw or insulate ourselves from our conflicted communities, from confused unbelievers, or from a paganized secular world. You never observe that in the book of Acts with the early church or in the Gospels with

2. Henderson, *Old Paths New Power*, 115.

3. For a book length treatment see, Helland and Hjalmarson, *Missional Spirituality*.

Jesus. Rather, the Holy Spirit will drive us into the wilderness and into the world to face the dominion of darkness and death— "to be in the world but not of it." Jesus's prayer to his Father in John 17 exposes the vital connection between the inner spiritual life and the outer missional life:

> I do not ask that you take them out of the world, but that you keep them from the evil one. They are not of the world, just as I am not of the world. Sanctify them in the truth; your word is truth. As you sent me into the world, so I have sent them into the world. And for their sake I consecrate myself, that they also may be sanctified in truth. I do not ask for these only, but also for those who will believe in me through their word (John 17:15–20).

As sanctified sent ones we are a missional church—devout Christians sent out with God on his mission in our world. "The church exists by mission," stated Emil Bruner, "just as a fire exists by burning. Where there is no mission, there is no church."[4] Think of your workplace, neighborhood, social networks, and schools as your mission field. God is at work out there in those spheres of your influence. He calls you to be an obedient, spiritually fed, sent one. Jesus taught, "My food is to do the will of him who sent me and to accomplish his work" (John 4:34).

However, there are those who label Pietism as a spirituality that withdraws into anti-intellectual, subjective, feel-good emotions and otherworldly experiences, preoccupied with the inner life, driven by sterile rules, and detached from social concern and mission. Yes, there are so-called pietist aberrations or extremes, as even radical Pietism was known for at times. It is also possible to overlook one's inner life and focus on Christian social activism or a social gospel. We can feed the homeless, volunteer at a women's shelter, or offer so-called "kingdom work" at an orphanage in China—but never read our Bibles or pray, and never share the gospel with them. Classic church Pietism embraced a doctrine of justification with sanctification rooted in a love theology for God and neighbor expressed in spiritual *and* social service. Pietism was *missional.* Dale W. Brown comments: "The Pietist milieu resulted in desires to transform the living conditions of the poor and oppressed, reform prison systems, abolish slavery, remove class distinctions, establish a more democratic polity, initiate educational reforms, philanthropic institutions, and missionary activity, obtain religious liberty, and propose programs for social justice."[5]

4. Bruner, *The Word and the World*, 108.
5. Brown, *Understanding Pietism*, 86–87.

It is unbiblical for us to study the Bible and pray, worship God, and foster spiritual formation and Christian community merely for our sake or for church renewal as an end. The goal is not merely to seek another holiness, charismatic renewal, or Toronto Blessing movement—as useful as they were. These can focus inward. *Spirit*-ual formation results when the Spirit forms us into Christ's image for the sake of the gospel and mission. As Jeffrey Greenman defines it: "Spiritual formation is our continuing response to the reality of God's grace shaping us into the likeness of Jesus Christ, through the work of the Holy Spirit, in the community of faith, *for the sake of the world*."[6] The Pietists connected their living faith and piety with love. This informed their virtue ethics—how they treated people. Their ethic was Galatians 5:6: "all that matters is faith active in love."[7]

SPIRITUAL AND SOCIAL FORMATION

What do you think of this idea: "The more spiritual you are the more missional you will also become?" Or put another way: "The more you love God the more you will love people?" Or what about: "The more you become like Jesus, the more you will become like the Good Samaritan?" Or: "The more you live a life worthy of the gospel, the more you will spread the gospel?" Classic Pietists saw an interrelation between the spiritual, social, and physical needs of people. Spener, who was "considered a pioneer in public relief and care for the poor," also "taught that the Christian life is devoted to world-formation, that is, to contribution to the well-being of society."[8] In addition, Francke's work at Halle "made that city a center not only of spiritual renewal of church and society but also of social transformation."[9]

Pietists prized spiritual and social formation. Spener in *Pia Desideria* addressed many issues of his day such as drunkenness, lawsuits, trade, the crafts, and begging. He yearned for a formational impact of the gospel on the ruling class, clergy, and the laity. According to Michelle Clifton-Soderstrom, "Wherever he ministered, Spener demonstrated his knowledge of and advocacy for widows, orphans, peasants, unemployed, refugees, migrants, beggars, and invalids. He encouraged his parishes to work as Christians in partnership with the government to provide things like aid,

6. Greenman, "Spiritual Formation in Theological Perspective," 24.
7. Clifton-Soderstrom, *Angels, Worms, and Bogeys*, 2–3.
8. Stein, *Philipp Jacob Spener*, cited by Olson and Winn, *Reclaiming Pietism*, 101.
9. Olson and Winn, ibid.

jobs, relief, homes, and medical care."[10] Spener sought spiritual renewal in the church that would also activate social renewal in the community.

His postmillennial version of the end times (eschatology) drove his missional spirituality with "hope for better times for the church" in view of the coming millennial kingdom of Christ on earth (Rev 20:1–10; Luke 18:1–8). He saw Pietists as "those who await in hope the fulfillment of the promise, which the church awaits, even the conversion of the Jews, the fall of Babel, and afterwards the glorious spread of the kingdom of God."[11] He believed that our anticipation of the future kingdom must affect the present church in spirituality, ethics, evangelism, and social reform. In Pietist fashion, the Apostle Peter directly connects our piety with eschatology in a practical way: "But the day of the Lord will come like a thief, and then the heavens will pass away with a roar, and the heavenly bodies will be burned up and dissolved, and the earth and the works that are done on it will be exposed. Since all these things are thus to be dissolved, what sort of people ought you to be in lives of holiness and godliness?" (2 Pet 3:10–11) In view of the cataclysmic end of the universe and the earth as we know it, we ought to express the devout life in a present tense lifestyle of holiness and godliness or piety (*eusebeia*).

The realities of Christ's kingdom are both future (full) and present (partial), just as his rule as lord and king are both present and future. As citizens of the kingdom who serve under his rule, we are also citizens of our society called to live out the gospel of the kingdom in both word and deed as workers sent into the lord's harvest field. This is not a call to merely volunteer at an inner-city gospel mission, food bank, pro-life society, school board, or youth drop-in center, or to lobby for political action, serve with World Vision, sponsor a Syrian refugee family, or rally for human rights and the elimination of prostitution, child exploitation, and poverty in the world. I like how Eric Swanson and Rick Rusaw put it: "When Jesus asked us to pray for laborers for the harvest field, is putting more volunteers in the community the answer to his prayer for laborers?" They conclude, "A volunteer in the community becomes a laborer in the harvest field when he or she combines the good news with good deeds."[12] In addition they write, "Good deeds create goodwill, and goodwill is a wonderful platform

10. Clifton-Soderstrom, *Angels, Worms, and Bogeys*, 45.

11. Brown, *Understanding Pietism*, 85.

12. Swanson and Rusaw, *The Externally Focused Quest*, 156.

for good conversations about the good news"[13] (for example, see 1 Peter 1:12 and Colossians 4:5–6).

The motto, "preach the gospel, and if necessary use words," is flawed. In the Gospels and Acts, when Jesus and the disciples preached the gospel it involved *verbal announcements* of "good news," often accompanied by good works of healing, deliverance, mercy, generosity, inclusion, and service to the oppressed and outcasts of society through all strata of Jewish, Gentile, and Roman society. Unlike a Constantinian approach, our mission is not to coerce our secular society through politics to Christianize culture. Our mission is to be Spirit-filled witnesses who proclaim and live out the gospel in both word and deed and make disciples of all who will follow king Jesus and submit to his righteous rule in all sectors of society. Pietism became not simply a spiritual force in the church but also a cultural force in the world. A prime Pietist example of this is Spener's pupil and protégé August Hermann Francke (1663–1727), whose spiritual and social influence surpassed Spener.

Francke, who encountered Johann Arndt's *True Christianity* and Puritan devotional works during his childhood, enrolled in 1684 at Leipzig University (which became an early outpost of Pietism) to study Hebrew and theology as a master's degree student and to eventually lecture on oriental languages and biblical interpretation. In July 1686, he formed a *collegium* to offer academic seminars that met on Sunday afternoons, at which he aided students in Greek and Hebrew exegesis on biblical passages. As this grew it moved to the home of a fellow professor. Spener heard of it and encouraged Francke to focus on devotional study not just academic study of Scripture, to focus on a living encounter with the text. This led to his dramatic conversion experience that emerged after he preached a sermon in Lüneberg in 1687, on John 20:31: "This is written that you might believe that Jesus is the Christ, and by faith have life in his name." The text convicted him that he did not experience this truth for himself. A week later this led to his hard-won struggle of repentance—*Busskampf*. This proved to be a key innovation in later Pietism—the call to a crisis decision of repentance and faith with the certainty of the new birth. He spent a year in Hamburg and two months with Spener in Dresden, as "a new man completely filled with a burning piety"[14] and then returned to Leipzig in late February 1689.

13. Ibid., 161.

14. For this quote and for the core content of this paragraph I credit Shantz, *An Introduction to German Pietism*, 107, 102–11.

During mid-1689 he lectured on Paul's epistles with a devotional approach followed by a time for discussion. It attracted three hundred students as well as local townspeople. Francke and two other professors held lectures on Bible books as they shared a common approach where the study of Bible and theology was to equip students in piety, prayer, and the Christian life. This led to citywide revival as students began to hold Bible studies and prayer in homes and conventicles.

In a sense, like Paul and Silas in Thessalonica, these Pietist professors "turned the world upside down" with their new teaching. This did not go over well with the Leipzig city council, theology faculty, and clergy. In the fall of 1690 Leipzig authorities banned Francke as well as Pietist students from the University. Many of the students left for other places and took their Pietist practices with them, which sparked similar conflicts in Germany. Eventually in early 1692, Francke became the pastor at St. George's Church in Glaucha, a small suburb south of Halle, near Leipzig. At the newly formed University of Halle, at Spener's request, he also became the professor of Greek and Oriental languages, and in 1698 professor of theology. He went on to establish the "Halle Foundations" to change the world through piety-driven spiritual and social service. In fact, "The story of the social reforms and institutions associated with Halle Pietism," writes Douglas Shantz, "is one of the most dramatic in Christian history."[15]

In 1695 Francke's initial venture was a school for poor children in Glaucha, which evolved into a world-class orphanage that trained students in piety and Christian intelligence through Bible reading, prayer, catechism instruction, study, and work. In many ways, the Glaucha orphanage was a rigorous monastic style Bible school designed to train a new generation of Pietist pastors and leaders who would spread worldwide spiritual and social formation. The Halle center grew to nearly 3,000 people. Francke founded a missions society, soup kitchens, a publishing house, a hospital, a widow's home, and a teacher's training institute. Between 1711 and 1719, Halle printed more than 100,000 New Testaments and 80,000 Bibles.[16] Francke "used his influence to place Halle graduates in key positions with the Prussian state, creating a highly successful Pietist network."[17] His vision was to "change the world through changed people."

15. Ibid., 118.

16. Ibid., 208.

17. Ibid., 143.

The influence of Halle Pietism reached into England, America, Hungary, Estonia, Siberia, India, and Scandinavia, particularly through teachers and students who reproduced Pietism in other settings, and where institutions in other parts of the world sought to copy Halle. Francke sent money, Bibles, and Pietist literature to Swedish prisoners in Siberia, where "they enjoyed a great amount of freedom from the Russians and established schools after the Halle pattern. A pietistic awakening resulted among the prisoners. Pietism penetrated quickly into Sweden through the returned soldiers from Siberia and students from the German universities."[18] In the eighteenth century many Swedish, Lutheran, Reformed, Mennonite, and Moravian Pietist immigrants came to America and eventually to Canada in the nineteenth century. These often-persecuted Pietists who had experienced profound renewal and revival in their homelands, imported their spirituality and sense of mission. This deeply impacted American Christianity and culture and many of them also began to focus on their own countrymen who emigrated later.

One of Francke's students who studied at Halle for six years was Lutheran Pietist and future Moravian leader Count Nikolaus Ludwig von Zinzendorf (1700–60). As you know, he went on to establish *Hernnhut* with a band of persecuted refugees who fled from Moravia as the Hussite church (followers of John Hus) known as the *Unitas Fratrum* (United Brethren). An important feature of Pietist missional spirituality was their practice of powerful, extemporaneous, private and public prayer. The *Herrnhut* community became conflicted until Zinzendorf drew up a *rule of life* called the "Brotherly Agreement." He divided the community into bands of two or three people of the same gender to meet and pray for one another. The community elected twelve elders and night watchmen. They established a twenty-four-hour continuous prayer watch, originally with twenty-four men and twenty-four women who prayed in pairs for one hour, seven days a week, to ensure that the "fire shall be kept burning on the altar continually; it shall not go out" (Lev 6:13). Known as the "Hourly Intercession," that prayer inferno blazed for over a century. Powered by devotion to prayer, the Moravians plunged the depths of spiritual renewal and produced the first large-scale Protestant global missionary movement with dramatic results.

Herrnhut was a strict experiment in organized Pietism that led to a movement of modern missions and the establishment of over thirty settlements globally on the *Herrnhut* model. It spawned hundreds of small

18. Brown, *Understanding Pietism*, 101.

renewal groups that operated within the existing churches of Europe, known as *Diaspora societies*. These groups encouraged personal prayer and worship, Bible study, confession of sins, and accountability. Pietist Moravian community was one of the most dynamic and fruitful expressions of Christian community ever seen since the book of Acts. Moravian missionaries were the first large-scale Protestant missionary movement comprised mostly of laypeople, which were peasant farmers and tradesmen. In 1732, the first Moravian missionaries ventured to the West Indies. By 1760, no less than 226 Moravian missionaries had ventured to the Caribbean, North and South America, the Arctic, Africa, Egypt, and the Far East. They were the first to send non-clergy laypeople, the first to reach black slaves, and the first missionaries in many countries of the world.[19] Pietist Moravian missional spirituality also greatly impacted Anglican priest John Wesley and the Methodist movement.

By 1739 John Wesley set out to promote practical religion and spread Scriptural holiness. After being rejected in Anglican churches he preached to the poor in open-air field meetings, and taught that justification by faith imputed righteousness and "intended that sanctification should be a disposition of the mind or a condition of the heart from which spring all good works."[20] For Wesley, the Christian life is a *via devotio*—way of devotion—the consecration of the whole person to love God and neighbor. Wesley viewed discipleship as *devotion* to the Christian vocation to love God and neighbor. He championed fights against slavery, prison reform, social issues, and the disadvantaged. As a "reasonable enthusiast" his theology and spirituality stoked his burning heart for mission, evangelism, and social formation from a postmillennial position. He preached the gospel to coal miners, smelters, quarrymen, shipyard workers, farm laborers, prisoners and women industrial workers. He believed that salvation included spiritual and social holiness—holiness of character and culture.

Methodism was largely a lay movement of non-ordained preachers and pastors held together through a tight network of classes, bands, and societies. It grew among members of England's working class who did not fit into the refined Church of England culture. Methodist spirituality emphasized hospitality, music, Bible study, prayer, confession, and discipline

19. "The golden decade of 1732–42 stands unparalleled in Christian history in so far as missionary expansion is concerned. More than 70 Moravian missionaries, from a community of not more than 600 inhabitants, had answered the call by 1742," from "The Rich Young Ruler Who Said Yes," Christian History Institute.

20. Tuttle Jr., "The Wesleyan Tradition," 1167.

in inward and outward holiness for mission. In addition, "As purveyors of hospitality, deaconesses, visitors, evangelists, prayers, exhorters, testifiers, class leaders, and preachers, women largely defined the character of the Methodist movement . . . Whatever you make of him, Wesley founded one of the most dynamic and fast-growing movements in the history of Christianity."[21] An Anglican clergyman his whole life, Wesley was a small man of not quite five feet six inches tall and weighed 122 pounds, who achieved large results. According Snyder, by the time Wesley died in 1791, there were 72,000 Methodists in Great Britain and Ireland and 57,000 in America. He is often cited as an example of a warm-hearted evangelism tied to active social action.[22]

> He did not teach "sinless perfection" but he did teach that love could, and must, become the primary motivating force in the Christian's life . . . Christians were not saved *out of* battle, but were rather *called into it* to wrestle with principalities and powers . . . There was no split between personal salvation and social engagement . . . Love was the key dynamic in Wesley's whole life and theology. The Christian's life was to be one of active faith—faith working by love.[23]

John Wesley "did more to transfigure the moral character of the general populace, than any other movement British history can record."[24] In addition, Elaine Heath comments, "Methodism became the largest Christian movement in North America by the mid-nineteenth century because of the power of its class and band meetings to form Christian disciples . . . whose social justice advocacy reformed American culture."[25]

DEVOTION TO THE GOSPEL AND MISSION

Where does this all lead? While I applaud the vast amount of attention that many give to gospel-centered ministry, missional leadership, and missional church, we must first plunge the depths of spiritual renewal to invigorate missional renewal. If the Spirit and the word of the gospel do not transform me, how can I expect it to transform others? If I do not live by the gospel,

21. Lindberg, *The Pietist Theologians*, 262, 268.
22. Snyder, *The Radical Wesley*, 3.
23. Ibid., 84, 86, 88.
24. Bready, *England: Before and After Wesley*, 327.
25. Heath, *The Mystic Way of Evangelism*, 33.

how can I proclaim the gospel? When you read about Spener, Francke, Zinzendorf, and Wesley, you will note that *their lives of devotion compelled their lives of mission*. The transformational vitality of Scripture and prayer in their lives, infused with their ardent passion for Jesus Christ, combined with their hardy commitment to personal and social holiness and community, endowed their devotion to the gospel and mission. Pietism embodies a missional spirituality.

Jesus announced, "My food is to do the will of him who sent me and to accomplish his work" (John 4:34). Jesus made this theological statement to his disciples after his noon hour conversation with a Samaritan woman at Jacob's well near Sychar. His disciples had gone into town to buy lunch. When they returned, they marveled that Jesus was talking with her. She left her water jar, went into town, and witnessed to the townspeople about this man who told her all that she ever did. Meanwhile, the disciples urged him to eat. His reply was consistent with the one recorded in Matthew's gospel when the devil tempted him to turn stones into loaves of bread, "Man shall not live on bread alone, but by every word that comes from the mouth of God" (Matt 4:4). Our spiritual life *in* God will feed our missional life *for* God. Many Samaritans believed in him because of her testimony, and others heard him for themselves first-hand and believed his word. A divine necessity compelled his cross-cultural mission where he "had" (*dei*) to pass through Samaria (4:4). Should we embrace the necessity of his mission as well?

What is the *mission* of the church? Is it to love God and neighbor? It is to proclaim the gospel? Is it to evangelize the lost? Is it to make disciples? Is it to transform the world? A few years ago, I served on a task force for our denomination to forge a new mission statement. After we compiled two years of research, meetings, and surveys, this is where we landed: the mission of the Baptist General Conference of Canada is "to build a network of churches that make disciples, who live out and spread the gospel of Jesus Christ in their communities, Canada, and the nations." On a broader scale, the mission of the church is "to announce and demonstrate the good news of God's kingdom regarding Jesus the Messiah, who died for our sins and was resurrected, and call people to repent, believe, and follow him as Lord and King." Given the whole structure of biblical theology, these capture the core mission of the church.

In a nutshell, our mission is to proclaim and practice the gospel and make disciples of the Lord Jesus Christ (Matt 28:18–20; Mark 16:15–16;

Luke 24:45–49; John 20:21–23). As sent ones on the Lord's mission into the world, we are missionaries and ambassadors who witness to the gospel of God. We are to proclaim and spread the word (message) of the gospel of the kingdom (check all the references in the Gospels and Acts for yourself). We are also to live our lives in such as way as to be worthy of the gospel (Gal 2:14; Phil 1:27). God saves, sanctifies, and sends us by his Spirit.

Our mission is not to transform the world, make culture, eradicate poverty or AIDS, eliminate human trafficking, establish social justice, or build the kingdom of God. Our primary mission is not humanitarian social service. There are numerous agencies that offer social services. As Christians and churches should we care about social issues? Yes, of course. This is core to Pietism. In fact, "evangelism produces a true act of social action."[26] Our devout life will inspire us to do good to everyone (Gal 6:10), be a neighbor to those in need (Luke 10:36–37; 1 John 3:17), visit orphans and widows in their affliction (Jas 1:27), remember the poor (Gal 2:10), and seek the welfare of the city (Jer 29:7). God "anointed Jesus with the Holy Spirit and with power. He went about doing good and healing all who were oppressed by the devil, for God was with him" (Acts 10:38). Jesus taught that we are the salt of the earth and the light of the world (Matt 5:13–14), to glorify God by our good works (Matt 5:16; 1 Pet 2:12). Paul said: "In Christ Jesus, then, I have reason to be proud of my work for God. For I will not venture to speak of anything except what Christ has accomplished through me to bring the Gentiles to obedience—by word and deed, by the power of signs and wonders, by the power of the Spirit of God so that . . . I have fulfilled the ministry of the gospel of Christ" (Rom 15:17–19).

Let us cultivate two expressions that partner together: (1) *proclamation* (announce the gospel); (2) *practice* (live the gospel) in both words and works. These will also gain boundless traction when empowered by signs and wonders and the power of the Spirit of God. Our spirituality is social, but our mission is primarily spiritual—we announce the gospel so that people can experience the forgiveness of sins and the regeneration of the Holy Spirit. However, we must devote ourselves to both evangelism (mission) and social responsibility (ministry). We call this *integral mission* or holistic mission committed to proclaim and practice the gospel, "show and tell" the Good News, accompanied by the power of the Holy Spirit, with a faithful *incarnational presence* in the world. *The Lausanne Covenant* describes the nature of evangelism:

26. Stiles, *Marks of the Messenger*, 63.

> To evangelize is to spread the good news that Jesus Christ died for our sins and was raised from the dead according to the Scriptures, and that as the reigning Lord he now offers the forgiveness of sins and the liberating gifts of the Spirit to all who repent and believe. Our Christian presence in the world is indispensable to evangelism . . . The results of evangelism include obedience to Christ, incorporation into his church and responsible service in the world.[27]

To investigate how the book of Acts portrays spell-binding evangelism and proclamation of the gospel and what their central concerns were, read: Acts 2:14–39; 3:12–26; 4:8–12; 7:2–53; 10:34–43 with 11:4–18; 13:16–41; 14:15–17; 17:22–31. What electrifies me in these accounts is how Christ-centered they were, saturated with Scripture, biblical history and theology, apologetics, contextualization, and reports of the filling of the Holy Spirit and boldness, with calls to repentance, faith, and baptism. Paul's speeches also offer rich material: Acts 22:1–21; 24:10–25 and 26:1–29. His conversion narratives always point unmistakably to Jesus Christ.

When the early church leaders proclaimed the gospel, and made disciples of many people, they engaged both Jewish and Greco-Roman culture and penetrated all sectors of society with people who came under the rule of God in Christ. Members of the church were a dispersed presence in the culture as witnesses of Christ. Mission was Christian truth and love in dynamic action led by the Spirit. We read of a fantastic cross section of people who became believers: many Samaritans and a black finance minister of Ethiopia (Acts 8); Cornelius a Roman centurion and others in Caesarea (Acts 10); Hellenists in Antioch (Acts 11); a Roman proconsul in Paphos and Gentiles in Pisidian Antioch (Acts 13); Lydia a businesswoman and her household and a Roman jailer in Philippi (Acts 16); some men, Dionysius the Areopagite, a woman named Damaris, and others in Athens (Acts 17); Crispus the Jewish ruler of the synagogue and his household, many Corinthians, John's disciples, and others in Ephesus (Acts 19). The gospel through power encounters freed a slave girl from a spirit of divination, which caused a commotion in Philippi with her owners who lost their ability to profit through her fortune-telling (Acts 16). Many believers in Ephesus who had practiced magic arts brought their books and burned them at great cost, and the gospel caused profound cultural tensions in Ephesus with Demetrius and other craftsmen who sold silver shrines of the goddess

27. *The Lausanne Covenant*, 4.

Artemis (Acts 19). In fact, the gospel spread to Roman provinces and triggered dramatic cultural formation in key cities such as Thessalonica, Philippi, Corinth, and Ephesus. Read the letters Paul wrote to these centers to understand the issues he addressed with the gospel. Also read Romans, Galatians, Colossians, Philemon, and Revelation to study the relationship between the gospel and integral mission. *The Lausanne Covenant* offers theological insight into our social responsibility:

> We affirm that God is both the Creator and the Judge of all people. We therefore should share his concern for justice and reconciliation throughout human society and for the liberation of men and women from every kind of oppression. Because men and women are made in the image of God, every person has an intrinsic dignity because of which he or she should be respected and served, not exploited . . . The message of salvation implies also a message of judgment upon every form of alienation, oppression and discrimination, and we should not be afraid to denounce evil and injustice wherever they exist. When people receive Christ, they are born again into his kingdom and must seek not only to exhibit but also to spread its righteousness in the midst of an unrighteous world.[28]

In *How Christianity Changed the World*, Alvin J. Schmidt documents enormous amounts of history where ordinary people accomplished extraordinary things for God as they proclaimed and practiced the gospel, through spiritual and social impact. People transformed by Christ became a shaping force that inspired some of the greatest achievements in Western civilization outside church walls. Christians and Christianity were behind the early formations of the YMCA and YWCA, hospitals, mental institutions, orphanages, the Red Cross, Braille, colleges and universities, the abolition of slavery in England and the USA, women's rights and the rights of the unborn, labor and social welfare, and various gifts of music, literature, art, architecture, holidays, symbols, and words. Gabe Lyons founded Q "to educate church and cultural leaders on their role and opportunity to embody the gospel in public life." He sees seven channels of cultural influence: media, arts and entertainment, business, education, government, the social sector, and the church. He covers four themes: culture, future, church, and gospel. "The seven channels of culture touch every citizen in a society. It is historically proven that when leaders from each channel work together

28. Ibid., 5.

toward a common goal, cultural change is possible."[29] I would add law and healthcare as significant channels of culture as well. I agree with Gabe Lyons, "The next wave of Christian influence will come from the pews, not the pulpit."

VOCATION FOR "GOD'S GLORY AND NEIGHBOR'S GOOD"

I have always sought to proclaim and practice the gospel in evangelism and social service. I have served on a hospital board and volunteered at a cancer agency. I have traveled abroad on mission trips to visit orphanages and prisons and distribute Bibles. I have supported a pro-life society, volunteered with Samaritans Purse for flood disaster relief and the Salvation Army for Christmas donations, and contributed to both secular and Christian charities to promote social projects. My wife and I have opened our home to foreign students and welcomed other people to live with us when they needed a place to stay. I have voted for Christian leaders for public office; signed petitions that oppose the redefinition of marriage, assisted suicide, and abortion; and donated food and clothing to various share shops. I have sought to understand and love LGBTQ people, and offer money, meals, and gospel messages to homeless people. I have helped my unsaved neighbors, prayed for and befriended unsaved people, shared the gospel with and discipled many people. By God's grace I intend to continue.

My experiences are unremarkable and are likely not much different than yours. I think numerous Christians try to live by the Golden Rule and share their faith from time to time or invite people to church. And yet I know we need to leverage the spiritual priesthood of all believers and our sense of vocation in the community and culture. My Christian worldview sees evangelism and cultural formation through God's work of saving grace and common grace. *Saving grace* is God's special favor granted to people to come to Christ by faith for salvation. *Common grace* is God's universal favor granted to all people through his providence and care. Steve Garber states, "Vocation is integral, not incidental, to the *missio Dei* [mission of God] . . . this vision of vocation is being lived by men and women, younger and older, who are committed to a faith that shapes vocation that shapes

29. Q: Ideas/about.

culture."[30] You and your church will serve people and shape culture as you proclaim and live out the gospel through *vocational stewardship*.

People spend significant amounts of time each week in the workplace. The paradigm for many Christians, however, is to serve God on Sunday at church and then enter the real world at work on Monday. How can we foster an identity that Christians are missionaries as businessmen, bankers, carpenters, schoolteachers, and waitresses? Who can best influence police, secretaries, computer techies, and supermarket cashiers? Is it not those who work in those sectors?

Key biblical characters practiced vocational stewardship as they held secular jobs where God was active in their work: Joseph was a prime minister, Amos was a fig farmer, Nehemiah was a wine taster, Luke was a doctor, Lydia was a merchant, and Philemon was a businessman and slave owner in Colossae. Paul mentions numerous lay-leaders with significant ministries in the church and community (cf. Rom 16; Col 4). There is also a biblical place for some people to leave secular jobs and commit themselves to full-time ministry as a vocation or bi-vocationally. Moses left shepherding; Jesus left carpentry; but Paul was a bi-vocational tentmaker.

A missional spirituality will inform one's journey of vocation and the implications for career choices. As mentioned in chapter 7, we must listen to the "call," the voice of vocation, and how God places us in the world to make a difference. A missional spirituality enjoys a home field advantage where you have natural bridges to embody the gospel with people in your field of work. Builders influence other builders; artists and musicians influence other artists and musicians; those in law enforcement influence others in law enforcement; and so on. All vocations are sacred when you serve according to your "call" from God. If He calls you to the fields of medicine, education, or technology, do not sell the farm to grab a call in the field of pastoring, Bible translation, or worship. All service offered as a response to your call or vocation from God to meet human need is *ministry* connected to the gospel and mission. The Pietist motto, "God's glory and neighbor's good," will beam into tangible missional service in the world.

PRAYER, PROCLAMATION, AND PIETY

In some ways, as I write, I have this gaunt feeling that to inspire devotion to the gospel and mission will continue to be an uphill hike. Like a toothless

30. Garber, *Visions of Vocation*, 18.

lion, the church in the Western world largely poses a diminished threat to the kingdom of darkness and presents a faded voice in the cultural marketplace of public ideas and values. Like Paul in Athens, a Greek city overrun by a forest of pagan idols, our postmodern culture is overrun with the pagan idols of the media and the mall. Paul had few converts and no church plant in Athens. The gospel was another new teaching tossed into the smorgasbord of other philosophies. In our day, nominal Christians unchanged by the gospel will not have the commitment or staying power for devotion to the gospel and mission. It is merely one store in the mall. David Kinnaman and Gabe Lyons write:

> Pastors are feeling the tension too. They want to help people follow Jesus, but it is hard to disciple with lasting effect when many churchgoers show up only once or twice a month. Furthermore, churchgoers are immersed in entertainment and media-saturated culture shapes their lives and lifestyles in deep, irresistible ways. Pastors tell us they worry about the commitment level of their people and their willingness to be disciples. And they confess they feel inadequate to untangle the complexities of teaching people to follow Christ in today's culture . . . The morality of self-fulfillment is everywhere . . . Too many Christians have substituted comfortable living for a life changed by the gospel.[31]

We are quick to cite Peter who advises, "Always be prepared to make a defense to anyone who asks you for a reason for the hope that is in you" (1 Pet 3:15). But there are two issues. First, perhaps we do not really carry that hope in us. Second, perhaps we do not do what Peter says in the first part of the verse, "But in your hearts honor Christ the Lord as holy." Without the inner renewal of the heart where we first honor Christ the Lord as holy, as a Pietist would do, it is hard to make an outer missional defense and offer a reason for a hope that is supposedly in us. Perhaps, as Karl Barth proposed in January 1963, "What needs to take place today in the interests of peace is in the first place . . . a spiritual Reformation and thus a conversion of Christians and of the Christian churches themselves—a conversion to the truth of their own message."[32]

What enabled the early church leaders in Acts with such power were their lives of piety yielded to the power of the Spirit. Stephen was a man of good repute, full of the Holy Spirit and of wisdom, grace, and power (Acts

31. Kinnaman and Lyons, *Good Faith*, 53, 57, 59.

32. Cited by Miller, *The Vanishing Evangelical*, 65.

6:3, 8). Barnabas was a good man, full of the Holy Spirit and of faith (Acts 11:24). Paul, Silvanus, and Timothy embodied the Spirit's power in their proclamation and personal proof of the gospel: "Our gospel came to you not only in word, but also in power and in the Holy Spirit and with full conviction. You know what kind of men we proved to be among you for your sake" (1 Thess 1:5). They also shared their lives incarnationally:

> So, being affectionately desirous of you, we were ready to share with you not only the gospel of God but also our own selves, because you had become very dear to us. For you remember, brothers, our labor and toil: we worked night and day, that we might not be a burden to any of you, while we proclaimed to you the gospel of God. You are witnesses, and God also, how holy and righteous and blameless was our conduct toward you believers. For you know how, like a father with his children, we exhorted each one of you and encouraged you and charged you to walk in a manner worthy of God, who calls you into his own kingdom and glory (1 Thess 2:8–12).

We must first plunge the depths of spiritual renewal to oxygenate missional renewal. It will not work to simply launch an Alpha program to beef up evangelism, or bolt on a missions week, or read a book on the missional church or gospel-centered ministry, if we hope to incite our devotion to the gospel and mission in our churches. They can help, but it begins with spiritual fervor. Paul writes, "Never be lacking in zeal, but keep your spiritual fervor, serving the Lord. Be joyful in hope, patient in affliction, faithful in prayer" (Rom 12:11–12 NIV). Let me suggest one final pungent text that showcases the soul of the devout life.

Colossians 4:2–6

> Devote yourselves to prayer, being watchful and thankful. And pray for us, too, that God may open a door for our message, so that we may proclaim the mystery of Christ, for which I am in chains. Pray that I may proclaim it clearly, as I should. Be wise in the way you act toward outsiders; make the most of every opportunity. Let your conversation be always full of grace, seasoned with salt, so that you may know how to answer everyone (NIV).

In October 2015, I attended a three-day Church Renewal retreat at Southland Church in Steinbach, Manitoba, a small community an hour

South of Winnipeg. This church of 4,000 in a community of 16,000 has become a refreshing oasis on a Canadian prairie. Ray Duerksen is the founding pastor, and leader of Church Renewal Canada. It is an artesian well of spiritual renewal. About a hundred of us from a dozen denominations from across Canada journeyed together through a *Set Free* seminar similar to Neil Anderson's *Freedom in Christ*. It helped us practice confession and repentance to refurbish our souls. We then attended the weekend service and tour of the facility, followed by their monthly evening prayer summit attended by 1,200 men and women, young adults, youth, and children. The weekend retreat concluded on Monday with a *Hearing God* seminar. Throughout the weekend, we practiced the teaching and experienced God in a Christ-centered, humble atmosphere aflame with Scripture and the Spirit. I received an impartation. Acts 6:4 and Colossians 4:2–6 now drive my philosophy of ministry.

Paul's final instruction to the Colossian church contains practical teaching on the devout life, centered in a missional passion for the gospel. God calls us to practice persistent and specific ongoing prayer with an alert mind that sees where he is at work, invigorated with a thankful heart. The prayer is missional, that God would pry open the closed doors of hardened hearts, and that we would make the gospel clear to people. We need gospel literacy and boldness as we seize the opportunities that arise to share our faith. And, our character must match our message and our conversation must be winsome, so that we will know how to answer inquiring unbelievers.

That same fall, after I attended the Church Renewal weekend, I was in Edmonton, where I often travel to for my work. For several years, I stayed in the basement suite of Celia and Gerald, an elderly couple who I had known for years. One morning when I arrived, Celia mentioned that her neighbor who had just retired was on chemotherapy after his surgery for prostate cancer. The cancer had spread and now he had to fight for his life. She asked if I would visit him, as she knew that I also had prostate cancer several years ago and would be able to identify with him. I felt nervous to do so but sensed God's voice nudge me to have her contact him and see if I could come over that night to pray for him.

When I returned that evening she said, "Well it's on!" Now I really felt nervous, but I prayed right through Colossians 4:2–6. My goal was to pray for him and to also share the gospel, as I knew he and his wife were unbelievers. That evening the three of us went over to meet Celia's neighbors

Dave and Amy. After we chatted briefly, Dave blurted out, "Well I understand you had prostate cancer!"

I described my journey of fear and faith through what became a successful surgery, and mentioned that I believed that Jesus sometimes chooses to heal people. Amy, through tears, choked out her reply that his situation was not so successful. I asked if I could pray for Dave. They affirmed that "they believed in God" and open to prayer. I got up, walked behind Dave, anointed his forehead with a small portion of oil, and then with Celia placed my hands on his shoulders. I explained the ritual to him. As I began to pray for his healing, everyone began to weep. The presence of the Lord was so thick I could hardly stand or talk. I recall Luke 5:17, where "the power of the Lord was with him to heal." I also felt led to pray for their daughter Sarah who was in a wheelchair next to Dave. She recently had to undergo dialysis treatments for kidney failure. I wanted to share the gospel but sensed the Lord say, "Not now; the timing is not right."

Two months later, while in Edmonton again, I invited Dave out for lunch to see how he was doing. He said that the cancer was in remission, that he did not need chemotherapy anymore, and that he was now on hormone treatment and felt normal. The doctors said he might have three to seven years left with his type of cancer. His darting eyes and wavering voice disclosed the ominous uncertainty in his soul. I prayed quietly in my heart that God would open a door of opportunity for me to share the gospel, but waited until he offered questions that I could answer.

We chatted and then he asked, "So what do you do?"

For the next hour, I told him what I did as a pastor and he then asked, "Why?"

That opened the door for me to tell him my complete conversion story and the message of the gospel, and how I went from a Californian pagan to a Canadian pastor. He zeroed in on every word I said with a spellbound attention. I felt the Lord say in my heart, "That's enough for now."

As it turned out, a month later Dave and Amy's daughter died! I could not attend the funeral, but sent a sympathy card. The next time I was in town, I visited Dave and Amy with Celia and Gerald and expressed my compassion and care and prayed for them. We all wept together as they struggled to assemble the pieces of their broken lives back together. That next fall, I contacted Dave and we went for lunch again. This time I said to the Lord, "I want to share the gospel as clearly as I should and call him to repent and believe." Half way through our lunch I asked, "So are you secure with your future if things do not go the way we want, though we'll continue to pray for your healing. Can you face eternity with the bold confidence that I have because of my faith in the Lord Jesus Christ?"

"Well I've been pretty good all my life," was his reply.

"That could be, but being good is not good enough for God," I replied. I went on to describe why sin is a vast issue between God and us, and why it was necessary for Christ to die as our Savior. He teared up as I explained the bad news as we considered the good news. As we sat in my car in front of his house before I dropped him off, I prayed for his healing and for his heart toward Jesus.

He said, "Thanks Roger, let's get together again!"

Three months later I learned that his cancer had spread. He was to face another round of chemotherapy. We met and talked again over coffee at McDonalds and then we went to a park. As we sat on a picnic table in mid-May 2016 under stately trees and a sunny blue sky, he agonized over his struggle to face death and leave his family and wife behind in early retirement years. Before we met I had prayed Colossians 4:2–6 again. As we sat at that picnic table, through his tears, Dave called for hope. The Lord opened the door of his heart. I asked if there was any reason he could not believe the gospel.

He said, "No, I guess not." He repented and believed. We prayed as he committed his life to Christ. Ten months later, I sat with him for the last time, two weeks before he met his lord. Dave died as a new believer in March 2017. Read Colossians 4:2–6 again, then go and live it out:

> Devote yourselves to prayer with an alert mind and a thankful heart. Pray for us, too that God will give us many opportunities to speak about his mysterious plan concerning Christ. That is why I am here in chains. Pray that I will proclaim this message as clearly as I should. Live wisely among those who are not believers, and make the most of every opportunity. Let your conversation be gracious and attractive so that you will have the right response for everyone (NLT).

THE INFLUENCE OF PIETISM

Pietism was a powerful tributary that converged with at least two others, English Puritanism and High Church Anglicanism, which together unleashed a torrent of church renewal that flowed into an ever-widening missional river that helped irrigate the great awakenings into what would become evangelicalism.[33] Mark Noll writes:

> Almost as important in preparing the way for later evangelicalism were events taking place in central Europe. As historian Reginald Ward has demonstrated persuasively, a great range of connections—literary, personal, pastoral, hymnic—linked the spirituality of Continental Pietism to almost every phase of the British and American evangelical awakenings. The Pietists, who had themselves greatly benefited from the books of English Puritans, returned the favor many times over by pointing English-speaking evangelicals to ideals of true religion, models of organized philanthropy, a specific way of talking about conversion and a new focus on the assurance of salvation.[34]

As a Spirit-energized renewal movement, the dominant themes of the inner life of faith and its fruits, through the regenerate life, are foundational to Pietism. The devout life as I have developed it, consists of a posture with practices centered in piety. The devout life is broader than the Pietist tradition per se, but my goal has been to explore and expand on ten key features of Pietism and apply them to spiritual renewal today.

May you explore and experience devotion to biblical piety, heart religion, pure doctrine and life, continuous Christian conversion, and a transformational use of Scripture. May you also explore and experience devotion to heart-felt prayer, the spiritual priesthood, Christian life in community, a peaceful spirit, and the gospel and mission. Perhaps you or your church will spark another revival in our day. The Pietist impulse or ethos set a vigorous course for British and American revivals and evangelical Christianity particularly through John and Charles Wesley, Charles Whitefield, and Jonathan Edwards in the early eighteenth century. "In this sense, Pietism was the fountain of all modern revivals. It set the experience of new life in Christ at the center of the Christian message and the Christian ministry. For this reason, it is impossible to think of evangelical Christianity without the imprint of Pietism."[35] Stoeffler concludes:

33. Noll, *The Rise of Evangelicalism*, 50–68. Hutchison and Wolffe, suggest Scottish Presbyterianism as a third tributary along with the ones mentioned here in, *A Short History of Global Evangelicalism*, 26–32.

34. Ibid., 60.

35. Shelley, *Church History in Plain Language*, 348.

> There can be no longer any doubt that the evangelicalism which became the dominant pattern for the individual and corporate religious self-understanding of American Protestants is heavily indebted to the Pietist tradition. Hence Pietism touched all segments of American society, as well as all geographical areas. And, furthermore, its influence continues to be felt, not only among sectarian groups, but among the broad majority of Protestant denominations in America.[36]

In addition, Pietism has also impacted Canada and other nations across the globe. If you ask, "What is an evangelical?" The simplest answer that I would offer is, "One who proclaims and practices the gospel (the *euangelion*)." Would I overstate if I said that an evangelical should be a classic church Pietist, in the tradition of the Apostle Paul and Philipp Jakob Spener, who practices the devout life? Spener's potent book *Pia Desideria* helped unleash a deluge of revitalization that propagated evangelical spirituality and mission that influences us even today. His subtitle reveals his passion and goal: "Heartfelt Desire for a God-pleasing Reform of the true Evangelical Church, Together with Several Simple Christian Proposals Looking Toward this End." This captures my heart for you as a Christian leader or Christ follower to embrace, live, and equip others in the devout life to plunge the depths of spiritual renewal.

FOR REFLECTION AND PRACTICE

1. How would you describe the primary mission of the church? What is the relationship between spiritual and missional renewal, and how would you define a missional spirituality? Reflect on the statement, "our spiritual life *in* God will feed our missional life *for* God."
2. Describe the meaning of integral mission and the relationship between the proclamation and the practice of the gospel. Read through the statements of the Lausanne Covenant and seek ways to practice evangelism and specific areas that you are concerned for in social responsibility. How do the accounts of Francke, Zinzendorf, and Wesley support integral mission?

36. Stoeffler, *Continental Pietism and Early American Christianity*, 267.

3. How does vocational stewardship fit into devotion to the gospel and mission directed to God's glory and neighbor's good? Pray and practice Colossians 4:2–6 on a regular basis.

FOR PASTORS AND CHURCH LEADERS

1. Review or revise your church or denominational mission statement with your understanding of the biblical mission of the church. How do you approach social issues from the standpoint of the gospel and evangelism without reducing it to social action or a social gospel?
2. Read and reflect on Francke's exhortation concerning ministers in their preaching. What are your thoughts? Would you see value in incorporating his ideas into your regular preaching?
3. Develop a plan to equip people in vocational stewardship and integral mission and draw principles and practices from Pietism and from the book of Acts. How can you stimulate devotion to the gospel and mission?

CONCLUSION

Dimensions of Spiritual Renewal

"Behold, I am doing a new thing;
now it springs forth,
do you not perceive it?
I will make a way in the wilderness
and rivers in the desert"

(Isa 43:19).

As I sat down to type my final words for this book, I had just returned from a mid-July Sunday afternoon outing at our local city park with my wife, my daughter, and her three young daughters. In our conversation at the picnic table, my daughter Melissa quizzed me about the Holy Spirit, the supernatural, hearing from God, the demonic, and how you can know if something is from God or not. She had conversations with some people in her church that hold a strong view of Scripture and a conservative view of the Spirit, which restricts miraculous "sign gifts" to the early church. She remarked how close friends of hers were also switching to another church that is on a vibrant path of spiritual renewal—where the exercise of all the gifts and the embrace of the Spirit, healing, and prayer are profuse in transformational ways. I offered some answers.

My heart raced. Our chat stirred my resident passion for *Spirit*-ual renewal. I recalled my own profound experiences of spiritual renewal when I pastored in the Vineyard and from other more recent experiences, together with two initial books that I wrote to defend and tutor renewal: *Let the*

River Flow and *The Revived Church*. Interestingly, before my wife Gail and I met Melissa at the park, we had just attended the worship service at our own church where pastor Jeff has been leading our church this past year in renewal. In his message, he cited Isaiah 43:19 above. His key point was, "Our land needs strong churches and vibrant believers as never before." He outlined the challenges and then concluded, "Let's continue with church renewal!" When you think of church renewal or revitalization, think of the prefix *re*. To *re*-new is to make new again. To *re*-vitalize is to make vital again. Let us plunge the depths of spiritual renewal and watch God *re*-shape and *re*-vive us. However, challenges, changes, discomfort, and opposition will accompany the dive. What is a way forward?

LEADERSHIP RENEWAL

A way forward is to first embrace *leadership* renewal. Church leaders can become like bottlenecks or logjams and restrict or restrain renewal. When leaders long for or experience a deluge of God's empowering presence first-hand, they can become catalysts for corporate church renewal. Dissatisfied leaders, such as the Pietists, jam the pages of church history as spiritual entrepreneurs who paved the way and paid the price to release the rivers of renewal and revival. Form a church renewal leadership coalition in your context that generates fervent prayer and personal piety, and activates ardent ministry by the Spirit and the word. Over a twelve-week period read my book and discuss the questions and practices together. Pray for, practice, preach, and plan the devout life for the personal and corporate dimensions of your church, school, district, or conference. Adopt William Carey's counsel, "Expect great things from God; attempt great things for God."

CONCEPTUAL RENEWAL

A way forward is to also embrace *conceptual* renewal. Years ago, during one of my own seasons of renewal, a very accurate prophetic person announced to me, "Roger, God is re-arranging your dome!" Howard Snyder writes:

> Renewal may also come conceptually, as God gives new vision for what the church can and should be . . . for its life and mission. It comes primarily in the area of our thoughts, ideas, and images of the church. Each of us has a set of ideas—a certain 'model' or 'paradigm'—of what we feel the church should be. Our models

> are a combination of our experience and our study of Scripture. Conceptual renewal comes when our models are challenged, and we are forced to rethink what the church is really about.[1]

Books that have shaped my conceptual renewal and my capacity to discern genuine works of God, include: Philipp Spener, *Pia Desideria*; Johann Arndt, *True Christianity*; Jonathan Edwards, *The Distinguishing Marks of a Work of the Spirit of God*; John White, *When the Spirit Comes with Power*; Richard Lovelace, *Dynamics of Spiritual Life*; Howard Snyder, *The Problem of Wineskins* and *The Radical Wesley*; Donald Bloesch, *The Crisis of Piety*; John Wimber, *Power Evangelism*; Jack Deere, *Surprised by the Power of the Spirit*. Also: Darrel L. Guder, *Missional Church*; Roger Olson and Christian Collins Winn, *Reclaiming Pietism*; Gordon T. Smith, *Beginning Well*; J. D. Greear, *Jesus, Continued*; Daniel Henderson, *Old Paths New Power* and *Transforming Prayer*; John Piper, *The Supremacy of God in Preaching*; and Craig Keener, *Spirit Hermeneutics*. First dive into the book of Acts. Consult a commentary such as John Stott's *The Spirit, The Church, and The World: The Message of Acts*. In preaching, consider John Piper's idea of concept creation: "We must also labor to bring about, in the minds of our listeners, conceptual categories that may be missing from their mental framework . . . God [by the Spirit through us] brings about this new seeing and understanding and believing."[2]

STRUCTURAL RENEWAL

A way forward is to finally embrace *structural* renewal. Many leaders focus on improved structures to revitalize their churches. They might read bestselling books on leadership and assume that if they simply craft compelling mission and values statements, build collaborative teams, generate alignment with all departments, and re-design worship services, their church will experience renewal. Do we have a compulsive fascination with human leadership principles to "succeed"? We need effective organizational leadership and structures, but without the crackling fire of *spiritual* renewal, we might construct a clean and efficient fireplace, but one that provides little heat or light.

1. Snyder, *Signs of the Spirit*, 288.

2. Piper, *The Supremacy of God in Preaching*, 128. For the full discussion, see pages 127–31.

This is not contradictory to what I just discussed, but complementary. We need to engineer the best forms and structures that will serve the spiritual. Howard Snyder writes: "It is the question of the best wineskins for the new wine. Renewal often dies prematurely for lack of effective structures . . . Structural renewal is simply finding the best forms, in our day and age, for living out the new life in Christ."[3] In my book, I offer many ideas adapted from Pietist structures that can facilitate a transformational use of Scripture, heart-felt private and public prayer, the spiritual priesthood, Christian life in community, and so on. The Pietists used conventicles and the University of Halle. The Methodists used lay preachers, bands, and classes. The Moravians used twenty-four-hour prayer watches and daily Bible readings. What will you use? Let the river flow as renewed leaders with renewed concepts and renewed structures stream into missional renewal. Through the devout life, may you plunge the depths of spiritual renewal. Selah!

DEVOTIONAL EXERCISE FOR PRAYER AND SINGING

O breath of life, come sweeping through us,
Revive Your Church with life and power;
O breath of Life, come, cleanse, renew us,
And fit Your Church to meet this hour.

O Wind of God, come bend us, break us,
Till humbly we confess our need;
Then in Your tenderness remake us,
Revive, restore, for this we plead.

O Breath of Love, come breathe within us,
Renewing thought and will and heart;
Come Love of Christ, afresh to win us,
Revive Your Church in every part.

Revive us Lord! Is zeal abating,
While harvest fields are vast and white?
Revive us, Lord, the world is waiting,
Equip Your Church to spread the light.[4]

3. Snyder, *Signs of the Spirit*, 290.

4. Head, "O Breath of Life."

BIBLIOGRAPHY

Addison, Steve. *Movements That Change the World*. Smyrna: Missional Press, 2009.

Ames, William. *The Marrow of Theology*. Grand Rapids: Baker Academic, 1997.

Anderson, Brian. "How Did God Speak in the Book of Acts?" www.StoneBridgeMinistries.net.

Arbinger Institute, The. *The Anatomy of Peace*. San Francisco: Berrett-Koehler, 2006.

Arndt, Johann. *True Christianity*. Translation and Introduction by Peter Erb. New York: Paulist, 1979.

———. *True Christianity*. Christian Classics Ethereal Library. https://www.ccel.org/ccel/arndt/true.pdf.

Arthurs, Jeffrey D. *Devote Yourself to the Public Reading of Scripture*. Grand Rapids: Kregel, 2012.

Baptist Catechism. http://www.desiringgod.org/articles/a-baptist-catechism.

Barna Update. "What People Experience in Churches" (January 8, 2012). https://www.barna.com/research/what-people-experience-in-churches/.

———. "New Research on the State of Discipleship" (December 1, 2015). https://www.barna.com/research/new-research-on-the-state-of-discipleship/.

———. "The State of the Bible: 6 Trends for 2014." https://www.barna.org/barna-update/culture/664-the-state-of-the-bible-6-trends-for-2014#.VhlH5db6Rbw.

Bayly, Lewis. *The Practice of Piety*. http://www.ccel.org/ccel/bayly/piety.html.

Bengel, John Albrecht. "Gnomon of the New Testament 1742." In *Pietists: Selected Writings*. Edited by Peter C. Erb. New York: Paulist Press, 1983.

Bennett, David W. *Metaphors of Ministry*. Eugene: Wipf & Stock, 1993.

Blackaby, Henry and Richard. *Hearing God's Voice*. Nashville: B&H, 2002.

Bloesch, Donald G. *The Crisis of Piety: Essays Toward a Theology of the Christian Life*. Colorado Springs: Helmers & Howard, 1988.

———. *The Paradox of Holiness—Faith in Search of Obedience*. Peabody: Hendrickson, 2016.

———. *Spirituality Old and New*. Downers Grove: IVP Academic, 2007.

———. *The Struggle of Prayer*. Colorado Springs: Helmers & Howard, 1988.

Bonar, Andrew A. *The Biography of Robert Murray M'Cheyne*. Grand Rapids: Zondervan, n.d. Kindle edition.

Bounds E. M. *The Possibilities of Prayer*. In *The Complete Works of E.M. Bounds on Prayer*. 2015. Kindle edition.

———. *Power Through Prayer*. 6th ed. London: Marshall Brothers, n.d.

Bready, J. Wesley. *England: Before and After Wesley*. New York: Harper, 1938.

Brown, Dale W. *Understanding Pietism*. Revised ed. Nappanee: Evangel, 1996.
Bruner, Emil. *The Word and the World*. London: Student Christian Movement, 1931.
Burns, Bob, Tasha D. Chapman, and Donald C. Guthrie. *Resilient Ministry: What Pastors Told Us About Surviving and Thriving*. Downers Grove: IVP, 2013.
Calvin, John. *Institutes of the Christian Religion*, 1. Edited by John T. McNeill, Vols. XX and XXI, Library of Christian Classics. Philadelphia: Westminster, 1977.
Canadian Bible Engagement Study. "Are Canadians Done with the Bible?" http://www.bibleengagementstudy.ca.
Carlson, Kent, and Mike Lueken. *Renovation of the Church*. Downers Grove: IVP, 2011.
Carlson, William G. "Pietism." In *Dictionary of Christian Spirituality*, Glen G. Scorgie, general editor, 673–74. Grand Rapids: Zondervan, 2011.
Carson, D. A. *Praying With Paul*. 2nd ed. Grand Rapids: Baker Academic, 2014.
Christian History Institute. "The Rich Young Ruler Who Said Yes." https://www.christianhistoryinstitute.org/magazine/article/the-rich-young-ruler/.
Cleveland, Christina. *Disunity in Christ: Uncovering the Hidden Forces That Keep Us Apart*. Downers Grove: IVP, 2013.
Clifton-Soderstrom, Michelle. *Angels, Worms, and Bogeys: The Christian Ethic of Pietism*. Eugene: Cascade Books, 2010.
Craddock, Fred B. *Preaching*. Nashville: Abingdon, 1985.
C.S. Lewis Institute. "Christianity Makes Sense of the World." In *Reflections* (Dec. 2013). http://www.cslewisinstitute.org/Christianity_Makes_Sense_of_the_World.
Dark, David. *The Sacredness of Questioning Everything*. Grand Rapids: Zondervan, 2009.
Davids, Peter H. *The Letters of 2 Peter and Jude*. The Pillar New Testament Commentary. Grand Rapids: Eerdmans, 2006.
Dawn, Marva, and Eugene Peterson. *The Unnecessary Pastor: Rediscovering the Call*. Grand Rapids: Eerdmans, 2000.
Deere, Jack. *Surprised by the Voice of God: How God Speaks Today Through Prophecies, Dreams, and Visions*. Grand Rapids: Zondervan, 1996.
Eastwood, Cyril. *The Priesthood of All Believers*. Eugene: Wipf & Stock, 2009.
Edwards, Jonathan. *A Treatise on Religious Affections*. Grand Rapids: Baker, 1982.
Elwell, Walter A., general ed. "Heart." In *Baker Encyclopedia of the Bible*. Grand Rapids: Baker, 1988. Logos Bible software edition, 938–39.
Ferguson, Sinclair B. "Preaching Christ From the Old Testament." *PT Media Paper* 2. London: Proclamation Trust, 2002.
Fernando, Ajith. *Acts: The NIV Application Commentary*. Grand Rapids: Zondervan, 1998.
Flavel, John. *A Saint Indeed or the Great Work of a Christian in Keeping the Heart in the Several Conditions of Life*. Christian Classics Ethereal Library. http://www.ccel.org/ccel/flavel/saintindeed.pdf
Flourishing Congregations Institute. "Defining a Flourishing Congregation." http://www.flourishingcongregations.org/defining-a-flourishing-congregation.
Foster, Richard. *Celebration of Discipline*. Revised ed. San Francisco: Harper & Row, 1988.
———. *Prayer: Finding the Heart's True Home*. HarperSanFrancisco, 1992.
Francke, August. "The Foretaste of Eternal Life." In *Pietists: Selected Writings*, edited by Peter C. Erb, 149–58. New York: Paulist Press, 1983.
———. *Guide to the Reading and Study of the Holy Scriptures*. 3rd ed. London: 1819.
———. "A Letter to a Friend Concerning the Most Useful Way of Preaching." In *Pietists: Selected Writings*, edited by Peter C. Erb, 117–27. New York: Paulist Press, 1983.

———. "Rules for the Protection of Conscience and for Good Order in Conversation or in Society." In *Pietists: Selected Writings*, edited by Peter C. Erb, 108–13. New York: Paulist Press, 1983.

Fuqua, Dennis. *United and Ignited: Encountering God Through Dynamic Corporate Prayer*. L\P Press, 2012, Kindle edition.

Galli, Mark, and Ted Olson, eds. "Nikolaus von Zinzendorf." In *Christian History* (August 8, 2008), from *131 Christians Everyone Should Know*, Holman Reference: 2000. http://www.christianitytoday.com/ch/131christians/denominationalfounders/zinzendorf.html?start=2.

Garber, Steve. *Visions of Vocation: Common Grace for the Common Good*. Downers Grove: IVP, 2014.

Garland, David E. *2 Corinthians*. The New American Commentary. Broadman & Holman, 1999.

George Whitefield's Journals. Edinburgh: The Banner of Truth Trust, 1960.

Greenman, Jeffrey P. "Spiritual Formation in Theological Perspective." In *Life in the Spirit: Spiritual Formation in Theological Perspective*. Jeffrey P. Greenman and George Kalantzis, eds. 23–35. Downers Grove: IVP Academic, 2010.

Grenz, Stanley J. *Theology for the Community of God*. Grand Rapids: Eerdmans, 2000.

Grenz, Stanley J., and Roger E. Olson. *Who Needs Theology? An Invitation to the Study of God*. Downers Grove: IVP, 1996.

Guthrie, George H. *Read the Bible for Life*. Nashville: B&H, 2011.

Hardin, Michael. "The Authority of Scripture: A Pietist Perspective." *Covenant Quarterly* (February 1991) 3–12.

Hartley, Fred. *Living in the Upper Room*. Terre Haute: Prayer Shop, 2013.

Head, Bessie Porter. "O Breath of Life." In *The Cyber Hymnal*. http://www.hymntime.com/tch/htm/o/b/r/obreathl.htm.

Heath, Elaine. *The Mystic Way of Evangelism*. Grand Rapids: Baker Academic, 2004.

Helland, Roger. *Magnificent Surrender: Releasing the Riches of Living in the Lord*. Eugene: Wipf & Stock, 2012.

Helland, Roger, and Leonard Hjalmarson. *Missional Spirituality: Embodying God's Love From the Inside Out*. Downers Grove: IVP, 2011.

Henderson Daniel. *Old Paths New Power: Awakening Your Church Through Prayer and the Ministry of the Word*. Chicago: Moody, 2016.

———. *Transforming Prayer*. Minneapolis: Bethany House, 2011.

Heschel, Abraham. *Man's Quest for God*. New York: Scribner, 1954.

Hillman, Os. *The 9 to 5 Window: How Faith Can Transform the Workplace*. Ventura: Regal 2005.

Hunter, Todd. *Christianity Beyond Belief*. Downers Grove: IVP, 2009.

Hutchison, Mark, and John Wolffe. *A Short History of Global Evangelicalism*. New York: Cambridge University Press, 2012.

Johnson, Terry L., and J. Ligon Duncan III. "Recommendations for Improving Public Prayer." http://9marks.org/article/recommendations-improving-public-prayer/.

Jones, E. Stanley. *A Song of Ascents*. Nashville: Abingdon, 1979.

Josephus, Flavius, and William Whiston. *The Works of Josephus: Complete and Unabridged*. Peabody: Hendrickson, 1987.

Keller, Timothy. *Prayer: Experiencing Awe and Intimacy With God. New York*: Dutton, 2014.

Kinnaman, David, and Gabe Lyons. *Good Faith: Being a Christian When Society Thinks You're Irrelevant and Extreme*. Grand Rapids: Baker, 2016.

Kuruvilla, Abraham. *A Vision for Preaching: Understanding the Heart of Pastoral Ministry*. Grand Rapids: Baker Academic, 2015.

Lausanne Covenant, The. https://www.lausanne.org/content/covenant/lausanne-covenant.

Law, William. *A Serious Call to a Devout and Holy Life*. Grand Rapids: Baker, 1977.

Lencioni, Patrick. *The Five Dysfunctions of a Team*. San Francisco: Jossey-Bass, 2002.

Lindberg, Carter, ed. *The Pietist Theologians*. Oxford: Blackwell, 2005.

Lovelace, Richard F. *Dynamics of Spiritual Life*. Downers Grove: IVP, 1979.

Matthaei, Sondra Higgins. *Making Disciples: Faith Formation in the Wesleyan Tradition*. Nashville: Abingdon, 2000.

McHugh, Adam S. *The Listening Life: Embracing Attentiveness in a World of Distraction*. Downers Grove: IVP, 2015.

McIntosh, Gary. "The 6 Top Factors in Growing Churches." http://www.biblestudytools.com/blogs/the-good-book-blog/top-factors-in-growing-churches.html.

McKnight, Scot. *Turning to Jesus: The Sociology of Conversion in the Gospels*. Louisville: Westminster John Knox, 2002.

McLean, Max, and Warren Bird. *Unleashing the Word*. Grand Rapids: Zondervan, 2009.

Miller, Calvin. *Letters to a Young Pastor*. Colorado Springs: David C. Cook, 2011.

———. *The Vanishing Evangelical: Saving the Church From Its Own Success by Restoring What Really Matters*. Grand Rapids: Baker, 2013.

Murray, Andrew. *The Prayer Life*. Chicago: Moody Press, n.d.

New City Catechism. http://www.newcitycatechism.com.

Nikolaus Ludwig, Count von Zinzendorf. "Brotherly Union and Agreement at Herrnhut." In *Pietists: Selected Writings*, edited by Peter C. Erb, 325–30. New York: Paulist Press, 1983.

Noll, Mark A. *The Rise of Evangelicalism: The Age of Edwards, Whitefield and the Wesleys*. Downers Grove: InterVarsity, 2003.

Nouwen, Henri J. M. *Reaching Out*. New York: Doubleday, 1975.

O'Connor, Elizabeth. *Call to Commitment*. New York: Harper & Row, 1963.

Ogden, Greg. *Unfinished Business: Returning the Ministry to the People of God*. Grand Rapids: Zondervan, 2003.

Olson, Roger E. "Pietism: Myths and Realities." In *The Pietist Impulse in Christianity*. Edited by Christian T. Collins Winn, et al., 3–16. Eugene: Pickwick, 2011.

———. "Reclaiming Pietism." http://www.patheos.com/blogs/rogereolson/2011/03/reclaiming-pietism/.

Olson, Roger E., and Christian T. Collins Winn. *Reclaiming Pietism: Retrieving an Evangelical Tradition*. Grand Rapids: Eerdmans, 2015.

Owen, John. *On the Mortification of Sin in Believers*. Christian Classics Ethereal Library. http://www.ccel.org/ccel/owen/mort.pdf.

Packer, J. I. *Knowing God*. Downers Grove: InterVarsity, 1973.

———. *Rediscovering Holiness*. Ann Arbor: Servant, 1996.

Packer J. I., and Gary A. Parrett. *Grounded in the Gospel: Building Believers the Old-Fashioned Way*. Grand Rapids: Baker, 2010.

Peterson, Eugene H. *Eat This Book: A Conversation in the Art of Spiritual Reading*. Grand Rapids: Eerdmans, 2016.

———. *Working the Angles*. Grand Rapids: Eerdmans, 1987.

———. Twitter@PetersonDaily, August 1, 2015.

Pierson, Arthur T. *George Muller of Bristol and His Witness to a Prayer-Hearing God*. Kindle edition.

Piper, John. *A Godward Heart: Treasuring the God Who Loves You*. Colorado Springs: Multnomah, 2014.

———. "How to Pray for a Desolate Church." (January 5, 1992). www.desiringgod.org.

———. *The Supremacy of God in Preaching*. Revised and expanded. Grand Rapids: Baker Books, 2015.

Q. http://qideas.org/about/.

Rande, Ken. *The Peace Maker: A Biblical Guide to Resolving Personal Conflict*. Grand Rapids: Baker, 2004.

Rowe, David L. "Wisdom." In *Dictionary of Christian Spirituality*, Glen G. Scorgie, general editor, 840–41. Grand Rapids: Zondervan, 2011.

Schmidt, Alvin J. *How Christianity Changed The World*. Grand Rapids: Zondervan, 2001, 2004.

Scorgie, Glen G. "Religion of the Heart: The Enduring Value of Pietism." *The Baptist Pietist Clarion*, Vol. II, No. 1 (March 2012). https://cas.bethel.edu/dept/history/Baptist_Pietist_Clarion/edit/Baptist_Pietist_Clarion_Issues/BPC_March_2012.pdf.

Shantz, Douglas H. *An Introduction to German Pietism*. Baltimore: Johns Hopkins University Press, 2013.

Shelley, Bruce L. *Church History in Plain Language*. Dallas: Word, 1982.

Smith, Gordon T. *Beginning Well: Christian Conversion & Authentic Transformation*. Downers Grove: InterVarsity, 2001.

———. *Called to be Saints: An Invitation to Christian Maturity*. Downers Grove: IVP Academic, 2014.

———. *Transforming Conversion: Rethinking the Language and Contours of Christian Initiation*. Grand Rapids: Baker Academic, 2010.

———. *The Voice of Jesus: Discernment, Prayer, and the Witness of the Spirit*. Downers Grove: IVP, 2003.

Smith, James K. A. *You Are What You Love: The Spiritual Power of Habit*. Grand Rapids: Brazos, 2016.

Snyder, Howard A. *The Problem of Wineskins: Church Structure in a Technological Age*. Downers Grove: IVP, 1975.

———. *The Radical Wesley: Patterns for Church Renewal*. Grand Rapids: Zondervan, 1980.

———. *Signs of the Spirit: How God Reshapes the Church*. Eugene: Wipf & Stock, 1997.

Spener, Philipp Jakob. "From The Necessary and Useful Reading of the Holy Scriptures." In Pietists: Selected Writings. Edited by Peter C. Erb, 71–5. New York: Paulist Press, 1983.

———. "God-Pleasing Prayer, John16: 23–30." In *Pietists: Selected Writings*. Edited by Peter C. Erb, 88–93. New York: Paulist Press, 1983.

———. *Pia Desideria*. Augsburg: Fortress, 1964.

———. "The Spiritual Priesthood." In *Pietists: Selected Writings*. Edited by Peter C. Erb, 50–64. New York: Paulist Press, 1983.

Spurgeon, Charles. *Twelve Sermons on Prayer*. Grand Rapids: Baker 1971.

Stein, James K. *Philipp Jakob Spener: Pietist Patriarch*. Chicago: Covenant, 1986.

Steinke, Peter L. *Congregational Leadership in Anxious Times*. Herndon: The Alban Institute, 2006.

St. Francis of Sales. *Introduction to the Devout Life*. Christian Classics Ethereal Library. http://www.ccel.org/ccel/desales/devout_life.pdf.

Stiles, J. Mack. *Marks of the Messenger*. Downers Grove: IVP, 2010.

Stoeffler, F. Ernest, ed. *Continental Pietism and Early American Christianity*. Grand Rapids: Eerdmans, 1976.

Strom, Jonathan. "The Common Priesthood and the Pietist Challenge for Ministry and Laity." In *The Pietist Impulse in Christianity*. Edited by Christian T. Collins Winn, et al., 42–58. Eugene: Pickwick, 2011.

Swanson, Eric, and Rick Rusaw. *The Externally Focused Quest*. San Francisco: Jossey-Bass, 2010.

Sweeting, George. *Great Quotes and Illustrations*. Nashville: Word, 1985.

Taylor, Jeremy. *Holy Living and Dying*. London: Forgotten Books, 2012.

———. *Holy Living*. Anglican Library. http://anglicanlibrary.org/taylor/holyliving/24chap4sect4.htm.

Telford, John. *The Life of John Wesley*. London: Epworth, 1947.

Thomas à Kempis. *The Imitation of Christ*. Christian Classics Ethereal Library. http://www.ccel.org/ccel/kempis/imitation.pdf.

Torrance, T. F. *Karl Barth: Biblical and Theological The*ologian. Edinburgh: T&T Clark, 1990.

Tuttle Jr., R. G. "The Wesleyan Tradition." In *Evangelical Dictionary of Theology*. Edited by Walter A. Elwell, 1165–67. Grand Rapids: Baker, 1984.

Vogt, Peter. "Nikolaus Ludwig von Zinzendorf." In *The Pietist Theologians*. Edited by Carter Lindberg, 207–23. Malden: Blackwell, 2005.

Wallmann, Johannes. "Was ist Pietismus?" In *The Pietist Theologians*. Edited by Carter Lindberg. Malden: Blackwell, 2005.

Webber, Robert E. *The Divine Embrace: Recovering the Passionate Spiritual Life*. Grand Rapids: Baker, 2006.

Weborg, John. "Reborn in Order to Renew." In *Christian History*, Issue 10 (1986). http://www.christianitytoday.com/ch/1986/issue10/1017.html?start=3.

Wesley, John. *A Short Account of Christian Perfection*. Christian Classics Ethereal Library. http://www.ccel.org/ccel/wesley/perfection.pdf.

Wesley, John. *The Works of John Wesley*. 3rd ed. Vol. IV. Peabody: Hendrickson: 1872, reprint, 1984.

Wessel, Walter. *Mark*. The Expositor's Bible Commentary. Edited by Frank E. Gaebelein. Grand Rapids: Zondervan, 1984.

Westminster Confession of Faith. http://www.reformed.org/documents/wcf_with_proofs/index.html.

Westminster Shorter Catechism in Modern English. http://matt2819.com/wsc/.

Wilkins, Steve, and Mark L. Sanford. *Hidden Worldviews*. Downers Grove: IVP Academic, 2009.

Willard, Dallas. *The Great Omission: Reclaiming Jesus's Essential Teachings on Discipleship*. San Francisco: HarperCollins, 2006.

———. *Hearing God: Developing a Conversational Relationship With God*. Downers Grove: IVP, 2012.

———. *Living in Christ's Presence*. Downers Grove: IVP, 2014.

———. *Renovation of the Heart: Putting on the Character of Christ*. Colorado Springs: NavPress, 2002.

———. *The Spirit of the Disciplines*. San Francisco: Harper & Row, 1988.

CPSIA information can be obtained
at www.ICGtesting.com
Printed in the USA
LVOW10s2330020318
568565LV00006B/39/P

9 781532 636646